RAYMOND BLANC mange

RAYMOND

BLANC

mange

The mysteries of
the kitchen revealed

Photographs by Graham Kirk

BBC BOOKS

Published by BBC Books,
a division of BBC Enterprises Limited,
Woodlands, 80 Wood Lane, London W12 0TT

First Published 1994
Reprinted 1994

© Raymond Blanc 1994

ISBN 0 563 37016 5

Designed by Harry Green
Photographs by Graham Kirk
Styling by Helen Payne
Set in Baskerville by Selwood Systems,
Midsomer Norton
Printed and bound in Great Britain by
Butler & Tanner Ltd, Frome, Somerset
Colour separations by Radstock Repro,
Midsomer Norton
Jacket by Lawrence Allen Ltd,
Weston-Super-Mare

Contents

Acknowledgements

Firstly, I would like to thank my editor, Susan Fleming for her continued patience (this is the second book Susan has edited for me) and to Nicholas Kurti and Hervé This-Benkhard for their invaluable scientific input.

I would also like to thank the BBC Books editorial team of Suzanne Webber and Deborah Taylor who were so understanding when faced with the deadlines (which I did manage to meet – for the first time ever). My thanks to Graham Kirk, photographer and Frank Phillips, Art Director for the stunning food photographs. I would also like to thank Harry Green, the designer and Anita Bean, the nutritionist.

My heartfelt thanks to Le Manoir team led by Clive Fretwell with special thanks to Nicolas Jambert, Jonathan Wright, Alex MacKay, Anita Springall, Thierry de Meo, Freddie Forster and my assistant, Elena Giacomelli.

Many thanks to Albino Barberis who helped we write the material on oils, Peter Kromberg for the Stilton soufflé recipe, Felicity Bryan, my literary agent and Maria Pedro, my business agent.

Peter Lewis of Villeroy & Boch who provided a lot of the beautiful china used in both the book and the television series, Miele for the kitchen used in the series and Braun. Also thanks to Waitrose who are making available in their stores most of the produce mentioned in the book.

I feel it is appropriate to also mention the BBC Television team who were responsible for making the series – George Auckland, Producer, Martin Gorst, Director and Helena Powell, Production Assistant – special thanks to them for their patience and making the filming of the series such good fun, also.

Introduction

You may wonder why I would want to get involved in exploring the mysteries of food chemistry, let alone write a cookery book about them. After all, most chefs use their intuition primarily and their experience secondarily – but chemistry? Hardly ever. I actually left school *because* of flunking chemistry and other science subjects.

So why should I have an interest at all? And why should I believe you too may have an interest? The reason is that I am self-taught and, as such, have great empathy with people who start from scratch and struggle in much the same way as I used to. I vividly remember my naïve introduction to the kitchen in the guise of a chef, flanked by two English Cordon Bleu chefs. There were fifty hungry customers waiting for their meal in the restaurant, and all I had to rely on were memories of my mother's simple dishes. They saved the day, and thus began my slightly masochistic progression into chefhood.

I have never had a mentor, I have never worked under a great chef, so I have had to learn through trial and error. I am actually rather grateful for this lack of guidance as chefs are mostly a bunch of autocratic, egocentric despots! (Have I become one too?) I must, though, have been handed down a small gift from my various ancestors who took their food extremely seriously, but I can assure you, talent alone is not enough. This I discovered through my own blunders, failures, frustrations and hardships. I had to find the answers to many questions in order to improve my technique and my understanding of cooking!

My bedside reading was a different type of thriller. I devoured cookery books written by famous chefs and food writers, and I felt utterly bewildered and helpless while wading through them. They all assumed that the readers were experienced chefs, home economists or highly trained Cordon Bleus, no less! The recipes were a succession of techniques and operations totally incomprehensible to the novice. They did not tell me the reason for the rise or fall of a soufflé; why a sauce would curdle and separate; what magic governed the creation of puff pastry or brioche. Only hard facts stared at me and me at them. Why? Because most chefs are craftsmen working under masters whose effect is often that of a sculptor working on wax. They followed and perpetuated the blueprint of their own education, and found it easier to carry on traditions and tried and proven techniques. This created definite boundaries of which I was ignorant and, later on, intolerant.

Food chemistry books were my saviour, despite my general ineptitude for chemistry. Applied to food, chemistry took a different and magnificent direction. It enabled me to delve into the mysteries and dark secrets of the denaturing of food through cooking as I stumbled on revelations about, say, the miracles of egg yolk and white. Their incredible relationship provided me with the great joy and pride of my first successful soufflé.

Of course, I was not always that interested. The root of my particular fascination is not dissimilar to that of most French people: the 'table' and all it represents. I was brought up to love food, not only because my mother was the best cook (as all French men will tell you!), but because in the days of my childhood in rural France, the table represented a fusion of many aspects of life.

So, although I was not taught, I *lived* food and my specific passion grew from the associations it carried throughout my life. This is probably why food is still a passion more than a profession, a vocation rather than a career. This passion fuels an enormous curiosity about all related subjects: I am fascinated by the history of food; by its connection with the arts, with religion, economics and psychology etc.; by the way we assess its importance and properties; by how we relate to it; by the powers it carries; by what happens when we view it as just a primary physiological necessity, or from an aesthetic, artistic viewpoint. After all, the food with which I am currently preoccupied is not the basic hunger-appeasing variety, more a somewhat complex representation of creative ideas.

This being so, why chemistry, you may cry? Chemistry is to do with the basic nourishing aspects of food, or food manufacturing, not with the art! But not so. When I started cooking, the rules were established, as were the quantities, measures, methods and techniques. As I encountered one after another of these rules, I needed to know *why* I had succeeded or failed.

You might think this approach boring, especially if you too hated chemistry in school. A cookery book, with molecules appearing on every page would trigger yawns, not enthusiastic adventures in the kitchen. Ah, but you *would* want to know why your soufflé does its collapsing act in front of your most esteemed guests, wouldn't you? To understand the reason why might help prevent the collapse of your confidence as well. It would also come in handy to know why a sauce can turn into light magic as opposed to heavy sludge. You might also care to understand why that meat you bought on the butcher's recommendation and which looked so succulent, turned into leather despite your faithful following of the recipe!

Well, I am hoping to unravel some of the mysteries behind these everyday occurrences, and they are all to do with simple chemistry.

In our over-specialized and diversified lives, uniting such seemingly alien fields as cooking and chemistry may seem debatable. But let me explain. For years chefs have written cookery books which did not incorporate a basic understanding of chemistry; chemists have written about food, too, although concerning strict experiments in laboratory conditions. *They* have the knowledge, while I am very well aware that the expression of my craft is born out of intuition and creativity. Both

of these have spurred me on to gather scientific knowledge so that I may be able to better understand the 'science' of food. I hope that this book, which binds both intuition *and* knowledge, will give the reader understanding, control and confidence. For this book is my attempt to get the arts and sciences to speak the same language eventually, because they do, after all, describe the same phenomena.

Although I wish to preserve the sanctity of the table – the focus of union, family, communication and love – I aim to show how to retain these very special attributes in our hurried present-day lives. I wish to demonstrate that, with a little help from chemistry, you may buy and cook more effectively, prepare relatively complex and delicious dishes in a short time, and still have time for conversation. All this despite the fact that, like most people, you will not want to spend as much time in the kitchen as your grandmother did, while still getting food which both you and your guests can enjoy.

My new knowledge of some of the chemical changes involved in cooking neither devalued nor detracted from the pure magic I found in the processes; on the contrary it enhanced my creativity and provided me with much needed confidence. Furthermore, it proved conclusively to me that some of the cooking principles and techniques associated with food and which have been considered sacrosanct throughout the ages, were in fact incorrect and badly interpreted. I believe also that knowledge of food chemistry has helped me to become a better teacher, as I shout my way through my kitchen, trying to instil a firm understanding of my craft into my long-suffering team. It has shown me the way towards a lighter style and given me a better knowledge of nutrition and food hygiene.

For all these reasons, I really believe that some essential knowledge is a must for every cook, domestic or professional. Of course, this does not mean that we must turn our kitchens into laboratories (in my case, a highly unlikely event).

Cooking remains an inexact science, a mixture of experience and intuition, and creativity and keen tastebuds will always remain the main assets of chefs. But I cannot help thinking that a little understanding of what is going on will only help to advance our craft, and will equip our students with more confidence, leaving the magic intact.

Knowing and understanding what causes a sunset does not in any way diminish our experience of it. No, instead it empowers us to appreciate its magic for what it is. Similarly, applying chemistry to cooking can turn out to be a wonderfully enlightening experience – you have more *control* to apply to your craft and creativity.

NOUVELLE CUISINE

It was chefs, not scientists, who were the first in the early 1970s to introduce new ideas and concepts about food, principally that it should be lighter and more healthy. We all know that '*nouvelle cuisine*' is a misnomer. Newness implies the death of an old establishment and the birth of a new one. This is both dangerous and pretentious; 'modern cuisine' would have been much more appropriate.

Why am I discussing *nouvelle cuisine* anyway, when most people firmly believe that it died about fifteen years ago? Because, in short, I think it is very relevant to what is happening today.

It is very clear that the '*haute cuisine*' of the late nineteenth and early twentieth centuries simply did not fit the different needs of nowadays. *Haute cuisine* did not allow any flexibility or room for experimentation: in Escoffier's days, rules were rules, they were strictly laid down and followed, and these rigid restrictions stifled curiosity, the very essence of creative endeavour. Cooking sank into conformity; it was static, routine and repetitive, wrapped in cobwebs.

But as the world and our physiological needs changed, young chefs started to query the established rules and value-systems, and they reacted

somewhat violently. This was the dangerous part of the change, the aspect in common in all revolutions – the very negative emotion of anger. The problem with anger is that it makes you do all sorts of silly things. By making such a sudden and drastic move away from tradition, 'new' meant the denial of the past and practically anything which replaced old and well-tried methods counted as '*nouvelle*'.

Unfortunately, if one cuts the roots of a tree, the plant will simply die, and no branches or fruits will grow. If, however, one prunes and chops off the dead branches, the crop will be of better quality and still plentiful. Blinkered to this, however, chefs started hacking merrily away at the roots of the tree of cooking. For a while, in a paranoid search for new creation, all sorts of Frankenstein dishes were born. The raspberry saw itself happily associated with the white flesh of turbot; the slice of kiwi on all dishes meant 'light' and 'original'; the fish which should have been cooked to medium, often ended up half-raw, as did the vegetables. Appearance became all; the minimalism and geometry of the dish, its colours, even the choice of plate, took more time and effort than the food it contained. However, the reproachable heaviness of classical cooking was actually replaced by a deceitful lightness. Cream and butter still played their part, although hidden in the sauces, so the guest felt just as ready to fall off his chair after eating, as he was accustomed to in the past.

Some journalists and food writers, unwittingly perhaps in their enthusiasm, helped encourage this confusion. At one stage, cooking and eating became highly intellectual pursuits and demanded an effort of reflection before the tasting of a new dish, not to mention the analysis afterwards. Needless to say, a new vocabulary was introduced to the often disoriented guests who, when confronting a dish, had to murmur 'Oh, how interesting', 'How eclectic', or 'What a genius'.

Thereafter, other clichés and trends afflicted cooking, and truly excessive absurdities materialized on the menu, turning cooking into more of a 'visual' art than one of taste.

Man has never learned much from history, and we are still unable to initiate any sort of change without all sorts of upheavals ... What happened to *nouvelle cuisine* is no different, and, as in the wider historical sphere, some of the ideals involved in, and the benefits resulting from, a revolution are recognized much later.

Today, many claim that *nouvelle cuisine* is dead. I disagree. It took fifteen years of mistakes in order to find the way back to the very heart and core of the discipline. We have now moved away from those pretentious clichés, and deal with tradition in a more respectful way. The roots of cooking are not now interfered with; we trim only, and create new, healthy, strong branches, which yield beautiful fruit.

We have rediscovered honesty and this is the most important spice in cooking (as it is in any art form or in behaviour). First one must use the best ingredients and achieve a basic harmony, after which one must build up taste and texture. Only then is an emphasis on presentation justified.

What we have witnessed in these last ten years is hardly believable. The world has shrunk and there is a cross-fertilization of distant ideas and cultures. There are no frontiers any more: we now use spices from every continent, and are influenced by the cuisines of the tropics, Asia, South America, Japan etc. We are so privileged: imagine how a painter would react if you gave him two more primary colours to work with, or a musician two more notes. The priorities have been re-established, and appearance has been relegated to secondary status.

INGREDIENTS

Good food – which equals good nutrition – starts with good and healthy ingredients. Well, are these easily available?

As we all know, man is a creature of extremes,

and is very predictable in the spheres in which he operates. He has to go through extremes and excesses before retreating with great panic to a more acceptable base. Farming is a typical example, especially in Great Britain. Here, intensive farming has been practised for so long, using fertilizers, pesticides and growth promoters, that agriculture has now become agro-chemistry, and the farmer a technocrat.

In order to produce more at any cost, farming has seen some nightmarish scenarios, as demonstrated by the recent BSE scare. Cattle once used to graze in the fields, eating a natural diet. Of course the growth of these cattle was not spectacular, but then man discovered soya. This was rich in protein and produced swifter growth, so was widely grown and fed to cattle. Then, man discovered a way to manufacture soya chemically which helped reduce costs and once again increased cattle growth. Subsequently, man's disregard for certain basic rules led him to create a food much richer in protein – the ground carcases of dead animals – which led directly to mad cow disease, or BSE. We know too well the results of this, and although the practice is now under control, it happened horrifyingly recently.

European legislation has introduced new rules concerning the use of chemicals in food production, and is still tightening them up to prevent abuse. But in Britain we are still a long way from producing chemical-free vegetables and meat. We are now able to produce extremely beautiful and large but extremely tasteless tomatoes, fruit and vegetables to garnish a cotton-wool-fleshed, brittle-boned chicken dish, which tastes of fish meal! Intensive farming has had a terrible effect on the quality of all our food. It is governed by greed and profit, not by a love of taste or of the land.

PROCESSING

After the food has been grown or reared, it is delivered to the food manufacturer and a team of technologists. It is then refined, processed and re-designed, using colourings, anti-oxidants, flavourings, synthetic vitamins etc. All this so as to lengthen shelf life, improve appearance and tempt purchase.

Today it seems that looking good is more important than feeling good. This also applies to produce. These chemically altered foods, so beautifully wrapped in their glittering packaging, are then promoted on our television screens accompanied by Vivaldi or Beethoven. Do not be seduced by this glitter. We have a right and a duty as consumers to be more demanding and critical – after all, we *eat* the food. Politicians and the food industry may be very sensitive and wary these days, but change can only happen through consumers being critical, selective and demanding . . . You are the channel. Let us demand better food, starting with better ingredients.

COOKING

The problem with raw ingredients is that you have to cook them. We live in the era of the microwave, and we seem to have lost the simple art of cooking and giving. I hope that this book will entice you to rediscover the joy of cooking, creating and sharing healthy food, as well as, once in a while – and why not! – something quite naughty.

The table is a natural place in the home to meet, talk, relate, and discover each other. My mother's cooking was not just wholesome food, it was a catalyst for conversation, an exchange of opinions, celebrations and occasional arguments. These were the other ingredients which went into every ladle of soup, each plate of *cassoulet* and each spoonful of dessert.

In my family, you could just about read the menu by listening to the conversation. A light starter with drinks, and the crossing of bread by my atheist father, would be followed by the main course of massive discussions on religion, garnished with politics. And, of course, the topic for dessert

was sex, at which point my extremely devout Catholic mother would hurriedly leave the room.

Cooking and giving are an integral part of family life. I believe that the family is the very heart of society, and if one creates a caring and loving family, one is likely to create a more loving society.

DIET AND NUTRITION

Thank God I was not born in the nineteenth century, for I could never have become a chef. The famous words of the equally famous chef, Fernand Point, still resound with strong prejudice. 'Never trust a thin chef!' he declared. To have a sizeable belly and cauliflower cheeks were the prerequisites. Even quite recently, big was still equated with success. That fat post-war babies would turn into fat people was not a worry.

Luckily, the late twentieth century has brought some essential changes. We now have a very different concept of both good health and good food. Now, in fact, they must go hand in hand.

Scientists, doctors and nutritionists have all given us their learned opinions as to what constitutes a good diet. The tangible result is that it has left us more confused and more fearful than ever about the food we eat. The outcome has been that what should be an extremely enjoyable, sensual, social and family activity – eating – has turned into a nightmare. We are as concerned about our weight as we are about our health. What to eat for breakfast, lunch and dinner creates stress, guilt and panic attacks.

No longer does the boiled egg conjure up an appetizing breakfast image. First of all we feel guilty about the poor hen in a tiny cage under merciless, ultraviolet lights. Then we think about the cholesterol content, and the dreaded bacteria, salmonella.

What a lifestyle. What a way to start the day. Actually, the latest finding is that cholesterol in eggs does not cause you much harm.

It is fair to say that the Western diet has been poor, particularly that in Great Britain. The abuse of salt, unsaturated fats, sugar and cheap 'junk' food has created all sorts of disorders such as obesity, heart disease, high blood pressure, dental caries, strokes and cancer. But, at the same time, the message about better diet relating to better health has been slow to filter through from above, and when it did so, it was confused and contradictory, making us paranoid about what we ate.

Why *do* we have to go to the extremes which we know, by nature, are bound to be detrimental? Why is it that the views of orthodox medicine are still clouded and limited by their own teaching? Why are these views so irremediably linked with the pharmaceutical industry? As a result, pills, not food, would seem to be the answer to all our problems. Of course high blood pressure is not caused by a deficiency of beta-blockers, nor migraines by a lack of aspirins – yet sometimes current medical prescribing would have us believe so.

We are finally discovering how the food we eat is linked to the health of mind and body – something the Chinese have known for thousands of years. We can now see nutrition as a day-to-day medication, keeping us away from sickness and disease.

The difficulties concerning advice on nutrition lie in the complexities of the individual food and its recipient (us). There can only ever be nutritional guidelines, there is *no single magic answer*, for every-one has a somewhat different bio-chemistry and metabolism. What may suit one person may well disagree with another. That means that we are each unique and should be treated so. I believe, maybe naïvely, that unless one has a recognized medical condition, the answers lie in common sense (or, perhaps we should call it *rare* sense). A little bit of self-discipline, a basic knowledge of nutrition and a shrewd awareness of one's own need and greed are all needed to enable one to design a personal nutritional guide.

It is not by chance that the Mediterranean diet has become so popular and has been widely adopted in Britain and many other countries. Olive oil, as the cooking medium, is versatile and is monounsaturated. The ingredients used in this diet – the finest vegetables, fruit, and limited protein – are also healthy. The dishes do not contain either cream or butter, and the emphasis is on an enjoyable moderation.

So, eating a healthier diet does not mean we have to become hardened vegetarians, or lead extremely austere lifestyles. Extremes are usually dangerous and often create other disorders.

Let us enjoy what the good Lord has given us without abusing it. *Bon appétit.*

Truly yours,

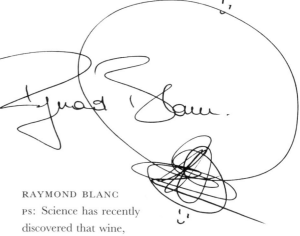

RAYMOND BLANC

PS: Science has recently discovered that wine, particularly red, holds some anti-oxidants which prevent and help alleviate heart disease. Let's cheerfully raise our glasses to a better today and a healthier tomorrow.

A Pinch of Science

When we cook we are not usually aware that we are working in terms of physics and chemistry. But a roast in the oven changes colour on its surface because of chemicals in the meat reacting together and generating a brown and aromatic crust. Oil and water do not usually mix, but add a little egg yolk and you create an emulsion, and a sauce.

Of course you need no scientific training in order to be a competent or even a superb cook, but it is useful to know what is going on so that you can predict the results of cooking operations or processes. For example, it helps to know *which* chemical reactions are producing the taste of the crusty part of a roast, and that fats take part in those reactions. Understanding what happens in the saucepan, frying pan, under the grill or in the microwave will not thwart but expand your creativity.

We shall explain only those facts and concepts of physics and chemistry which are relevant to cooking.

THE BUILDING BLOCKS OF ALL MATTER

Ultimately all matter is composed of *atoms*. There are about a hundred of these, and they are called the elements. The most common in all living matter are carbon, hydrogen, oxygen, nitrogen, phosphorus and sulphur. Atoms are very small indeed. Fifty million of them – the population of any major European country – would encircle, in a single row, the head of a pin.

Although the Greek word *atomos* means indivisible or unsplittable, it has been known for over a century that each atom is like a miniature solar system with a positively charged nucleus at its centre (the 'sun'), and negatively charged electrons (the 'planets') swirling around it in one or several layers. In the real solar system the planets are drawn towards the sun by the force of gravity, but in atoms the forces are electrical. You can get an idea of these forces when you rub a plastic ruler or comb against your shirt or jumper and then place it very near a small piece of tissue paper. The paper jumps towards the ruler because of electrical forces. Such forces draw electrons towards the nucleus of atoms.

Only one aspect of the structure of the atom need concern the cook, namely the role of these electrons. The outer electrons of an atom act as a kind of glue, or like tentacles, and they can grab electrons belonging to neighbouring atoms. When they do this, they form *molecules*, which thus consist of one or more atoms closely bound together. For instance, the water molecule (H_2O) consists of one oxygen atom and two hydrogen atoms. Ethyl alcohol (C_2H_6O) comprises nine atoms: one oxygen, six hydrogen, two carbons. Starch molecules and cellulose molecules are built from tens of thousands of atoms! By using children's building blocks of varying sizes and shapes, you can form endless differing structures. Thus it is with atoms, which can form innumerable types of molecule.

Molecules are electrically neutral, because the positive electrical charge of the nucleus equals the sum of the negative charges by the electrons. However, there are certain molecules called 'polar', in which the charges are not distributed symmetrically and therefore can be set in motion by electro-magnetic waves. This is the basis of water and microwave cookery (see pp. 40–41).

THE FOOD MOLECULES

Most food ingredients are composed of only a few different types of molecule, and food chemists distinguish primarily between water, proteins, fats and carbohydrates (starch, sugar, etc.).

WATER

Water is the preponderant constituent of all living organisms – the human body, for instance, consists of about 60 per cent water. As stated, water molecules are very simple: an oxygen atom is bound to two hydrogen atoms. Water is denser than oil because of the hydrogen atoms, which pack the molecules tightly together, thus oil will sit on top of water. We all know that water is transparent, that it is liquid at room temperature, that it boils at 100°C (212°F), and that it solidifies at 0°C (32°F). In the kitchen it is important to know that water is the primary molecule in most foods: up to 95 per cent in fruit and vegetables, about 87 per cent in wine, about 50–75 per cent in raw meat. Only pure oil contains no water molecules.

That water retains its volume but not its shape – i.e., it is liquid and moves about – is a property common to all liquids. This indicates that the forces of attraction between the molecules is strong enough to keep them together, bouncing against one another, but still allows them relative freedom of movement. Some of the molecules near the surface of the water, if they move fast enough, can escape, but this process is limited as they have to battle against air molecules. It is heat which increases the movement of molecules in water – think of the increasing agitation of water as it is heated through a simmer to a boil. The higher the temperature, the faster water molecules move, and when the temperature is higher than boiling point, the water molecules vaporize or turn to steam. The movement energy of the molecules is high enough to let them escape up into the air, and 'defeat' the air molecules.

The boiling point of a liquid is defined as the temperature at which the pressure exerted by the escaping molecules equals the pressure of the air in the atmosphere. The boiling point of water can change, therefore, depending on air pressure. Most of us live at or near sea level, so the boiling point is 100°C (212°F). But this decreases one degree

for every 300 metres (985 feet) gain in elevation above sea level. So the boiling point of water in Mexico City (elevation, 2000 metres/6560 feet) is 93°C (199°F), and that in Quito (elevation, 3000 metres/9840 feet) is 90°C (194°F). Cooking techniques and even ingredients may have to be adapted to these conditions. Cooking *over* pressure, for instance, is the principle of the pressure cooker.

When water is cooled to 0°C (32°F), it freezes and turns into ice, a crystalline solid in which the water molecules, instead of being free to move as when liquid, become anchored in fixed positions. As the water molecules move less and less, they increase the distance between them instead of bonding (as when liquid), so water actually expands as it freezes. This explains why frozen pipes burst, why bottles of wine explode in the freezer, and why cells of plant tissue can turn to a mush when frozen and defrosted – the cell walls have been ruptured by expanded ice crystals.

The freezing point of water and other liquids can be lowered by dissolving in it other substances such as sugar and salt. The addition of rock salt can reduce freezing point to about − 25°C (− 13°F), a principle which is used in making ice-cream. (Salt can also *raise* the boiling point of water.) Some substances such as glycerine or sugar syrup do not crystallize when frozen, but instead, as the temperature is lowered, become more and more viscous.

Another quality of water is that it is a very good solvent. Because the hydrogen atoms in water molecules are able to establish chemical bonds with atoms from neighbouring molecules, water can dissolve salt, sugar, alcohol and a lot of other molecules of food importance. Fats and oils cannot dissolve other substances, but 'coat' them instead, which is why any seasoning included in a vinaigrette should be dissolved in the vinegar first, before adding the oil.

PROTEINS

Proteins, the basic stuff of which we are composed and on which we 'run', were largely unknown until this century. Our bodies are composed of protein and water, and in a dietary sense protein is vital: we need to eat 'complete' proteins such as meat, eggs and dairy produce, and 'incomplete' proteins which are largely of plant origin (although soya bean protein is very nearly complete).

Protein molecules are very complex, long chains linked together by amino acids, the building blocks of life. Some of the amino acids can interact with water molecules, and other amino acids cannot. The protein molecules are coiled in on themselves like balls of wool, with their water-hating (hydrophobic) parts inside, protected from the watery environment, and the water-loving (hydrophilic) parts on the outside. But if the proteins are heated, they uncoil, because heat increases the movement of the molecules. These uncoiled, extended proteins are said to be 'denatured', and this is one of the two principal processes involved in cooking. As the protein molecules unravel like wool, the long strands start to link together to form a network. If this goes far enough, the food becomes semi-solid. This is a one-way trip, because once the strands are cross-linked the process is not reversible. But if the process is stopped while the proteins are still unravelling, the denaturing is partially reversible.

This could all be best illustrated by examining egg white, for example. Egg white is mostly a solution of proteins in water, about 50/50. In raw egg white the proteins are coiled up, but heating the white denatures the protein. Atoms that were linked together in the coiled molecules can now link up with the atoms in other molecules and form a more rigid network. This is the process responsible for the coagulation and change from transparent to opaque white when egg white is cooked. And it is this ability of egg to coagulate that makes it so vital in quiches, mousses, custards, soufflés, etc. (See also pp. 24–25.)

Carrying the illustration further, egg white can also be denatured simply by being whipped to a foam. The agitation of the molecules changes the nature of the egg white by introducing millions of bubbles of air, and the air itself to a certain extent 'sets' some of the protein molecules. If the egg white is beaten until stiff it becomes a stable foam – a necessity in many dishes – while if it is not beaten enough, the proteins are not fully unravelled, and the denaturing process can partially reverse, with part of the foam becoming liquid again.

The same applies to meat protein. Meat is composed of cells, small bags which are visible under the microscope, containing very many small structures and with a membrane round the whole lot. These membranes and their contents are all composed of molecules, which in turn are made of atoms. Heat coagulates the protein molecules, so that they form a network of neighbouring, denatured proteins.

FATS AND OILS

Fats are a group of molecules which store energy, twice as much as that stored by carbohydrates (see below). Plants, for instance, are largely carbohydrate, but their seeds, which require more energy, often contain fat as well (think of the cooking oils from seeds – soya, corn, safflower, grapeseed, groundnut or peanut, etc.). Fat is stored for energy by humans too, part of the reason why, in a more sedentary world, it is not used up and the result is overweight or obesity.

Oils are liquid at room temperature, fats are solid. The more saturated the fat, the harder it gets: lamb and beef fats are solid, chicken fat is soft. Fats are said to be insoluble in water – oil and water do not mix for long, and the oil just floats back to the top. Particular molecules from egg yolks have to be added to an oil and water mixture to make it form a smooth emulsion such as mayonnaise (see p. 17). But it is rare for anything to be completely insoluble. That is the reason why one has to prepare a stock with a large quantity of water: in a lot of water, more of the fatty or lipid molecules of the stock base (chicken bones, for instance) will be extracted, dissolved and retained in the stock after it has been reduced.

Fats are frequently blamed for health problems, but they bring a wonderful smoothness when added to many dishes, and the fats *within* meat contribute to the mouth-feel of juiciness. Fats also dissolve aromatic molecules, in particular flavours called terpenes, which are found in food. Terpenes are also found in fragrant flowers – their names include geraniol, nerol and linalol – and a process involving fat, known as *enfleurage*, is used to extract the aromatic molecules of flowers in perfumery. The same process can be used in the kitchen, in a herb butter for instance: by heating together butter with some minced herb leaves such as sage, the aromatic molecules of the sage dissolve into the butter. The fat of meat also contains the essential flavour of the meat – lamb fat tastes strongly of lamb, as does beef fat of beef. Different oils contain different flavour molecules: some are bland, and therefore good for cooking with if no extra flavour is required; some are highly scented with the nut or fruit of their origin, like walnut and olive oils. Types of cuisine can virtually be characterized by the fats used in cooking: the butter of northern France, the olive oil of southern Italy and the sesame oil of China.

Fats and oils also contribute to the Maillard reactions which are so important in creating flavour in food (see p. 19). They can do this because they are able to be heated to a much higher temperature than water, most of them upward of 200°C (392°F). But fats and oils have a smoke point (or 'boiling point') beyond which the oil will break down, will taste less good and *be* less good. The smoke point of fat is lowered every time it is used. An oil such as olive, which contains a lot of natural material because it has not been refined in any way, will have a lower smoke point than a more refined oil or fat.

CARBOHYDRATES

Carbohydrates – sugars, starches, etc. – are used by living organisms as energy storage, but less efficiently than fats.

Sugars are the simplest carbohydrates, and there are many different sugar molecules. Glucose is the main sugar of life: it is the fuel for our bodies, circulating with the blood. It is captured by cells and chemically modified to provide energy. Other sugars related to glucose are sucrose (table sugar), fructose (fruit sugar) and lactose (milk sugar).

In the plant world the trouble with glucose and other sugars is that they dissolve all too readily in water. For plant seeds such as wheat, barley, etc., such soluble instant-energy molecules are useless: when the seeds were planted, the first rain would wash the sugar away. As a result, evolution came up with a marvellous answer, and the simple sugar molecules were linked together in long molecules which are known as the starches (complex carbohydrates).

Flour, which is made from grains, is a starch composed of two kinds of carbohydrate molecule, amylose and amylopectin. Unlike sugars, these do not dissolve in cold water, but can dissolve in hot water – which is why a roux of butter, flour and milk is more successful when quickly made with hot milk.

Amylose and amylopectin play a part in the 'gelling' of starches – the ability of flour, for instance, to absorb liquid, thicken and become denser in something like a simple white sauce. This is the second of the important cooking processes – the gelatinization of starch. Raw starch, such as that in potatoes, is not very pleasant to eat, but cooking comes to the rescue. At temperatures in the range 55–70°C (131–158°F), the starch starts to soften or gelatinize. The starch starts to absorb water, swell to a large size and burst. The starchy food is then good to eat.

Cellulose too is made up of glucose sugars, and it forms the framework for storage of starch, generally the 'hard' outer part of plant cells. This is largely indigestible in the human gut, and is what we know as fibre. Some forms of cellulose, such as that in dried beans, pass through into the lower intestine unchanged, where bacteria 'digest' them, giving off methane gas in the process and giving rise to the embarrassing phenomenon of flatulence (see also the Scientist's Note on p. 82).

WHAT'S LEFT?

With water, proteins, fats and carbohydrates, the description of food and food molecules is not complete. It is well known that vitamins are important for a healthy life, but are they useful in the kitchen as well? Yes, they can be. When you chop an apple, the cut surface soon browns, but if you sprinkle it with lemon juice (which contains ascorbic acid or vitamin C), the chemical process that creates the brown molecules (due to enzyme activity, see p. 20) is stopped. The same process could be said to happen in the human body, for vitamin C, a very powerful anti-oxidant, is believed by doctors and nutritionists to prevent much degenerative disease.

Emulsifiers are another important group of molecules in the kitchen. They are also known as surface active compounds or molecules and include everything from washing-up liquid to mustard and egg yolk. They are usually long molecules which can attach themselves to water at one end and to oily and fatty molecules at the other. Thus they bring about one of the many miracles of cooking: emulsifiers make oil and water mix together, egg yolks in mayonnaise and mustard in a vinaigrette. Butter, itself an emulsion of fats and water, can also help sauces emulsify.

In mayonnaise, the surface active molecules of the yolk form layers around the oil droplets, preventing them joining together as they want to, separating them from the water, and stabilizing them. Similar molecules help to stabilize foams because the hydrophilic (water-loving) part binds to water, and the hydrophobic (water-hating) part binds to air.

SOME PHYSICAL AND CHEMICAL PROCESSES

Most but not all food preparation involves heating, or increasing the temperature. But what is heat, and what do we mean by temperature? And what chemical reactions does the application of heat bring about?

HEAT AND TEMPERATURE

Let us begin with heat. We know from everyday experience that if something hot is put in contact with something cold, the hot body cools and the cold body heats up: heat flows from hot bodies to cold bodies. For example, if we immerse a metallic spoon with a long handle into hot liquid, to begin with the end of the handle will be just as warm or cold as the surrounding air. However, it will gradually get hotter as heat travels out of the liquid along the handle, and finally the end of the handle may even become too hot to touch. It will never get quite so hot as the liquid, because some of the heat will be dissipated in the surrounding air. If we use a wooden spoon, the end will barely get warm: heat travels less easily in wood than in a metal.

What then is temperature? In simple language it is the degree or intensity of sensible heat of a body in relation to others as perceived, for instance, by touch or, more generally, by the sensory nerve endings in the skin. The end of a wooden spoon, which does not conduct heat, feels colder and has a lower temperature than a hot liquid in which it sits; sitting in front of a blazing fire, our body feels its high temperature. Touch is the earliest form of thermometer, and is still used widely, even predominantly, by cooks.

Let us examine how we perceive heat and temperature. Normal blood temperature, which is also the temperature inside our body, is about 37°C (98.6°F). However, the temperature of our skin is lower: at the tip of our fingers it is usually below 30°C (86°F) because, just as in the case of the wooden spoon in the liquid, heat is flowing slowly from the inside of our body towards the air; the skin is giving off some of its heat before it can flow from the inside to equalize the temperature of the inside and outside of the skin.

If the skin is exposed to a material – air or

water or some solid – which has a temperature below that of the skin, it feels cold, while if the temperature is above, it feels warm. What does this mean in molecular terms? As we said before, molecules are in incessant motion: the faster they move, the higher their energy. In a simplified way we can say that higher energy means higher temperature. If the molecule which hits the skin is 'hotter' than those of the skin, it will give some of its surplus energy to the skin molecules and heat it. Conversely, if it is colder, it will remove some energy and cool it. Of course, thanks to the body's excellent thermostatic control, skin temperature is kept roughly constant, loss of heat being compensated for by increased blood supply, a gain of heat by increased perspiration. Put your finger in water at about 28°C (82.4°F), and it will feel pleasantly lukewarm (such water is hotter than your finger); but take a sip from the same water, and you will have a cool sensation (because your mouth is at blood temperature, i.e. hotter than the water sipped).

What happens if we place a piece of meat either in hot water (preferably a flavourful stock or broth) or hot air, in an oven for example? The 'hot' molecules of the water or air surrounding the meat collide with 'colder' molecules on the surface of the meat, and pass on to them some of their energy so that the surface molecules rapidly reach the same temperature as their surroundings. As they do so, the molecules near the surface pass on some of their energy to the molecules further in and, layer by layer, the piece of meat warms up. This process of heat propagation from molecule to molecule is called *heat conduction* and it takes place in solids, liquids and gases alike.

In any solid or mainly solid material, conduction is the only way heat can be transported. In a liquid, and also in a gas or vapour, another mechanism, called *convection*, plays an important, usually dominant, part. The density of a liquid depends on temperature: it expands as it is heated (water between 0 and 4°C/32 and 39.2°F is the only

exception), so if you heat a liquid at the bottom it will tend to rise to be replaced by the colder heavier liquid descending from the top. Convection currents are powerful equalizers of temperature. The strength of convection depends on viscosity. A bowl of hot clear soup will cool much more rapidly than a similar bowl of thick soup; in the thick soup, convection equalizes the temperature very slowly.

In conduction and convection the transport of heat is via the atoms and molecules, individually in the former and *en masse* in the latter. There is a third mechanism, namely *radiation*, or electromagnetic waves which can travel through empty space. It is radiant heat that you experience when sitting in front of a blazing fire, or in the sun. This method of heating is used mainly in grilling or in roasting on a rotating spit in front of a fire. Only some of the energy is carried by the visible radiation; most of it is in the form of invisible infra-red light which, unlike visible light, can penetrate many of the food materials to the depth of a few millimetres.

Cooking by radiation differs fundamentally from cooking in an oven or a casserole. In an oven the joint receives heat on all sides from the surrounding air, whereas radiated heat is received only by the side facing the source of radiation. Hence the need for turning over when grilling, and for rotating the spit.

The intensity of radiation depends strongly on the temperature of the emitting body, and also on how near or far the heat is to or from the food.

Microwaves, another form of electro-magnetic radiation, are also used in the kitchen. They are short radio waves which can penetrate many foodstuffs several centimetres deep and, by acting on molecules whose electrons are not symmetrically distributed, such as water, pass on to them some of their energy, which is then converted into heat by friction. (See also pp. 40–41.)

CHEMICAL REACTIONS

To return to our piece of meat. If we put it in

boiling water, the proteins will coagulate and the meat will be cooked. Boiling water is a very useful medium in which to cook foods. It provides a constant temperature of 100°C (212°F) which is only slightly above the temperature needed to render raw materials safe and palatable for con- ~ sumption. But that heat is not high enough to generate, through culinary chemistry, the flavours and fragrances which elevate food from the palatable to the enjoyable and exquisite. Having tasted our boiled meat, we would not have found it particularly exciting, even if the water had some herbs or spices infused in it.

Let us repeat the experiment using oil. Until we get to 100°C (212°F), nothing much happens, but as we heat further – and remember, fats or oils can be heated way beyond water's boiling point – we can see bubbles escaping from the meat and hear sizzling. The bubbles are steam, because meat contains about 50 per cent water. As the oil warms up, the water turns into steam and vapour bubbles leave the meat. When the temperature of the oil is higher than 100°C (212°F), this evaporation becomes more intense, but in the parts of the meat where some water is still present, the temperature stays at 100°C. After some time the boiling will stop because all the surface water from the meat has been evaporated. There is still some water inside the meat, but its diffusion towards the surface is slow.

At the surface of the meat, a brown colouring indicates that one of the hundreds of chemical reactions between proteins and sugars is gathering momentum. These are what are known as the Maillard reactions, and they could probably be termed the third most important cooking process in the kitchen, for they produce masses of flavour. It is Maillard reactions that generate the delicious aroma of fried, roast and baked foods, for instance.

What is happening is a chemical conjunction between amino acids in the protein of meat, say, with sugars also present in the meat. When these are heated together they produce a whole range of colourful and highly flavoured molecules which are responsible for the brown colour and some of the distinctive taste of cooked meat. This Maillard reaction between the sugars and amino acids can happen at a much lower temperature than is needed to caramelize sugar.

Other foods also contain proteins and sugars. If you like a very rich-flavoured stew – which, of course, is basically a *water* cooking process – then after searing or browning the meat in a little oil, you should do the same to the vegetables (and indeed any wheat flour you may be using as a thickening agent).

The Maillard reaction that browns meat also produces the tasty crust on bread and toast. Wheat flour contains quite a lot of protein as well as starch, so it browns well when cooked (see also Bread-making, p. 48). Interestingly, Maillard reactions are also responsible for the smell and flavour of coffee and chocolate. The beans of both are roasted while being processed, and this again involves interactions between sugars and amino acids.

Given the complexity of both the protein and sugar molecules, it is not surprising that there are literally thousands of these Maillard compounds of varying tastes and fragrances. Why is it that these and many other chemical reactions occur only at relatively high temperatures? For two molecules to combine they must have an 'affinity' to each other, and they must prefer that state to solitary existence. The constituents of the molecules, the atoms or atomic groups, are strongly linked and have no 'arms' to grab another molecule when they collide. However, as the temperature rises so does the molecular motion – not only the speed of the molecule as a whole, but also the movements of the constituent atoms or groups. As a result the bonds get loose and once they are sufficiently weak there is an increasing chance of molecules reacting with each other on collision.

The reaction velocity and its temperature

dependency varies from case to case, but, roughly speaking, for most reactions important in the kitchen the velocity doubles for every 10°C (50°F) temperature rise. Thus, if at ordinary temperature the reaction would take a day, at 150°C (302°F), it would be over in ten seconds.

Increasing the temperature is not the only way to start or accelerate chemical reactions. There exist certain substances called catalysts which trigger chemical transformations without them-selves undergoing any change. Particularly import-ant for culinary science are a group of complicated protein molecules called enzymes. They are of varying shapes and compositions, and these deter-mine what particular chemical change they can activate. Certain enzymes are beneficial in cookery, for instance those which are responsible for the subtle changes in the chemical composition, texture and ultimate flavour of meat that has been hung well (see also pp. 21–23).

Among the useful enzymes special mention should be made of the proteolytic (protein-dissolving) enzymes, for instance papain in papaya and bromelin in pineapple. As their names indi-cate, they break up proteins and thus, by softening the muscle fibres and the connective tissues, can tenderize meat.

Some other enzymes are less popular with cooks, such as those present in the cells of fruit and vegetables. These can cause spoilage, and it is they, when exposed to the air by chopping or cutting, that cause unsightly browning. This is particularly noticeable in potato and apple.

IN CONCLUSION

The kitchen is indeed a wonderful laboratory that should be used more often by teachers of physics and chemistry, because in a kitchen you find the stuff of real life to illustrate the properties of the far from exciting gases, liquids and solids of our textbooks. The richness of the physics and chem-istry of food should encourage us to think more about it. Pierre-Gilles de Gennes, who received the Nobel Prize for Physics (mainly for his studies of liquid crystals and polymers), has in recent years extended his researches to the properties of 'soft matter' of foams, emulsions and to many of the processes described in this scientific introduction. So the food lover of the twentieth century can perhaps expect a clearer and more comprehensible explanation of many complicated culinary systems used by science. One consequence must surely be that we shall improve our recipes and our use of them!

NICHOLAS KURTI
HERVE THIS-BENCKHARD
GEORGE AUKLAND

Ingredients

Here we cover some of the major ingredients used in the book, from meat, fish and dairy products, through to peppercorns and vanilla.

MEAT

The quality of meat varies according to breed, diet and the farming techniques employed, so what different butchers sell as fillet of beef may be as different as lumpfish roe is from caviar. It would be helpful to know where the butcher gets his supplies, and thus have a vague notion of what to expect. All too often, you can buy what appears to be a prime cut of meat for Sunday lunch or a dinner party and, having followed a wonderful recipe with faith and precision, end up with something which is tough and flavourless. You will probably blame your lack of understanding of cooking – or the recipe – but have you ever considered blaming your butcher?

For, sadly, most British butchers (with some notable exceptions) have lost their skill, and butchers' shops in this country are a pretty dispiriting sight. Continental butchers spoil their customers for choice with arrays of neatly prepared and trimmed cuts; here, the choice is often dictated by how quickly you can escape the look and smell of the shop.

Most meat should be hung. Through hanging, the meat loses water and matures somewhat, thus improving in flavour and tenderness. Most butchers in Britain do not hang their meat properly, so most customers believe quality lies in the vivid redness of unhung meat. This lack of proper hanging is for the convenience of the butcher, not the customer: hanging meat requires space and investment in a larger cold room – and water loss translates into weight loss, hence money loss. The best beef, for instance, comes from an animal that has been hung for a minimum of two to three weeks, when it will be dark reddish-brown, almost dirty looking. Because customers still think good meat is *red* meat, there is little incentive to change this practice, unless they demand better quality and threaten to withdraw their custom.

It is important to realize how much power we have as customers; only by exercising this power can we alter and improve standards of service. For example, by 1980, veal rearing in France had become so intensive and hormone-ridden, and the meat so tasteless and unacceptable to the fussy, food-conscious French, that they decided to boycott all veal. This nearly bankrupted the veal producers, who were forced to re-think their farming policies and so, now, all hormones are thankfully forbidden by law. If other producers of meat were to adopt similar attitudes, perhaps butchers would once again become proud of their craft and the word 'butchery' would no longer carry such pejorative overtones.

Never feel shy about asking your butcher to trim off fat or prepare a cut to your requirements; if he is a professional, he will readily perform these services, and if he seems surprised or reluctant at first, remember that you are helping him to rediscover his craft.

SCIENTIST'S NOTES

Meat is animal muscle. As a rough guide, its composition is: 50–75 per cent water, 18 per cent proteins, 4 per cent non-protein solids and 3 per cent fats. One-quarter of the non-proteins, or 1 per cent of the total, is glycogen which is the fuel store of the muscle; it provides, in the form of glucose, the energy required for its work.

After the animal is killed and before rigor mortis sets in, the muscles are still active, and the glycogen still produces glucose as well as lactic acid. It is the latter which is important for the further changes in the meat, by acting as a preservative. If the animal arrives at the slaughterhouse in an exhausted or stressed state the glycogen supply would have been depleted, little or no lactic acid would be produced and the result would be dry, fibrous and 'dark-cutting' (purplish-black) meat of unattractive appearance. It is clear that the quality of the meat depends not only on the animal's quality of life, but also on the mode of its death.

HANGING OF MEAT

All meat benefits from a period of hanging. The muscle fibres slowly become more acidic and this has a partial preserving effect. The acidity arises from the production of lactic acid as the glycogen reserves in the muscles are used up. The lactic acid releases enzymes which in turn attack the proteins in the muscle fibres, and produce free amino acids. The amino acids when cooked combine with other molecules such as sugars to produce many strong-flavoured compounds. In large animals this enzyme activity can take quite a long time, and high-quality beef, for instance, is often aged for up to three weeks at about 2°C.

AGE AND TENDERNESS

Animal muscles which are used a great deal often contain large amounts of connective tissue such as collagen, and this makes the meat tougher. In grazing animals, for instance, neck and shoulder pieces are often tougher, because of the exercise they get as the animal bends to eat; the fillet, from the back, is *under-exercised*, therefore is free of collagen and very tender.

The amount of collagen in muscle does not increase with the age of the animal, but the long molecules in the collagen often start to cross-link, and therefore the collagen in older animals is less easily softened by the cooking process. So the meat gets tougher with the increasing age of the animal. But marbled fat also develops in the muscles as the animal gets older, and this can make a major contribution to the finished flavour. Paradoxically, older meat can be both tougher and tastier.

COOKING MEAT

Meat is made up of muscle fibres (lean), held together by connective tissues (collagen or gristle). There is also a certain amount of fat alongside and surrounding the fibres and of course a large amount of water. The muscle fibres and the connective tissues are all different kinds of protein and react in different ways when we heat them. As the temperature rises, the muscle fibres start to shrink and squeeze out the water. Too much heat,

and the meat will be tough and dry. But at the same time the gristle, which starts out very tough and chewy, begins to turn into gelatine, which is soft. The fat melts and helps to lubricate the muscle fibres. So the cooking of meat is always a compromise. Too much heat and it gets tough and chewy, too little heat and it stays tough and chewy.

How you cook meat depends on the proportion of muscle fibres to connective tissue. Young and fine cuts of meat with soft connective tissue will need very little cooking. Older meat needs longer cooking in the presence of moisture to soften the gristle and make the meat tender. Experiments have shown that if we don't like the mouth-feel and juiciness of the meat, we will never enjoy its flavour.

POULTRY

I find it a shame that more farmers in Britain have not taken the opportunity to breed quality, *real* free-range chickens. There are only a few farms and companies producing quality birds. 'Free-range' has a double meaning in Britain. One type of free-range chicken can roam at will outside and feed at will, but for a legal minimum of 28 days only; it is still contained in pens, and in the company of many other birds – I would hardly call this free-range. The other types of free-range chickens are traditionally reared in the farmyard, with access to the open air throughout their lives.

For consistent quality and availability, most of us still have to buy French chickens, and you can see these on all the supermarket shelves – Poulet de Bresse, des Landes, etc. They are full of flavour and do not have the cottonwool texture of a lot of British birds. The same applies to duck, turkey, guinea fowl, etc.

Chicken, like beef, always gains both in terms of texture and flavour by being matured, for up to four days.

SCIENTIST'S NOTES

One of the most obvious things about the flesh of chicken or turkey is the presence of light and dark meats. The dark meat is on the legs, which tend to get the most exercise, and whose muscles need to store more oxygen. The molecule that retains oxygen in the muscle cells is myoglobin, which is deep red. Muscles which are less active use less oxygen, and contain less myoglobin, so they are paler in colour.

The dark meat is usually more juicy but less tender than the white. The juiciness is due to a higher fat content.

GAME

Game is becoming extinct in France. This is due largely to the activities of little gum-booted men who shoot on sight anything that flies or moves, thus drastically reducing the wildlife population. Never trust a Frenchman with a gun!

In Britain, there is a staggering variety of game – wild duck, woodcock, teal, grouse, snipe, hare … Yet, despite this natural abundance, game farming has become big business. Farming spoils the quality, so never buy farmed game (the only exception being farmed venison). The delicate pink flesh of the red-legged partridge, for instance, has, through cross-breeding, become strong and resistant to disease – but at the expense of taste and texture, since it ends up much like chicken. Beware, too, of wild ducks built like chickens; they have done more running than flying and hence have long legs and strange bodies!

HANGING

Game usually has a distinctive, rather strong taste. Most must be hung for one to three days, so that the flesh relaxes, but, generally speaking, if it is hung for too long, the flavour becomes coarse and overassertive. The only game animals I hang for more than three days are venison, pheasant, partridge and wild boar. Grouse is so strong to start with that hanging would make it overwhelmingly pungent. Pheasant, on the other hand, which has white flesh and a rather faint taste, needs to hang for a few days – sometimes eight to ten in cold weather – before being drawn and plucked, or it

will taste like chicken. During hanging, the flesh develops a mature, distinctive flavour.

CHOOSING AND COOKING GAME

Fresh game should have an attractive appearance and hardly any smell – any odour should not be unpleasant. The skin should be dry, not moist. Never buy birds which were shot in the breast, as the flesh will be inedible.

All game birds are delicious simply roasted. Deglaze the caramelized juices in the pan with a little water, and you can hardly go wrong. Furred game, like venison or hare, always needs a sauce to match the original flavour.

SCIENTIST'S NOTES

Just as a domestic chicken or turkey's legs are darker in colour because it is the leg muscles that are used most by these birds, so the flesh of a game bird is darker in colour all over because of all the muscular activity involved in flying.

FISH

Before the health and diet revolution, fish eating was largely limited to Fridays. Now, however, many people are discovering how to cook this delightful source of protein. What better place to find it, you might think, than Britain, surrounded as it is by water and an abundance of fish?

However, in my experience, there are two types of fish available in Britain. One type is that from trawlers, which mode of fishing destroys marine life and threatens several species of fish with extinction. Just imagine the tons of bruised frozen fish of dubious freshness that come from those huge ships, often after four or five days' storage on ice. It is these fish which are most often found in shops in the guise of 'fresh fish'.

The other, less accessible type – but the truly *fresh* fish – come from the tiny number of small boats operated by individual fishermen who respect the sea and its bounty. Their fish arrives in the market within one day, fresh and unbruised.

Unfortunately, this type of fishing is considered too expensive, and most of the catch ends up in France (although I buy my fish from a small network of fishermen in Cornwall, the Isle of Wight and Scotland). With luck, and your help, these small suppliers – a new addition to the British market – will continue to flourish.

Another difference to be found in British fish is that between farmed and wild fish. When testing two turbot, one farmed and one wild, the difference was staggering. The flesh of the farmed fish was like cottonwool, soft, flaky and deadly white. The texture of the wild fish was firm, appetizing and creamier in colour. The *taste* of the former was undefined and bland.

The only successfully farmed fish is salmon, which offers the consumer a relatively good-quality fish at a very low price. Off season at Le Manoir we choose Glenarm salmon, which are kept free in locks and take their food naturally.

HOW TO RECOGNIZE FRESH FISH

In Japan, fish is only considered fresh when it jumps over the counter; our criteria are rather less stringent and so we must rely on other indications of freshness.

The appearance of a fish should be attractive; the eyes clear and bright, not glazed. The scales should be shiny, steely and undamaged, the gills should be bright red, and the flesh firm to the touch. There should be no unattractive odour. If the fish looks or smells unpleasant, do not buy it – and tell your fishmonger why; quality and service will only improve if you are critical.

HOW TO RECOGNIZE FRESH SHELLFISH

The shells must be tightly closed, or snap firmly shut at the slightest touch; if not, the shellfish are probably dead, so do not buy them. Dying shellfish close slowly and not tightly. Do not buy these either. Really fresh shellfish should be heavy with sea water. Less than fresh shellfish are not only unpalatable gastronomically, they can also cause food poisoning.

Crustaceans (especially lobsters and langoustines) should be bought alive, or the serum which holds the flesh together will slowly flow out, causing the flesh to quickly deteriorate and become like cottonwool when cooked.

SERVICE

A final word about fishmongers. If customers receive poor service, it is because they do not demand any better. A good fishmonger should clean and open scallops and oysters for you and should cater for special requirements such as boning, filleting, gutting and scaling – all at no extra charge. Always ask for special orders well in advance.

SCIENTIST'S NOTES

Fish live in a world where they are particularly free from the effects of gravity, therefore their muscles have developed in a way which is different from land animals. The muscle fibres are shorter than meat, they have very little fat, and very little connective tissue or collagen – the gristly stuff which can make meat chewy – so the flesh is very fragile. As a result, fish needs very little cooking, just enough to set or denature the protein of the muscle fibres.

Fish also need to be cooked when very fresh. Their flesh can go off very quickly because the temperature of the fishmonger's slab or your fridge is much the same as that of the water in which they lived. The enzymes therefore can continue working inside the chilled flesh, 'eating' or digesting the flesh.

Anyone who finds fishy odours off-putting can get rid of the offending smells by poaching fish in any bouillon containing an acid – in the form of wine, vinegar, lemon juice, beer and so on. Fishy smells are caused by simple molecules related to ammonia which are easily neutralized by acids.

EGGS

All the recipes in this book use standard or medium eggs, size 3.

In the kitchen, eggs are part of many cooking

processes and techniques; they are as versatile as they are magical, with thickening, absorbing, stabilizing, aerating and lifting capabilities. They also help to clarify a stock (see p. 42).

In the majority of cases, the fresher the eggs are, the better. Only when the eggs need to be whipped should you use older eggs. When eggs are older, some of their water content has evaporated, leaving the white more viscous, thus more whippable.

Always buy free-range eggs as they will lend the dish a better flavour and a more appetizing colour. Traditionally, cooks use only egg yolks to bind a sauce. But egg whites too are a binding agent, as they coagulate – as in quiches, meringues, mousselines and soufflés. Their flavour, however, is much weaker than that of egg yolks.

SCIENTIST'S NOTES

About two-thirds of the egg is the white which is composed of 10 per cent protein and 80 per cent water. The yolk is half water, about 35 per cent fats and 15 per cent proteins. So a size 3 egg (see below) weighing about 60 g (or 2¼ oz), consists roughly of 46 g water, 7 g fats and 7 g proteins. Among the fats (or lipids), are the lecithins (2 g), noted as powerful emulsifiers, and cholesterol (0.2 g) which has been regarded as harmful to health. However, it is now generally accepted that 'dietary' cholesterol is far less harmful than the cholesterol the body manufactures from saturated 'dietary' fats. There seems to be no longer a justification for the Draconian rule of 'one egg per week'.

Egg sizes: Size (0) 75g and over
       (1) 70–75 g
       (2) 65–70 g
       (3) 60–65 g
       (4) 55–60 g
       (5) 50–55 g
       (6) 45–50 g
       (7) under 45 g

Eggs contain a third component – air. A small pocket of air is responsible for the shell breaking when you are boiling eggs: if the eggs are heated too rapidly, the air has no time to diffuse through the tiny holes in the shell, and air expansion breaks the shell. On the other hand, this air pocket is useful when trying to assess the freshness of eggs. Put an egg in a large quantity of water: if the volume of air is small, as in fresh eggs, the egg will stay on the bottom of the container; but if it is not fresh, some water will have evaporated, the air pocket will have grown, and the egg will float.

EGG YOLKS

Egg yolk is often used as an *emulsifier*. Many recipes call for the intimate mixing of watery ingredients with oily or fatty ingredients. As a rule oil and water don't mix, and the oil just floats back to the surface. But egg yolks contain compounds such as lecithin which acts a bit like soap, enabling water and oil to be mixed. These emulsifiers tend to be large molecules, parts of which are attracted to water and other parts attracted to oil.

One theory is that the oil-loving parts of the emulsifier embed themselves into the oil droplets, leaving their water-loving parts sticking out. The 'sticking-out' bits prevent other oil droplets coming too close and joining together. With sauces such as mayonnaise you first of all add very small quantities of oil to the beaten egg yolks and vinegar. At the start there should be much more emulsifier than oil, so it can rapidly and completely coat the oil droplets and make a stable emulsion. Soon you can add larger amounts of oil because the well-dispersed tiny droplets, already present, help break up the larger drops as you beat.

EGG WHITES AND FOAM

Foams made from egg white or albumen are very popular, especially for creating dishes with a light and delicate texture. As a food, egg white is unusual in that it is alkaline, while most other foods are to some extent acidic. The proteins in the white are normally tight little balls. When they are beaten they unwrap, elongate and form a web-like structure. In a sense the proteins are being 'cooked' by the beating; they are losing their original nature. If you add a little acid such as cream of tartar or lemon juice, you will reduce the alkalinity of the egg white and make the foam more stable and less prone to lumpiness and draining.

MILK

Milk represents a major ingredient in our diet – poured over cereals, drunk in cups of tea and coffee – but it also enters the composition of many dishes, especially desserts such as ice-cream, custard, pancakes, rice puddings, etc. It is particularly high in calcium, but it is also fairly high in fat.

COMPOSITION

Protein	3.5%
Fats	2.6%
Minerals	0.9%
Carbohydrates	5.0%
Vitamins	1.0% (A, B and D)
Water	87.0%

There are many different types of milk to be bought. Most is cows' milk, but ewes' and goats' milks are also available. Cows' milk is mostly sold pasteurized, and contains about 4 per cent butterfat. Other milk types have varying degrees of fat content, ranging from the richest, Jersey or Channel Islands, with up to 8 per cent fat, to skimmed, with a fat content of about 0.1 per cent. Raw or unpasteurized milk (*lait cru* in France) is occasionally available, but only from farms which are registered for this purpose by the Ministry of Agriculture, Fisheries and Food. It can be sold either at the farm gate or through a licensed dairy retailer. Its flavour is good, but it is less safe for the vulnerable than pasteurized.

SCIENTIST'S NOTES

The fat in milk is in the form of globules ranging from 1–10 microns (thousandths of millimetres), and are dispersed throughout the water. Milk is an emulsion, but not a very stable one. The larger fat globules tend to rise to the top and after a day or two one finds a layer of thinnish cream containing 15–20 per cent fat. Before the advent of the centrifuge which could efficiently separate the oil globules from the other, higher density, components, this was the usual process for obtaining cream (see below).

In homogenized milk, in which all the fat globules have been reduced to 1–2 microns, the cream does not rise.

CREAM

Cream is the butterfat content of whole cows' milk, separated from the water. The principal difference between the various types of cream – whipping, double, clotted, single, soured and *crème fraîche* – is the balance of water and butterfat. This will make them liquid or of a very thick consistency. Other differences concern the way they have been made and for how long they have been matured, and these influence taste as well.

COMPOSITION

• *Single cream* contains not less than 18 per cent butterfat. It cannot be whipped due to there being too little butterfat and should not be used in sauces as it can separate whilst boiling.

• *Whipping cream* contains not less than 35 per cent butterfat. As its name indicates, it is perfect for whipping, which will change its volume and texture. Whipped cream, sweetened or unsweetened, can be used as a dessert accompaniment, and is very often added to mousse and charlotte mixtures to lighten them.

• *Double cream* contains not less than 48 per cent butterfat. It can be whipped, but not too much or it will turn into butter! It can enrich sauces and soups, but may curdle or separate if boiled or mixed with acid ingredients.

• *Clotted cream* contains not less than 55 per cent butterfat. It is already very thick, so is used just as it is, not whipped.

• *Soured cream* and *crème fraîche* are single creams which contain about 20 per cent butterfat, but have souring culture added to them, and they are matured.

SCIENTIST'S NOTES

Cream contains some protein molecules (called surface active molecules) which act a bit like washing-up liquid. If the cream is thick enough (with at least 30 per cent butterfat), it is possible to whip in lots of small bubbles: the more the better, because the forces which make the bubbles stable act over only very small distances. The tiny bubbles are surrounded by a film containing fat droplets, kept stable by the special surface active molecules.

BUTTER

All butters nowadays are made from pasteurized cream, and are manufactured under very strict health and safety regulations.

COMPOSITION

Fat	82%
Water	16%
Soluble ingredients from the milk	2%
Vitamins	A and D

I strongly favour unsalted butter as its flavour is more delicate and it can be heated to a high temperature.

Salted butter will keep better but has many drawbacks:

- the salty taste often does not suit pastry or savoury recipes – sauces, for instance
- it contains many more impurities than unsalted butter
- there are more solids in the whey of the milk, which impart a coarse taste to the butter
- the impurities and solids in salted butter are the reason why it cannot be heated to a very high temperature without burning.

Always wrap butter after using, as it will very easily absorb other flavours.

SCIENTIST'S NOTES

Butter is made by churning cream. Cream is an emulsion of fat droplets dispersed in water. As the cream is churned the fat droplets soften slightly and start to join up as they continuously bump together. Gradually larger lumps of fat form until the original arrangement of fat in water has swapped round leaving droplets of water dispersed in fat. Buttermilk, which is largely water, is drawn off and you are left with lumps of butter.

Why is it that butter left unwrapped in the fridge can pick up unpleasant and unwanted smells? It is related to a process used in the perfume industry, named 'enfleurage': freshly picked flowers are put on a fat layer for some hours or days, then the fat is distilled to separate out the volatile perfume molecules which have been trapped in it. This effect is due to the hydrophobic (fear of water) nature of many aromatic molecules: they dissolve badly in water, but easily in fat. The same effect can happen in your fridge: any strong smell, due to molecules, can be trapped in unwrapped butter (or indeed eggs or chocolate).

The technique of enfleurage can be used to good effect in the kitchen, though: utilizing the fragrance of herbs and other aromatics in savoury butters and oils, and in marinades.

GELATINE

Gelatine, in sheets or as a powder, is a substance produced by the boiling of cattle bones and other trimmings; in this process tough collagen dissolves into the gluey, water-soluble gelatine. This can actually be used as a glue, but is normally used culinarily to cause liquids to set. This gelatinization of collagen is the same process that makes cuts of stewing meats tender.

Young animals tend to have a greater amount of collagen in their muscles than more mature animals, so calf's feet are most often used to make the 'best' kind of gelatine, aspic. Veal stock is also the most unctuous.

Gelatine leaves, which are much easier to use, are stocked by Waitrose. Powdered gelatine is difficult to weigh, so I would suggest you use leaves – they're each 2 g in weight – and soften them in cold water before adding to the hot liquid called for in the recipe.

SCIENTIST'S NOTES

Collagen is often described as a coiled coil. When meat or bones are cooked for a long time in water, the triple helixes of proteins that make the collagen are dissociated and the protein molecules are separated. But they later tend to form triple helixes again. This is the basis of gelatine jellies, systems where a small quantity of gelatine molecules form a network capturing a lot of water molecules (and other molecules dissolved into the trapped water). Gelatine molecules dissolved in hot water stay apart, because of their molecular motion, but when the temperature is reduced, there comes a stage where the binding energy of the protein molecules is higher than the motion energy. Thus when the proteins meet, they stick.

A gelatine jelly is always better made at a medium temperature rather than a low temperature: when the same gelatine solution is heated, divided into two parts, and one kept in the fridge, one in the kitchen at room temperature, the jelly of the latter is firmer. Molecules that meet and bind loosely cannot move any longer when the temperature is too low; the binding is weak. On the other hand, at room temperature, loosely bound molecules have enough energy to unbind, then bind again more firmly.

YEAST

Yeasts are single-celled, microscopic fungi. There are many kinds of yeast, some good for us, some bad, but the ones we use in bread-, beer- and wine-making are known as sugar fungi because of their ability to digest glucose and produce alcohol, carbon dioxide and energy.

Yeasts can live with or without oxygen, but they only multiply (which they do by splitting in half) in the presence of oxygen. When a dried yeast, for instance, is mixed with warm water and some sugar (for food), it is activated, and begins to multiply in the freely available oxygen. The thick foam on top of the mixture attests to this growth. Once the yeast mixture is mixed into the dough, there is less oxygen available, so by and large the yeast moves into its anaerobic stage (surviving without oxygen). It still has enough energy to live, but it lacks the massive amounts of energy required to reproduce.

What it then does is produce carbon dioxide which fills and expands pockets of air in the dough (produced by gluten and by kneading). The more

and more finely the air and carbon dioxide are distributed through a dough, the smoother the final texture of the baked bread will be, thus the importance of kneading and proving. (See also the Scientist's Note on bread-making on pp. 49–50.)

The temperatures are important as regards yeast. Yeasts cannot sustain high temperatures because their proteins would coagulate; they are killed when the centre of the dough or loaf reaches about 60°C (140°F). Their metabolic activity is reduced, but not stopped, by a low temperature, so uncooked yeast doughs can be chilled, even frozen. Yeast metabolism comes from a lot of intertwined chemical processes, and as these processes increase in velocity with a warm temperature, so they are reduced by a cold temperature.

FLOUR

Most of the flour we use is made from wheat. For the cook, wheat flour has two vital components – starch or carbohydrates, and proteins. These latter form something called gluten when mixed with water, and without gluten there would be no such thing as a raised bread. Wheat is the only grain which has a gluten strong enough to produce raised breads: breads made from rye, for instance, are characterized by their dense, solid texture, and this is because rye contains very little and very weak gluten.

Gluten enables a wheat flour dough to change its shape while being kneaded and to resume its shape when allowed to rest. As the dough is kneaded the gluten molecules unfold and realign themselves into less random shapes, which accounts for a dough starting off rough and then becoming smooth and elastic. If worked for too long, though, gluten can make dough tough, which is why one should handle a pastry as little as possible.

Wheat flour is up to 75 per cent starch and the proteins (gluten) vary from about 7 per cent to 14 per cent. It is the amount of gluten protein which determines which flour you should use. Cakes and biscuits, which are crumbly, need a small amount of gluten, therefore a plain flour is called for. On the other hand, bread with its open springy texture (and indeed pasta) needs the higher amount of gluten, which can be found in strong flours.

OILS

OLIVE OIL

Olive oils are extremely healthy as they are mono-unsaturated, and most of them have a wonderful flavour. Buy carefully, though, as labelling is still not controlled strictly enough in Europe.

• *Extra virgin olive oil* consists of cold first-pressing olive oil from olives that have been freshly harvested, possibly by hand. This makes the olive oil very low in acidity (less than 1 per cent). It is normally sold either as a 'must' (unfiltered) or filtered. The best producers filter it naturally without further pressure, but this is not required by law. The legal specification requires that this olive oil has this kind of acidity and that it has not been chemically manipulated. It is not yet required that the oil comes from a specific region or country. Therefore it is normal that the industries sell (quite legally) some extra virgin oil 'bottled in Provence' or 'in Tuscany' that comes from Spain or Morocco, or elsewhere in the Mediterranean area, so beware.

Extra virgin olive oils are the ones with most flavour, and are best in dressings.

• *Virgin olive oil* is cold pressed, but has an acidity between 1 and 3 per cent. This higher acidity derives from a series of factors, like over-ripened olives, or too long a waiting time between harvest and pressing (olives ferment very rapidly).

Virgin oil is not so flavourful as extra virgin oils, but is good for cooking.

• *Olive oil,* plain and simple, is oil which cannot be sold in the two categories above, or it may be specifically produced in order to be sold cheaply.

It derives from a hot pressure, which squeezes out much more oil from the pulp, or from a third or fourth pressing of the pulp from the first cold pressing. It is normally refined chemically to make it edible and commercial.

Some people use it for frying or other purposes in the kitchen. I, personally, do not like it.

NON-SCENTED OILS

Non-scented oils are useful in the kitchen as they do not impart any flavour of their own to the food being cooked.

• *Groundnut oil* is a general purpose oil which can be used for vinaigrettes and frying. *Sunflower and grapeseed oils* are good, too; the latter is good to use in mayonnaise as it does not congeal when left in a cool place. *Vegetable oil* is the one to use for deep-frying as it can reach a very high temperature without smoking.

SCENTED OILS

These are useful in moderation. *Sesame oil* is the one to use in Eastern dishes. *Walnut and hazelnut oils* add their inimitable flavours to dressings, but they must be mixed with a non-scented oil, otherwise they will be too overpowering.

VINEGARS

• *Red and white wine vinegars* are the most commonly used for sauces and dressings. Always buy the best quality.

• *Sherry or xérès vinegar* is made from sherry wine, and can, of course, be used in dressings. It is also very good in sauces where Madeira or port are used.

• *Aceto balsamico,* or *balsamic vinegar*, originates from Italy, and it is made from grapes which are picked very late so they have a very high concentration of sugar; these are then crushed, cooked to stop the fermentation, and left to mature in oak and other wood casks for a minimum of 10 years and up to 50 years. Of course, the older the better.

Balsamic has a balance of sweetness and acidity which is very pleasant and unusual. Its colour is dark, mostly due to the ageing process. Some aged balsamic vinegars are so thick and fragrant they are like a sauce in themselves.

• *Raspberry, passion fruit and kiwi vinegars* are by-products of *nouvelle cuisine* and were invented mostly for their novelty value – and used for the same reason. If you use these highly flavoured vinegars, add only one part to five parts of white wine vinegar.

SCIENTIST'S NOTES

Vinegar is a 5–6 per cent solution of acetic acid in water, containing various naturally occurring or added flavours. It is usually made from alcoholic liquids by the addition of a culture of the bacterium *Acetofactor aceti*, which converts ethyl alcohol into acetic acid.

Other vinegars include malt vinegar (from fermented malted barley, which is beer, essentially), cider vinegar, Champagne and rice wine vinegar.

SUGAR

Culinary sugar is sucrose, a pure, simple carbohydrate, which is obtained from sugar cane or sugar beet. White sugar is refined, with its molasses entirely removed; brown sugar can be unrefined, or can be white refined sugar with a molasses coating. Sugar contains calories far in excess of its nutrients – virtually nil – and the carbohydrate energy boost it gives is instantaneous but brief.

Sugar is used primarily as a sweetener, but it also has other chemical roles to play in the kitchen.

SCIENTIST'S NOTES

First, as a crystal without water, sugar can draw water from meat or fruits by the phenomenon of osmosis. If you want to make fruit preserves, put the fruits in a syrup, not in pure water. If fruit were put in pure water, because of its sugar content, water would enter the fruits and make them explode. In too

concentrated a syrup, the water of the fruits would be drawn out and the fruits would be too firm. A medium syrup is best.

Sugar is also used to cure salmon, for instance: water from the surface of the fish is drawn out by sugar, by the same osmotic effect as above, and micro-organisms are killed because they are deprived of their water.

Sugar participates in many important culinary reactions such as Maillard browning (see p. 19). When heated with amino acids, it reacts and generates molecules that give a brown colour and taste. Maillard reactions are responsible for the culinary interest of meat crackling, of bread crumb, of chocolate and coffee (because of the roasting of the beans). It is not to be confused with caramel, which comes only from a complex degradation of sugar alone. In both cases there is a browning and the appearance of a pleasant taste, but the chemistry is completely different. To prove that Maillard browning is not just caramelization of sugar, heat together some chicken and a sugar syrup. The chicken will brown long before the sugar syrup (and at a lower temperature).

Finally, sugar is useful for ices, because the increased viscosity of the water solution limits the formation of ice crystals. A frozen syrup keeps its texture at low temperatures.

SALT

Salt is sodium chloride, and is available as rock salt (mined from dried-up underground saline lakes) or as sea salt (crystals of salt extracted from sea water). Table and kitchen salts are ground and refined rock salts.

Salt has various effects on our bodies. It is essential in the diet of all animals, including humans, but too much is said to be a contributory factor in high blood pressure and heart disease. To little – such as when salt and water are lost in the form of heavy sweating – may cause heat exhaustion. Salt is one of the most familiar tastes, and one of the most easily perceived by the sensory buds of the tongue and mouth. It enhances the tastes of foods.

Some people like more salt, some people like less, thus the usual recipe instruction, 'season to taste'. Salt is also used to cure foods (see p. 41).

Never salt a stock if the stock is going to be reduced – this would concentrate the saltiness. And never season a sauce *last*. If you add salt after pepper, spices, lemon juice, a red wine reduction, etc., you will have a mixture of flavours and it will be difficult to judge the amount of salt needed, and you could ruin the sauce by adding too much. Salt first, *then* add the other flavourings.

SCIENTIST'S NOTES

Salt in a solution modifies the temperature of boiling. Instead of boiling at 100°C (212°F), water with salt boils at a higher temperature, 105°C (221°F), for instance, depending on the salt concentration. In practice, this elevation does not change anything, but a corollary is that salt does not evaporate. As water with dissolved salt is heated, only the water is boiling and reducing, so that the salt concentration increases in the solution. If you added only 2 grams of salt to 1 litre (1¾ pints) of stock, after a tenfold reduction, the salt concentration would be 20 grams per litre – which is a lot!

Salt is frequently used in the kitchen for its osmotic effect: when salt touches wet mushrooms, for instance, or cucumber, meat, or anything containing a lot of water, the water molecules are drawn out of the food. This is very useful: if your mushrooms are too wet or soggy, cover them with salt for some 20 minutes or so: some of their water will be eliminated, and you can rinse them briefly before cooking. In this way, the mushrooms firm up slightly, but none of their perfume is lost.

PEPPER

Peppercorns are the fruit of a tropical vine, native to Asia. The fruit is picked when it is green and then dried (for black peppercorns) or brined (for green peppercorns). For white peppercorns, the fruit is allowed to mature on the vine, then it is soaked in water, its red skin removed, and the seed is dried. White is less pungent than black

and, unless stated otherwise, this is what I use in the recipes in this book.

Try to use freshly ground pepper rather than the already ground variety. All spices are at their most fragrant when newly ground.

VANILLA

Whenever possible, use the real thing. Before you buy, make sure that the pod is moist; pods that have dried out will have lost much of their flavour. Buy up to six at a time, and store them in sugar in an airtight container; this will give you vanilla sugar.

For the best results in cooking custards etc., split the pod lengthways, scrape out the seeds from the inside, and add these scrapings to the liquid. Chop and add the pod as well. This may not be economical, but it makes the most delicious custard.

For a lighter flavour, infuse a whole pod in the milk, then wash and dry it, and store it in caster sugar for later use. This way, a vanilla pod can be used at least two or three times. Split the pod when using it for the last time.

Never, never use vanilla flavouring. Please avoid, as it is too often associated with the worst kind of chemistry.

You may, however, be able to find good-quality vanilla *essence*. Check thoroughly before buying it, though it can never replace the sweet flavour of the real thing.

SCIENTIST'S NOTE

The characteristic smell of the vanilla pod comes from a variety of components, a major one of which is the chemical compound, vanillin. This latter can be synthesized, and vanilla 'flavouring' and cheaper extracts are probably based on this (and contain other ingredients such as sugar). Good vanilla 'essences' are likely to be extracted to an extent from real vanilla pods and thus contain some or even most of the other compounds present in small quantities which give the vanilla pod its full aroma. Thus, to use a cheap vanilla flavouring is like listening to one note instead of a full chord, to one instrumentalist rather than a complete orchestra.

WINES FOR COOKING

If you need white wine for a sauce, use a good-quality dry white, but not an expensive wine such as Chablis; this will be a waste of money as it will lose most of its characteristics whilst boiling. On the other hand, if you use a 'nasty' wine, the sauce will possess every single one of its characteristics.

The same applies to red wine. Try to obtain a wine which has lots of body and not too much tannin – for example, a Cabernet Sauvignon from Bulgaria or the Napa Valley, or a good French table wine from Corbières or Côtes du Rhône.

If using Madeira, choose a dry one for the best results. And if using a port, choose ruby port for the best results.

Cooking Techniques

Here, you will find helpful notes on all the techniques used in this book.

BOILING

Boiling involves food being heated by convection currents in hot water – at a maximum, of course, of 100°C (212°F). Water cooking – and this includes the variants of boiling, such as blanching, steaming, poaching and braising – is a moist method, and therefore there are no Maillard reactions (see p. 19).

Boiling is a technique rarely applied to animal proteins, and is more relevant to vegetables. They are cooked quickly in plenty of rapidly boiling salted water, and for a very short time. This gives a firm and pleasant texture, keeps the colour, and ensures that the vegetables will retain most of their nutrients. Most green vegetables (such as mangetout, broccoli, asparagus, French beans) are cooked in this way, as well as potatoes, Jerusalem artichokes, etc.

The amount of water used should always be four or five times the volume of the vegetables you are cooking, so that the water can regain its boil very quickly when the vegetables are plunged in. The amount of salt used is the reverse of what you might expect. For example, asparagus only takes 5–6 minutes' cooking, so because the salt does not have time to permeate the vegetable, the salt content of the water should be quite high – 20 g ($^3/_4$ oz) to the litre ($1^3/_4$ pints). The water should be kept at a full boil and the pan should always be uncovered; volatile acids contained in all green vegetables will escape and if the pan is covered these will be recycled in the water and discolour the vegetable.

SCIENTIST'S NOTES

The green colour of vegetables such as beans, cabbage or spinach is caused by chlorophyll, the molecule which allows plants to capture sunlight and make sugar from carbon dioxide in the air and water from the soil. But chlorophyll is easily damaged by heat, by acids and by enzymes. It loses its bright green colour and so cooked vegetables often look dull greyish-green. Acids and enzymes are present all the time in plant cells, but their bad effects are activated during cooking. In a large amount of boiling water, at a high temperature, the enzymes will be rapidly destroyed.

———

Vegetables such as green beans can be dropped into cold water as soon as they are cooked. They will then be stable and can be rapidly reheated just before you want to serve them.

BLANCHING

Blanching is a literal 'boiling', and could be said to be a 'technique for other techniques'. It involves boiling foods in water for minutes only, not necessarily to *cook* the foods, but to prepare them for the next step in their preparation or cooking.

Vegetables, for instance, are often blanched before they are frozen. This greatly reduces the activity of enzymes in them, an activity which can lead to spoilage or to the vegetable rotting. The vegetables are then plunged into cold water to stop the cooking process. Blanching in this case lengthens the safe storage period.

Pieces of offal are often blanched to remove the pungency of the smell, or to facilitate the removal of the outside membrane or skin: the blanching firms up the offal marginally, which coagulates the membrane. Blanching also reduces the activity of the enzymes which cause spoilage. Offal often benefits from the minimal firming of texture that is caused by the brief boiling. Always plunge into cold water to arrest the cooking.

A number of fruits are blanched in order to loosen their skins – among them tomatoes and peaches. Herbs are blanched mainly to tone down aggressively strong flavours and smells.

STEAMING

This cooking technique is intimately related to boiling. Food is cooked over water at a rolling boil, at boiling point – when the water molecules are changing to gas, or steam – and thus the temperature is slightly higher than the boiling point of water. This rise in temperature compensates for the slightly less efficient contact between steam and food (as opposed to water, which would wholly surround the food).

Foods such as vegetables and thin pieces of protein are cooked fairly rapidly by steam from boiling water or stock. It is a technique most suitable for delicate foods, as they remain stationary while being cooked instead of rolling around in liquid, so are less liable to break up.

Steaming does not involve Maillard reactions (see p. 19).

A proper steamer is not entirely necessary, as one can be improvised.

BRAISING

The technique of braising is a cornerstone of peasant and family cooking. The result is wholesome, and although cooking is usually lengthy, it is very easy to achieve and demands little attention or knowledge. The meat cuts used are usually the ones which cannot be roasted as they would be too tough. They require long cooking to tenderize them, but they can be as delicious as the prime cuts used in roasting. These include shin of beef, ox cheeks, hock of pork, shoulder and neck of lamb.

See Fish (p. 138), Poultry (p. 170), Meat (p. 190, 199, 201) and Game (p. 201).

Braising involves what I call 'cooking by exchange'. Basically the meat is cooked in liquid in the oven (or, occasionally, on top of the stove), at a very low temperature. The meat is enriched by the liquid, and the liquid – which becomes the sauce – is enriched by the meat.

There are two distinct methods of braising. One involves browning the meat or poultry first (see p. 36). This browning, in hot fat, gives colour and flavour, which in turn will lend flavour and colour to the sauce. Diced vegetables can also be browned to add extra flavour and colour.

Many braises do not have an initial browning or searing, usually because the dish should be paler in colour.

THE LIQUID
According to which meat you are using, you may need red wine, white wine, light or brown chicken stock or simply water.

MARINATING
Very often the meat to be braised is marinated with wines, aromatics and herbs etc., to give extra and more complex flavours. The meat is then strained, and patted dry to remove excess moisture.

The acidity of the wine will also help to tenderize the meat. When I use wine I prefer to first reduce it by half, which lends a more intense flavour and colour to the meat. Equally I find that the flavour is better and more gentle in taste, as a proportion of the alcohol has been removed.

HEAT
Braised food is cooked in the oven. The heat should always be low. As the meat protein will start to coagulate and cook from 55°C (131°F), a temperature of about 140°C/275°F/Gas 1 is perfect to cook the meat and produce the desired melting texture. All braises take quite a long time, but the results are well worth it.

So long as there is water in the casserole, the temperature will be 100°C (212°F), irrespective of the oven temperature. However, if the meat is cooked at too *high* a temperature, the effect is usually disastrous. The high heat will evaporate the water in the meat tissues, making the meat dry and hard. The meat nearest the sides of the casserole may caramelize as well.

PANS
Use thick cast-iron casseroles with lids. The cast-

iron conducts the heat well and also distributes it well. The lid will prevent evaporation and reduction of the liquid.

BINDING

Often it is recommended that flour be added at the very start, to coat the meat, or during the browning process. The addition of flour at this stage will absorb all the fat, and then this will be hidden in the sauce. It may give extra flavour, but it will be at the expense of lightness. Cooking juices *without* any form of thickening or binding will be thin, although delicious. The dish can, of course, be eaten as it is, but you might want to create a more full-bodied sauce, and this I prefer to do at the end. Remove any excess fat from the juices, dilute a little arrowroot or cornflour with water, and then add the mixture to the juices gradually, heating gently, until the sauce reaches the desired thickness.

LARDING

Many believe meat cuts for braising need to be larded (with strips of fat) to help moisten them and make them tender. I believe there is enough fatty connective tissue within braising cuts (they are not prime cuts, after all) which will gelatinize whilst cooking and make the meat tender and moist.

POACHING

The technique of poaching involves immersing food in barely simmering, usually salted, water or meat, vegetable or fish stock.

Fish, poultry, meat, vegetables, pasta and eggs can all be cooked in this way. Again, like braising, some types of poaching are examples of 'cooking by exchange'.

Fish or meat cooked in an aromatic broth at just under simmering point allows both food and liquid to enrich each other during the cooking process. Generally, though, for meat and fish, poaching is a quicker technique than braising partly because it is used on better quality fish and meat.

HEAT

The stock should reach barely simmering point, which is just below boiling point, 90°C (194°F). The heat will slowly permeate the cut of fish and cook it well; at the same time the flavour of the stock will be imparted to the fish. If the stock, however, is brought to a harsh boil, the flesh will tense up and as a result the fish will very likely be overcooked outside and undercooked at the centre.

SCIENTIST'S NOTES

The meat or fish cooked in a bouillon or broth is enriched by the aromatics infused in the broth. In the first stage of poaching, the proteins of the muscle cells coagulate: this expels the juices within the flesh, creating 'cavities' between the cells. As the cooking continues, these cavities are replenished by the aromatic cooking liquid.

COOKING IN A BAIN-MARIE

Certain foods cannot be cooked with direct heat, as they would either become grainy or curdle and spoil. So, to control the heat, we cook these foods in a water-bath or *bain-marie*. The foods involved are usually egg mixtures, such as crème brûlée, crème caramel and savoury or sweet mousses.

The food is first placed into buttered moulds, terrines or dishes which are then put into a tray of barely simmering water. The water should come two-thirds of the way up the height of the mould. This height is important because otherwise the foods in the moulds would be exposed to a dry heat in the oven, which would entirely defeat the object of the exercise.

The oven should be set at about 110°C (225°F or Gas $^1/_4$), which will mean that the temperature of the water around the foods in the moulds will be about 85°C (185°F). As most protein – whether fish, meat or egg – cooks from 63°C up to 76°C (145–168°F), this water temperature will be ample to allow the foods to coagulate and cook to a perfect set. Eventually the water would reach boiling point – 100°C (212°F) – but cooking in a water-bath is usually a short-lived process, so the heat remains gentler.

A sheet of perforated greaseproof paper placed over the moulds in the water-bath in the oven is useful. This will prevent the surface of the foods from drying. Ensure it is loose, though, otherwise the heat will build up under it and the foods will overheat and spoil.

You can also cook in a water-bath or bain-marie on top of the stove – custards and creams, for instance – and a water-bath is also useful for keeping delicate foods warm. A saucepan holding a bowl, whose bottom is touching simmering water, also serves as a water-bath.

SCIENTIST'S NOTES

The *bain-marie*, or Mary's bath, links cooking and the mysterious art of alchemy, for it was a third-century alchemist, Maria or Miriam of Alexandria, who is credited with its invention. She realized that water has some very unusual properties. It acts as a buffer to heat because it absorbs large amounts of energy and gives only a small rise in temperature. The same amount of energy needed to raise the temperature of a kilogram of water by 1 degree will raise the temperature of a kilogram of iron by 10 degrees. So, a *bain-marie* is a slow, gentle form of cooking.

SWEATING

This is an important technique involving fat, rather than water, and it should be more properly understood. It is usually applied to vegetables such as shallots and onions, when they are chopped. There is a minimal amount of fat, and the heat should be as gentle as possible so there is no coloration whatsoever. This gentle heat will slowly transform the harshness of the vegetables' raw flavours, and convert the starches into sugar, bringing out the hidden flavours. It will also change the texture of the vegetable from crisp to soft.

SCIENTIST'S NOTES

The purpose of sweating hard plant tissue such as onion is to make it tender, remove unpleasant odours and render it suitable

as a base for stews etc. When plants are heated to 70–100°C (158–212°F), the cells literally explode, the volatile compounds evaporate and the starch molecules gradually disintegrate into their basic units, the glucose molecules.

SEARING AND PAN-FRYING

Whether fish, meat or vegetable, only small pieces are truly pan-fried on top of the stove, on direct heat. Larger pieces are first pan-fried on top of the stove, finishing in the oven; they also are given a resting time (see the examples below).

Fat is the cooking medium; it prevents sticking and, once hot, it also helps the ingredients to have an intense flavour by browning them.

DOES BROWNING SEAR AND RETAIN THE JUICES?

For years, it was believed that sealing and browning of meat would prevent its juices from coming out. This was based on a theory posited by the German chemist, Baron Justus von Liebig. Modern scientists have other ideas, namely the Maillard reactions (see p. 19). I believe I have fair experience as a cook. I have found that by browning meat, the outside tightens up, and the albumen and the proteins coagulate to some extent, and in so doing prevent some juices from running out. I believe, despite the views of certain scientists whom I respect very much, that there is some truth in both theories!

HEAT

The degree of heat is extremely relevant for pan-frying: most often a medium heat is the best. The heat of the fat will brown the food too, lending delicious tastes and an appetizing colour. Any juices escaping will slowly be collected at the bottom of the pan and will caramelize; these help to create a delicious juice simply by diluting them with a little water.

COMMON MISTAKES

With too low a heat, the ingredient will not become brown. The juices will all escape, creating a messy beige food which would be half braised and half pan-fried.

Too high a heat will often cause the breakdown

of the fat, especially if you use butter. The fat will definitely brown the meat, but it will also, unfortunately, create a dryness which penetrates very deep into the fibres. This is due to the too-high temperature applied.

PANS

The pans for pan-frying should be just large enough to contain the ingredients, which prevents burning. I believe a thick-bottomed pan is preferable, as I have better heat conduction, hence more control. Non-stick pans are an ideal solution to the problems of sticking.

WHICH FAT TO USE?

According to which dish you are going to prepare, different fats can be used but, on the whole, I prefer either unsalted butter or olive oil.

If using butter, it must always be unsalted. It needs to be heated to the 'hazelnut' stage (170°C/338°F), when it foams and becomes a rich golden colour. This will help colour the meat or fish a rich brown. The main danger with butter is that you might overheat it; it will burn and lend a rather nasty taste to the ingredients. It will also be very indigestible.

If using olive oil, choose a good-quality one. An expensive extra virgin olive oil is not necessary as its chemistry and flavour will alter whilst cooking. While olive oil has many health qualities, it can also be heated up to 250°C (482°F) without breaking down. It imparts wonderful flavour to the foods cooked in it.

Other oils can of course be used. Sunflower, safflower, vegetable and sesame oil are all good, and all seed oils are polyunsaturated.

EXAMPLE: *Pan-frying a small cut of meat (escalope of veal)*

This can be done in one stage: pan-frying.

Heat unsalted butter until it foams and reaches the 'hazelnut' stage (see p. 58). Pan-fry the escalope for 3 minutes on each side until you have a good colour. Season with salt and pepper.

Put the escalope on a warm plate, remove most of the fat from the pan and add 4 tablespoons of water. Bring to the boil and scrape the juices caramelized in the bottom of the pan so they dilute and create a very aromatic juice. Pour on to the escalope.

EXAMPLE: *Pan-frying a thicker cut of meat (a beef medallion, 3.75 cm/1½ in thick)*

This is done in three stages: pan-frying, oven cooking, then resting.

The first stage is to brown the meat, the second is to complete the cooking in the oven, and the third, the resting time, which will allow the meat to relax and become more tender. During the resting process some juices will be released from the meat and thence can enrich the other juices.

Heat unsalted butter until it foams and reaches the 'hazelnut' stage (see p. 58). Pan-fry the beef for 3 minutes all over until you have a good colour on both faces of the meat, and the sides have been seared briefly. Spoon out most of the fat from the pan, season the meat with salt and pepper and place in the oven pre-heated to 220°C/425°F/Gas 7 for 3 minutes. Remove from the oven and from the pan, and rest the meat in between two warm plates for 5 minutes or cover with aluminium foil.

Add 4 tablespoons water to the cooking pan, bring to the boil, and scrape the juices caramelized on the bottom of the pan so they dilute and create a very aromatic juice. Add the juices that the meat has released to this. Pour over the medallion.

See also Fish (pp. 150, 154, 161–2), Poultry (p. 180), Meat (p. 210) and Offal (pp. 205, 214–15).

SCIENTIST'S NOTE

Pan-frying is based on the fact that oil and fats are very efficient in transferring heat from the pan to the food, and can be used in a wide temperature range up to about 250°C (482°F). The frying may be done in two stages: first at moderate heat, so that the heat may penetrate without the side in contact with the pan getting dry; then for the second stage, the temperature is increased so that the Maillard reaction may get under way. A sugar or starch molecule attaches itself to an amino acid, the resulting long molecule forms itself into a buckle and it is at this stage that the fat ceases to be a mere heat-transfer agent, and influences the properties of the meat, in particular the taste of the resulting Maillard compounds. (See also p. 19.)

SAUTEING

The principle of this technique is much the same as pan-frying, with or without browning of the food. Usually the foods sautéed are very small cuts of meat, fish or vegetables. The difference is that you stir the food whilst pan-frying it, so the heat is evenly distributed amongst all the pieces.

STIR-FRYING

This is more of a Chinese technique than a Western one, but it has now been adopted in our cooking. It uses very little oil, so is considered healthy. The meats and fish are cut into small slivers, the vegetables cut up small.

Stir-frying is done without browning. Pan-fry the food in hot fat (sesame or sunflower oil), shaking and stirring all the time, so that the food is cooked thoroughly but is still *al dente*.

DEEP-FRYING

Deep-frying is a technique which involves immersing foods in hot fat (groundnut or vegetable oil, or animal fat such as dripping or lard), to cook and brown them. Some very essential principles must be understood to obtain the best results.

- Clean fat must be used. Once a fat has been used, it should be strained for re-use.
- All foods must be thoroughly dried to remove extra moisture which may cause spitting.
- The amount of oil used must be at least three times the volume of food that you are deep-frying, so the heat loss of the fat is minimal.
- The temperature of the fat must be a minimum of 140°C (284°F) to colour and caramelize, but usually the frying temperatures are between 160 and 180°C (320 and 356°F). (See individual recipes in Starters, Fish and Desserts.) A tem-

perature of under 140°C (284°F) is too low, and will let the food absorb fat which will then become very heavy and unappetizing.

- The deep-frying pan must have very high sides so the fat is securely contained, and a basket and tongs or a slotted spoon must be used. Many fat fires are caused by pans with sides that are too low.
- The air over a deep-frying pan is very hot indeed, so avoid placing your hands or arms over the pan.
- The food should be carefully slid into the hot fat to prevent any splashes.

DEEP-FRYING WITH A COATING

Various coatings can be added to foods before deep-frying such as batter, breadcrumbs or flour. This is protective and provides a very moist interior and a crusty outside texture.

Most of these coatings contain both sugars and amino acids, and thus give rise to Maillard compounds. (See p. 19.)

DEEP-FRYING WITHOUT A COATING

A lot of vegetables can be deep-fried without a coating. With potatoes it is done in two stages, as for French fries or chips, and Pommes Soufflées. The chips are first deep-fried at a lower temperature in order to blanch them and basically cook them through. They are then cooled down (or they can be cooked on straightaway) and then browned in fat at a higher temperature so that they acquire a crusty texture and a pleasant appearance. This second frying evaporates all the water from the surface of the chips and makes them crisp.

Sprigs of herbs can also be fried without a coating. This should be done at a lower temperature to remove all the moisture and give the herbs a beautiful crispy texture. (See p. 243.)

SCIENTIST'S NOTES

It is vital to thoroughly dry any foods which are to be deep-fried. If the food is damp, the water which is suddenly heated to its boiling point of 100°C (212°F) will evaporate: when the steam occupies more space than the original liquid, this will force the oil outwards, making it spit. In addition, residual water on the foods will infiltrate the oil, reducing its temperature.

ROASTING

Roasts are rarely done better than at home, because the domestic cook does not try to add all sorts of exotic touches. True beauty often depends on simplicity.

Traditionally roasting was done on a spit, but today it is mostly done in an oven. Roasting is the cooking of prime cuts of meat by dry heat. Small and medium joints are first seared and browned on top of the stove, then they are roasted in the oven. They are seared first because the short cooking time would not allow the browning to happen otherwise.

Only large cuts are browned directly in a hot oven (220–240°C/425–475°F/Gas 7–9). The heat is then lowered to 160–180°C/325–350°F/Gas 3–4 which allows the heat to permeate the meat slowly, to break down and gelatinize the connective muscle tissues, and coagulate the meat proteins. Cooked in this way the joint will be moist and perfectly cooked.

HEAT

The oven should always be pre-heated well in advance, and whether it is high or low depends on the size of the joint, fish, poultry, etc.: small joints are cooked at a high temperature, large at a high, then a lower temperature.

TIMING

It is almost impossible to absolutely define the time necessary to cook a joint, as too many factors can intervene. Timing will depend on whether the meat has been hung or not, on how the meat has been cut, on the thickness of the cut, on how much collagen the flesh contains, on its source (whether intensively farmed or raised naturally, whether wild or farmed), and on whether it has been frozen or not. To some extent the same applies to fish or poultry.

WHICH FAT TO USE?

Butter is too fragile for such a long cooking and would burn; and oil by itself would not give good flavour. A mixture of butter and oil is good, but clarified butter or chicken fat or beef dripping would be even better. This retains the butter flavour, but can be heated to high temperatures without burning.

BASTING

There are very strong disagreements about whether one should baste or not. I feel that within most meats there is enough fat content to keep them moist. Some drier meats, such as poultry or game birds, need the extra help of barding fat, and this will liquefy over the meat as it cooks, thus eliminating the need for basting. I believe you should only baste large joints because this helps the browning process.

RESTING

A resting time of 20–30 minutes is crucial for small or large joints. If you serve a joint straight after being cooked it is very likely that the inside will be barely cooked or, worse, uncooked and cold. Resting prevents this.

- Wrap or cover the joint with a piece of aluminium foil. Place it in a warm place.
- The residual heat from the roasting will travel slowly to the centre of the meat, and cook it to a perfectly juicy medium. So long as the temperature is above 50°C (122°F), a joint continues to cook.
- During roasting, the fibres and muscles of the meat coagulate, which forces juices towards the exterior of the meat. During the resting period, the juices move back through the meat, moistening all the drier parts, thus giving the meat the tenderness desired.

So, effectively, for a large joint such as a leg of lamb, cooking it medium rare and resting it for 20–30 minutes will make it the most perfect medium with a pink slice right the way through.

This applies to smaller cuts of meat as well, although the resting time could be shorter.

• *Small roasts*   Partridge, quail, baby chicken: An initial browning, then oven-roasting at 200–220°C/400–425°F/Gas 6–7, plus resting time.

• *Medium roasts* (up to 900 g/2 lb) Chicken, guinea fowl and small meat joints: An initial browning, then oven-roasting at 180–190°C/350–375°F/Gas 4–5, plus resting time.

• *Large roasts* (over 1.8 kg/4 lb): No initial browning. Oven-roasting for the first 20–30 minutes at 220°C/425°F/Gas 7 until brown, then the heat is lowered to about 160–180°C/325–350°F/Gas 3–4, plus resting time.

MAKING THE JUICE

First, carefully remove all the fat from the roasting tray. The juices which have escaped from the meat will have caramelized on the bottom of the tray. Equally, the bones on which the roast was resting (if relevant) will have caramelized and will add an enormous amount of flavour. Simply add water to dilute all those deposits on the bottom of the tray, bring to the boil and then scrape together. Add the juices that the meat has released whilst resting. Bring to the boil, skim and remove fat, then strain, taste and season.

SOME ROASTING TIPS

1. When you remove the fat, you often remove lots of juices. A way to avoid that is to put both juices and fat in a bowl and then refrigerate or freeze. The fat will rise to the top and solidify, when it can be scooped off the jellied juices.

2. A few cloves of unpeeled garlic or herbs such as thyme, marjoram or rosemary could be added to the roasting tray.

3. Adding finely chopped bones to the roasting tray will support the meat whilst it roasts and will add extra flavour to the juice (see p. 197).

4. Cooking the meat on the bone lends a better taste to the meat and will prevent the flesh retracting. Contrary to common belief, a bone-in roast does not need extra cooking time, as the bone is an excellent conductor of heat.

5. I prefer to season roasting meat when the browning has been completed, then I season again at the end of cooking. The salt will not penetrate the meat during cooking. So give a few turns of salt and pepper after slicing it.

6. Do not pierce the meat when turning it.

See also Fish (pp. 147, 159), Poultry (pp. 174, 185), Meat (pp. 194, 197, 202, 218).

GRILLING

This is a cooking technique involving radiant heat (see p. 18). The food is placed under a pre-heated grill or source of heat (or *over* barbecue coals), and one side is cooked before the food is turned over for the second side to receive the radiated heat.

The grill should be pre-heated very well, and the heat should be high at first to produce Maillard reactions of browning (see also p. 19), then reduced in temperature if the food needs further cooking. Small pieces of meat and vegetables should require only brief, high heat.

The distance of the food from the source of heat is important: too near and the food could burn; too far away and the food will barely cook. Timing is very important as well, as grilling can be a very fast cooking technique.

Grilling is a healthy way of cooking as no added fat or oil is generally necessary: meats contain fat within them, and these drip off as the cooking proceeds. Some drier pieces of meat and most vegetables may need to be marinated in oil or a marinade to help them cope with the fierce heat (and this also adds flavour, of course).

Do not turn grilled foods over with a fork as piercing the food will allow juices to escape. Use kitchen tongs.

MICROWAVE COOKING

Microwaves are electro-magnetic waves like light, X-rays or radiant heat. Their wavelength (about

10 cm/4 in) is similar to that used in radar. They can penetrate materials which do not conduct electricity (non-metals), hence all foodstuffs. If the material contains polar molecules (see p. 14), these are set in motion by the microwaves and this kinetic energy is turned into heat by friction. The water molecule is polar and as most food contains water, microwaves can be used for cooking. Only a small fraction of the microwave energy is absorbed over a thickness of 5 cm (2 in), so heating is fairly uniform except for large volumes.

Solids, even if they contain polar molecules, do not on the whole absorb microwaves, as the molecules, being anchored in fixed positions, cannot be set into motion. This is the reason why thawing out deep-frozen food by microwaves is a slow process and is usually done at low intensity to allow 'wet spots' to grow. The same applies, in a less significant sense – but it's fun! – if you heat a chocolate-coated sweet with a liquid filling. The molecules in the solid chocolate casing don't move, but the liquid inside does, so the middle of the sweet can be hot while the chocolate casing is cool, unmelted and firm.

Since microwaves act mainly on the water molecules, they cannot, with a few exceptions such as sugar syrups, cook above 100°C (212°F), and consequently hardly any Maillard compounds are formed. This means foods do not brown (see p. 19). There are now, however, microwave ovens fitted with grills so it is possible to 'roast' a chicken without having to move it to a traditional oven or a grill in order to brown it. Foods could also be browned *before* being microwaved.

Microwave ovens have many uses. They are particularly good for reheating foods, because they do so instantly, without losing liquids within the foods, and for egg dishes. But beware, one must *never* try to cook an egg in its shell in a microwave oven (or indeed a whole tomato): they will explode!

CURING

This is one of the oldest preserving processes known to man. In salt-curing, the meat or fish is covered with salt or a brine solution for a period of time. The salt will kill most bacteria and germs which cause spoilage, and thus allows food to be preserved.

Curing can be achieved by smoking as well: the smoke inhibits bacterial and microbial growth as well as partly cooking the food. Some foods such as bacon and ham are salt-cured, then smoke-cured.

SCIENTIST'S NOTES

Curing or preserving food with salt or sugar works because the cell walls of both meat and vegetables allow water to flow through but retain the rest of the contents. (They are called semipermeable membranes.) Nature likes things to balance out, so if the food is placed in a solution of salt or sugar which is stronger than the contents of the cells, water will flow out, in order to try and dilute the outside. So the contents of the cells get drier and less liable to attack from bacteria – because bacteria like moisture.

PICKLING

This is also a food preserving technique, which uses vinegar, lemon juice, etc. as a medium. The acid present in these liquids will permeate the foods and kill most of the bacteria; they will also soften the texture.

SCIENTIST'S NOTES

Very few living organisms can survive in a strongly acid medium such as vinegar. It is difficult to give the exact figure for the minimum acidity or maximum pH for a safe pickling solution, but pH = 3.5 which corresponds to undiluted wine vinegar may serve as a guide. It is a wise precaution when pickling food with a high water content such as gherkins to extract at least some of the water by first 'curing' by sprinkling with salt or sugar.

The acetic acid in vinegar has been shown to be more effective at killing or preventing the growth of bacteria than any other acid at the same strength. This is fortunate for the cook, since it tastes quite pleasant and causes no injury in its dilute form.

SOUSING

This is a technique much the same as pickling, but it uses a lesser acid content. It is applied for a far shorter time than the acids of pickling. The main object is to give flavour to the food, rather than preserve it. Soused foods will keep for two to three days maximum.

MARINATING

Foods such as fish and meat are marinated to tenderize the flesh and to give extra flavour as a marinade permeates the flesh. Wine, oil or vinegar are the usual marinade basics, but diced vegetables, herbs and spices can be added for extra flavour. Marinades can also be based on raw pineapple or papaya juices, lemon or lime juices. During the marinating time, the acids of the liquids will also cause fluid loss from the flesh as they seem to be able to digest the animal protein and break it down.

Traditionally, meat is marinated with raw wine, but I prefer to boil the wine first to remove some of its acidity and some of its alcohol: this can interfere with the flavour. By boiling the wine, you may destroy some of the acids, but the benefit is a much better and rounder flavour. In cooked marinades, since the acidity is reduced, so is the tenderizing.

Tenderness of a marinated meat, for instance, is achieved through very slow and careful cooking.

CLARIFYING

This technique is sometimes necessary to produce the clearest possible stock for a consommé or jelly. Finely chopped raw meat, fish or vegetables (depending on the main ingredient of the recipe) are mixed with egg white, vegetables, herbs

and spices, and added to the stock. This is another demonstration of the great diversity of egg white.

Stock Clarification

INGREDIENTS

1 litre (1$^3/_4$ pints) stock (chicken, fish, etc.)
3 egg whites
100 g (4 oz) raw fish, lean meat, or vegetable, as appropriate, very finely chopped

herbs (according to taste and recipe) for flavouring
$^1/_2$ leek, finely chopped
$^1/_4$ celery stalk, finely chopped
1 tomato, finely chopped
1 carrot, peeled and finely chopped

METHOD

Place the stock in a suitable pan.

Place the egg whites in a bowl, and lightly break them with two or three movements of the whisk. Add the chopped meat or fish, herbs and vegetables, and mix thoroughly. Whisk all these clarifying elements into the stock.

Bring to the boil, stirring continuously, then lower the temperature and simmer for 30 minutes. Use a ladle to make a hole in the crust which forms on the surface, at the point where the bubbling is strongest. Take the pan off the heat and leave to rest for a few minutes.

Pour the clear stock through a fine sieve lined with damp muslin. Leave to cool, cover and refrigerate; keep in the fridge for five days, freeze for one month.

CHEF'S NOTES

The addition of meat or fish to the clarifying ingredients compensates for the loss of flavour *caused* by the clarifying.

SCIENTIST'S NOTES

When the clarification agents are whisked into the broth and heated gently, the coagulating proteins of the egg white and other ingredients capture the small solid particles floating in the liquid and form a microscopic mass of protein in a light crust at the top of the liquid, leaving a completely clear stock. The 'crust' is readily eliminated by filtering through muslin.

For the most efficient clarification, apply the heat to only a small part of the pan's base, for instance by placing it off centre on the hot plate.

SAVOURY MOUSSE-MAKING

Savoury mousses are very easy to make really, so long as you have a food processor or blender. The basic ingredients are fish, meat or vegetables; egg yolks, whole eggs or a mixture of both; whipping cream; and salt and pepper.

There are a certain number of steps, but once these are understood, the whole technique will become easier.

PUREEING THE MAIN INGREDIENT

The meat or fish should be chilled first, then puréed thoroughly. It is essential to purée thoroughly in order to break down the food's fibres and tissues, or the mousse may turn out grainy. Rub the mixture between your fingers; it should be perfectly smooth. When processing, stop the motor at least twice, and use a supple spatula to stir in any mixture trapped under the blade.

The entire process should last 2 minutes, no more, as the friction of the blade would warm up the purée.

ADDING THE SEASONING

I like to add some of the recipe's salt and pepper at an early stage. This distributes the seasoning well, but at the same time the salt causes the protein in the fish or meat to swell, firming up the consistency of the mousse mixture, which helps the subsequent incorporation of the cream.

ADDING THE EGG

Egg performs all kinds of miracles for the cook and in this case, the egg yolks have an enriching purpose. Add to the blender and mix in for no longer than 10 seconds. No egg white should be needed in fish or meat mousses, as there is already enough protein present to bind the mixture. In classical recipes many egg whites are used because they have a very strong binding power; I find this is unnecessary and damaging to the end result. The more egg white used, the larger the quantities of cream needed, hence a dilution of the essential flavour.

As far as I know, only lobster and langoustine mousses need the addition of egg white as there are not enough binding proteins.

CHILLING THE MIXTURE

If you are making a large quantity of mousse, the puréeing process will be much longer, and the friction of the food processor blade will cause the mousse mixture to heat up. It is essential therefore to chill it for about 30–60 minutes. If the cream were to be added to a tepid mixture, the liquids, fats and solids would separate. For a quantity of basic ingredients of up to 300 g (11 oz), the cream can be incorporated directly, without refrigeration, so long as all the other basic ingredients are cold.

ADDING THE CREAM

The cream should be chilled otherwise if it is at room temperature it is likely to split. Add the cream in a steady trickle, making sure each addition is absorbed before adding more. If you add too much at once, the cream may end up being whipped and the mixture will separate.

Half-way through puréeing, scrape out any purée trapped under the blade. This should take about 1 minute altogether.

The amount of cream may vary quite considerably. Each recipe has to give definite quantities: for example 300 g (11 oz) turbot, 3 egg yolks, 400 ml (14 fl oz) cream, 1 teaspoon salt and 2 pinches pepper. Then, having followed the recipe to the letter, you find that you have a disaster on your hands: the mousse is either too firm or it has collapsed.

The reasons are simple, but they need to be understood. According to the size, the age, the freshness of both fish and eggs, the amount of cream may vary greatly. Fillets from 3.6 or 5.4 kg (8 or 12 lb) turbots and 900 g (2 lb) turbots will be entirely different in chemical composition, hence may need more or less cream. A one-day-old turbot and a five-day-old turbot will also be different chemically. So you must always add four-fifths of the cream first, then test. Add more cream and seasoning if necessary.

TESTING THE MOUSSE

For the reasons above, the mousse mixture needs to be tested. Quarter-fill a small buttered ramekin with some mousse mixture. Cook in a *bain-marie* as in the basic recipe then release the mousse from the mould and taste to check seasoning and texture. The mousse should have a melting texture. If too firm, add the remaining cream to the bulk of the mixture, and correct the seasoning.

SIEVING THE MOUSSE

I only sieve the mousse after the cream has been added, when I find it absolutely effortless. Do so, using a fine-mesh circular sieve and a plastic scraper. Traditionally the basic purée is sieved before the addition of cream and eggs. I find this a waste of time and effort, as this involves wastage of good basic ingredients (and expensive sieves which collapse under the pressure!).

Sieving rids the mixture of all small fibres and nerves. Scallops are the only shellfish which do not need to be sieved as there is hardly any connective tissue.

GIVING EXTRA LIGHTNESS TO THE MOUSSE (OPTIONAL)

If you want to give the lightest texture to your mousse, place the sieved basic mousse mixture in a bowl, and beat with a wooden spoon in a circular motion, trapping as much air as possible.

PREPARING THE MOUSSE MIXTURE IN ADVANCE

The mousse mixture can be prepared one day in advance, but whilst this is very convenient, a little more cream will need to be added, as I find the mixture tightens up.

PREPARING THE MOUSSE MOULDS

Butter the insides lightly. Refrigerate so that the butter can harden and not be displaced when the mousse mixture is spooned in. This film of butter will ease the unmoulding of the mousses.

COOKING THE MOUSSES

The mousses are cooked in a *bain-marie*. Use a deep roasting tin lined with greaseproof paper.

Great care must be taken when cooking mousses as their structure is so delicate. The best way I have found for the lightest result is to pre-heat the oven to 110°C/225°F/Gas ¼, so that the temperature of the *bain-marie* water is about 85°C (185°F) which will be ample to set the mousse.

Place the ramekins into the *bain-marie* and pour boiling water into the *bain-marie* tray so it comes three-quarters up the sides of the moulds. This ensures that the temperature of the mousses is constant throughout. Cover the *bain-marie* with pierced foil or buttered paper. This allows the steam to hover above the mousses before escaping and keeps the surface moist. If the foil or paper were sealed too tightly, the heat would build up and the mousses would rise like soufflés, only to collapse miserably, especially if egg whites are used.

COOKING TEMPERATURE

Too often mousses are overcooked due to too high a heat. Egg proteins coagulate at around 63–65°C (145–149°F), and meat and fish proteins start coagulating at around 70°C (158°F), so the water temperature (lower than the oven itself) will cook the mousses perfectly.

The following little chart will give you the approximate water temperature of a *bain-marie* as related to oven temperature but, as outlined on p. 35, this water temperature depends on how long the water is in the heated oven.

Oven temperature	Water temperature
150°C/300°F/Gas 2	99°C (210°F)
140°C/275°F/Gas 1	95°C (203°F)
120°C/250°F/Gas ½	90°C (194°F)
110°C/225°F/Gas ¼	85°C (185°F)
100°C/212°F/lowest gas possible	76°C (169°F)

The following may also be helpful for when you are making fish mousses, giving you the quantities

I have found are needed for success. Needless to say, the fish and shellfish must be the freshest, and adult rather than young. Each starts off with 300 g (11 oz) fish or shellfish flesh, and gives the quantity of cream needed for that amount of fish.

A quenelle is a shaped mousse which is cooked directly in simmering water or stock (why it needs less cream).

Fish (all 300 g/ 11 oz)	Cream for mousse	Egg yolks	Cream for quenelles
Scallops	450 ml (15 fl oz)	3	100 ml (3½ fl oz)
Sea bass	500 ml (17 fl oz)	3	420 ml (14½ fl oz)
Turbot	600 ml (1 pint)	2 + 1 whole egg	500 ml (17 fl oz)
Brill	450 ml (15 fl oz)	3	400 ml (14 fl oz)
Salmon	750 ml (1¼ pints)	3	600 ml (1 pint)
Langoustine	650 ml (22½ fl oz)	3	550 ml (18 fl oz)
Lobster	500 ml (17 fl oz)	3	350 ml (12 fl oz)

SOUFFLE-MAKING

I vividly remember my despair when I first attempted to make a soufflé. Time and time again my efforts were a failure – such is the price of learning by yourself. There are many different ways to make soufflés, but with this one basic recipe you can make almost any variety.

A few items of equipment are necessary for making successful soufflés. You need a *mixing bowl* for beating the egg white. Use scrupulously clean china or stainless steel. Copper bowls (traditionally used to obtain the best bulk) are now thought to release tiny particles of dangerous copper into the mix. You also need a *whisk* if beating the whites by hand. A large, supple balloon whisk will make the beating easier, and give more bulk. But the use of an electric whisk, whether a table-top machine or a hand-held one, will produce the same volume but with much less effort. Another necessity is a supple *spatula* for folding the soufflé mixture into the pastry cream base.

Soufflé dishes should be made of ovenproof china, the finer the better for heat conduction. I prefer individual bowls to one large one, as they give you more control over the cooking. The heat permeates the soufflé mixture better and faster, leaving the soufflé just cooked outside and barely cooked inside. The presentation is better too. Some gourmets will argue that in a small mould the soufflé does not have time to obtain that luscious top crust; well, they have a point.

Your *oven* is most important in soufflé-making. Always check the accuracy of the oven thermostat with a thermometer. Cook soufflés at the bottom of the oven; if cooked higher up, strong heat is reflected off the top of the oven on to the tops of the soufflés, which impairs the rise and may cause the tops to burn.

SWEET SOUFFLES

The most effective way of describing how to make these is to give a recipe containing all the information.

Grand Marnier Soufflé

FOR 4 GUESTS
PREPARATION AND COOKING TIME: 55 minutes

SPECIAL EQUIPMENT: See above, and 4 small soufflé dishes, 10 cm (4 in) in diameter, and 5 cm (2 in) high.

INGREDIENTS
200 ml (7 fl oz) Pastry Cream (see p. 64)

2 egg yolks
2 tablespoons Grand Marnier
8 egg whites
40 g (1½ oz) caster sugar
1 teaspoon lemon juice
icing sugar to dust

FOR THE SOUFFLE DISHES
1 teaspoon unsalted butter, at room temperature
2 tablespoons caster sugar

METHOD
Pre-heat the oven to 190°C/375°F/Gas 5.

1 · Preparing the dishes
Using a pastry brush, evenly butter the inside of each of the soufflé dishes. Put all the sugar inside the first dish and rotate it until completely coated with sugar. Tip the excess sugar into the next dish and repeat.

This butter and sugar coating acts as a barrier between the dish and the soufflé, enabling the soufflé to rise without hindrance. Badly buttered dishes will produce an uneven rise or perhaps even prevent the rising altogether. The sugar fixes the butter in place and gives a delicious crust to the soufflé.

2 · Preparing the soufflé base

Put the warm pastry cream into a mixing bowl, add the egg yolks and Grand Marnier and whisk well together. Keep warm.

The pastry cream is the soufflé base, and holds the flavour. Check the degree of moistness; if it is too wet, the egg whites will not be able to absorb and lift it. The cream should still be warm when incorporated into the egg whites; this helps to prevent lumps and gives better lifting power.

Egg yolks are added for richness, not binding power; in some soufflés, such as raspberry and blackcurrant, they are not needed at all.

Many different flavouring liqueurs can be substituted for the Grand Marnier. Fruit coulis can also be used: some, among them raspberry, blackcurrant and apricot, must be reduced beforehand to concentrate the flavour and keep the base firm. Strongly textured and flavoured coulis, such as lime, lemon and passion fruit, do not need to be reduced.

3 · Adding the egg whites

Beat the egg whites at medium speed to a soft peak, then add the sugar and lemon juice. (The lemon juice will counterbalance the sweetness of the sugar, as well as prevent any separation from the egg whites.) Increase the speed and beat for a few more seconds until just firm but not too stiff. This will give the soufflé a wonderful melting texture.

During the whisking, the egg white will expand to create millions of tiny air bubbles which will expand during baking and cause the soufflé to rise. If the whites are beaten too stiffly, the mixture will be too close textured, making the soufflé too firm.

Week-old eggs are best; very fresh egg whites have a high water content and are prone to graining.

The mixing bowl must be scrupulously clean, as any trace of fat or yolk will severely reduce the bulk.

Whisk one-quarter of the beaten egg white into the warm pastry cream mixture for 2–3 seconds, until smooth. This brisk, brief whisking lightens the base mixture and eases the incorporation of the remaining egg white.

Using a spatula, delicately fold in the remaining egg white with large circular movements until just incorporated. Do not *over*-mix, or you will break down the air bubbles in the egg white and impair the rise.

4 · Filling the soufflé dishes

Fill the soufflé dishes with the mixture right to the top. Smooth the surface with a spatula, then push the mixture about 3 mm ($^1/_8$ in) away from the edge of the bowls with your thumb. This prevents the soufflé from catching on the lip of the dish as it rises.

5 · Cooking and serving the soufflés

Space the dishes well apart in the bottom of the pre-heated oven, allowing the heat to circulate freely, and bake for 12–13 minutes. After about 5 minutes, the soufflés will begin to rise. Check that they are rising evenly; if not, free the edges with a knife.

Dust the tops with a thin layer of icing sugar once or twice; this will melt and produce a delicious caramelized crust.

Remove the cooked soufflés from the oven, and serve immediately.

CHEF'S NOTES

Soufflés are not as fragile as you may think. You can open the oven door for a few seconds without them collapsing. Do not remove them as soon as they have risen, however, as the centres must also be cooked. If they are removed too soon, they will indeed collapse. Overcooking produces the same result, as the air bubbles will eventually burst open.

An ideal soufflé should have a melting texture, with a barely cooked, soft creamy centre. It will stand for at least 1 or 2 minutes without deflating.

A soufflé should have enough flavour of its own and should not need a sauce poured into the centre. This is unsightly, and immediately destroys the texture. I often serve a sorbet or slices of the same fruit used in the soufflé.

SAVOURY SOUFFLES

The technique is very much the same as sweet soufflé-making, but see the recipe for Stilton Soufflé on p. 120.

In savoury soufflés, the Pastry Cream is replaced by a béchamel sauce (based on a roux of butter, flour and milk, see Stilton Soufflé).

A mixture of breadcrumbs and finely chopped walnuts or hazelnuts could be used to coat the sides of the soufflé dish instead of the sugar. For a cheese or vegetable soufflé, finely grated Parmesan would give flavour and a wonderful savoury crust.

As we do not use sugar, more lemon juice should be added when the egg whites have reached soft peaks. The lemon juice will lift the flavour and the citric acid will make the foam more stable and prevent the egg whites graining.

For savoury soufflés, the egg white foam should be a bit firmer than those used in sweet soufflés.

Add salt to the egg whites when the egg white foam is at the soft peak stage. Do not add it earlier as this can retard the coagulation of the egg whites. Beware of adding too much salt to a cheese soufflé, as there will already be quite a lot of salt in the cheese.

SPONGE-MAKING

This method of making sponge, or *biscuit*, is not only easier and quicker than the conventional method, but it also gives a lighter result. If you have an electric mixer, this machine will do everything for you. It is less time-consuming and very gentle on the washing-up!

Sponge or Biscuit

PREPARATION TIME: 15 minutes

COOKING TIME: 10–15 minutes

SPECIAL EQUIPMENT: See individual recipes, but greaseproof paper, baking trays and cooling racks are essential.

PLANNING AHEAD: The sponge can be baked a day or so in advance and kept in an airtight tin.

INGREDIENTS
2 eggs, separated
40 g ($1\frac{1}{2}$ oz) caster sugar
40 g ($1\frac{1}{2}$ oz) plain flour

METHOD
Pre-heat the oven to 180°C/350°F/Gas 4.

Beat the egg whites until they reach soft peaks, then add half the sugar, beating continuously. Lower the speed, add the remaining sugar, and mix for about 30 seconds to allow the sugar to dissolve.

Add the egg yolks and mix for 30 seconds. Finally fold in the flour delicately; you don't need an absolutely perfect mix.

Prepare and pipe as defined in the individual recipes, then bake for the specified time – usually 8–10 minutes – in the pre-heated oven, until golden and firm. Leave to cool a little on the tray, then remove to a cooling rack using a fish slice.

VARIATIONS
The sponge can be caked in a pastry ring or cake mould. Depending on the size of these, and thus the thickness of the sponge mixture, the cooking time will vary. To check, test with a needle, which should come out dry if the sponge is cooked.

Grated orange or lemon zest can be added to the basic mixture, or any other flavouring such as ginger or vanilla essence.

The tops of the sponge shapes can be dusted

with icing sugar before baking – this gives a shine, a crunch and extra strength.

For a chocolate sponge, follow the basic ingredients and method exactly, but use only 30 g (1¼ oz) plain flour made up to the basic recipe 40 g (1½ oz) with 10 g (¼ oz) cocoa powder (*not* drinking chocolate).

CHEF'S NOTES

Use a large supple balloon whisk to make beating easier and give more bulk as more air is incorporated in the whites. Alternatively, use an electric mixer with a whisk attachment.

Greaseproof paper on the baking tray is very useful for several reasons.

- You will be able to lift the paper up from the tray when you think the sponge has cooked and see through the paper to check the degree of cooking. The sponge should be a light blond colour when cooked.
- It is far easier to remove the sponge from the tray. It will prevent overcooking and the base drying out from the heat generated by the tray.
- The paper keeps the tray cleaner.

___

Always check the accuracy of the oven thermostat with a thermometer. Cook the sponge on the middle shelf of the oven; if cooked higher up, strong heat is reflected off the top of the oven on to the top of the sponge, which impairs the rise and may cause the tops to burn.

___

Use egg whites that are three or five days old, as they will provide more volume when whipped. As eggs grow older, there is evaporation of water in the whites, giving more strength to the egg white and making it less prone to separation.

Make sure no fat whatsoever gets into the egg white (yolk or otherwise), or the sponge will fail miserably or will lose a lot of lightness.

___

Caster sugar is used as a sweetener in the recipe, and gives strength to the egg white.

Flour is used as a thickening agent which gives texture and helps the sponge to hold its shape.

___

Here the egg white shows off its magic and, when whipped, gives the sponge its rising ability, its lightness and its delicate texture.

Due to the high sugar content of this recipe, lemon juice or citric acid is not required. You must add up to half the amount of sugar.

Mixing for 30 seconds and lowering the speed allows the sugar to be gently incorporated and dissolved. A higher speed will 'meringue' the mixture: at the cooling stage this will simply make the sponge rise too much and then collapse during cooking.

___

Folding in the flour must be done delicately. Use a spatula and mix with a large movement until well incorporated. Do not *over*-mix as you will break too many of the little air bubbles.

BREAD-MAKING

Bread has been a symbol of nourishment, both spiritual and physical, from biblical times to the present day. In France bread has always played an important part in daily life, and no good meal is served without good bread, whether in a three-star restaurant or at home, on a day-to-day basis. In my childhood I remember that my father alone carved slices from the huge crusty loaf. This I could understand: it was surely a way of showing us that he was the provider. But then his ritual would extend to tracing a cross on the bread with the point of a knife. Knowing that my father was an atheist, this puzzled me. His explanation was clear and simple: that it was the only and best way he knew to show his respect for bread. I must say that it was beautiful bread, made by the village baker, following traditional recipes.

In the years since then, it has been a different story. Industrialization and machines took over, usurping the craft of proper bread-making, hence the poor quality on the shelves – more often than not anaemic loaves with dead white crumb, wrapped in plastic and, needless to say, tasteless. The last few years, though, have seen a revival of interest in 'real' bread. An interest in healthy eating has generated many organic flours which come from grains grown free of pesticides and soil additives. The direct result is a higher quality of flour, and this in turn produces better bread.

Bread-making demands time – a minimum of half a day – but it can be a most fulfilling, soothing, enjoyable and rewarding activity.

There is an incredible variety of flours you can use – plain, wholegrain, rye, etc. – and many different ingredients can be added to bread. Once you have mastered the basic techniques, you can explore many other varieties of flours, and ingredients such as carrots, herbs, walnuts, sun-dried tomatoes, currants, almonds, ham, smoked bacon and spices, etc. Bread is made from four basic ingredients: *water, salt, flour and yeast.*

FLOUR

People often ask me to define the difference between English and French flours. For a start they just *are* different, because they come from different wheats, or different mixtures of wheats. They are also treated differently in the milling process or at the bakery. The bread-making properties of a flour are much improved by prolonged storage – the flour able to produce more loaf volume and a finer, softer crumb after twelve months' storage. In the last twenty years or so, it has become common practice to simulate this natural ageing process by the use of oxidizing agents and improvers.

The use of many of these improvers gives the dough an excess of strength which, in my opinion, results in a loaf that has developed too quickly, very often giving a white and insipid crumb. After having tried many flours we have selected two brands which are more likely to give you good results (Allinson and Waitrose own brand), both of which are made from organically grown grain and

are unbleached. They can be found easily in many places.

When it comes to pâtisserie, use quite a strong flour for all pastries made with yeast, such as croissants, bread and brioche; for everything else, use a medium-strength flour.

WATER

The dough temperature should not go over 24°C (75°F). Above this temperature, the strength of the gluten will be affected; the dough would also prove too fast, and the taste and texture of the bread would not be as good.

So the water added to the flour should be cold – 8–10°C (46–50°F).

YEAST

We have used fresh moist yeast which is available from your delicatessen or local bakery (though in the latter your request might prove less popular!). Dry yeast can also be used, but the flavour of the bread will be affected.

The main function of yeast is to produce carbon dioxide which causes the dough to grow in volume and give bread its light texture. See also p. 28.

SALT

Salt is obviously used to give flavour to the bread. It must never be mixed with the yeast, though, as salt has a retarding effect on yeast fermentation because of osmosis. It tends to draw the water out of the yeast cells and dehydrate them. It is much more effective in this respect than sugar. Salt should be added to the bread dough at quite a late stage.

SPECIAL EQUIPMENT

The most important piece of equipment for home bread-making is an electric mixer fitted with a dough hook. You will also need a thermometer, a spatula, a sieve, a razor blade or scissors, bowls and cloths to cover the dough while it is proving.

SCIENTIST'S NOTES

The ingredients for traditional bread are strong (high protein) flour, water, yeast, a little salt and air. Most recipes forget to mention the air, but it is vital. Most people know that yeast ferments the sugar and produces large amounts of carbon dioxide gas and alcohol. Although sugar may not be included in the recipe, it occurs quite naturally as starch grains are broken down into simpler sugars (glucose), by a naturally occurring enzyme (amylase). The problem is that the carbon dioxide produced by fermentation is very soluble and just diffuses through the mixture. It cannot, by itself, form the little pockets of gas we need in the dough, but it can inflate *existing* small pockets. That's why we have to mix lots of pockets of air into the dough, so that they will provide sites for the carbon dioxide to accumulate. The kneading of the dough is thus doubly important: first of all it works or extends the gluten to form a complex web, but at the same time it also mixes in lots of air, on which the yeast can work its magic.

Carbon dioxide and alcohol are not the only products of yeast fermentation: many highly flavoured compounds are made in small quantities. If you use a fermented dough starter in your bread-making, not only will the yeast have plenty of time to produce gas and develop the gluten, but more tasty molecules will be formed.

Fermented Dough Starter

Using a fermented dough starter is the traditional way to make better, lighter and tastier bread. Fermented dough is composed of flour, water and a small quantity of yeast which is left to ferment, then added to the other ingredients of the recipe. The living yeast cells will reproduce during the fermentation and, when mixed into the basic ingredients of the bread, they will activate the other yeast cells in the fresh dough, giving a light acidity which is important to the taste of the bread. One can, of course, make bread without this dough starter but it will be less tasty and of a heavier texture.

INGREDIENTS
100 g (4 oz) white
   unbleached flour
60 ml ($2^{1}/_{4}$ fl oz) cold water,
   at 22°C (71.6°F)

5 g ($^{1}/_{8}$ oz) fresh moist
   baker's yeast

METHOD
Knead the flour and water in the bowl of the electric mixer at a low speed, no. 1, for 3–5 minutes. Crumble in the yeast and knead on medium speed, no. 2, for 10 minutes. Remove the bowl from the mixer, and cover with a cloth. Prove the dough for 3 hours at room temperature.

Break or knock back the dough by lifting it. This will remove the fermentation gases from the dough. Replace in the bowl, cover with the cloth and prove for another 3 hours for a second fermentation.

This fermented dough can be made one to two days in advance. If you do this, omit the second fermentation as the dough will go on fermenting slowly in the fridge.

When making bread with the fermented dough, the dough must be removed from the fridge at least 2 hours in advance, to allow it to prove.

Country Bread

MAKES 3 LOAVES OR 20 ROLLS
PREPARATION TIME: About
20 minutes

PROVING TIME: 1 hour +
$1–1^{1}/_{2}$ hours

COOKING TIME: 8–30
minutes, depending on
whether loaves or rolls are
being made.

PLANNING AHEAD: The
Fermented Dough Starter
must be made in advance.

INGREDIENTS
500g (18 oz) plain
   unbleached flour
   (Allinson), at room
   temperature, and sifted
350 ml (12 fl oz) cold water,
   about 8°C (46°F)
12 g (slightly under $^{1}/_{2}$ oz)
   fresh moist baker's yeast
15 g ($^{1}/_{2}$ oz) salt
165 g ($5^{1}/_{2}$ oz) Fermented
   Dough Starter (see
   above)

METHOD

1 · Mixing the dough
Place the flour in the bowl of the electric mixer. Pour the water in, and start mixing on speed no. 1 for 3 minutes. Then crumble the yeast in and knead at speed no. 2 for a further 8 minutes. Add the salt and fermented dough starter and mix on the same speed for a further 5 minutes.

2 · Proving the dough

Take the dough out of the bowl and shape it into a big ball on a lightly floured working surface. Cover with a cloth and leave to prove at room temperature, approximately 1 hour.

Divide the risen dough into 3 equal pieces for loaves – or 20 for rolls – and shape them according to personal taste (oblongs, rounds, etc.).

Place a cloth on a tray and lift the dough pieces on to it, separating each with a fold in the cloth so they don't stick to one another. Cover again with a cloth and prove the dough for about another 1–1½ hours, depending on room temperature. The dough will be ready when it has doubled in volume, and if, when you press the surface with your finger, it springs back.

The dough is now ready for baking. With a fine sieve, dust the loaves with a little extra flour.

3 · Baking the bread

Meanwhile, pre-heat the oven to 250°C/500°F or as high as your oven will go, and put a tray of boiling water at the bottom of the oven.

Lightly flour a baking tray and very delicately lift the pieces of risen dough on to the tray, leaving as much space as possible in between them. Then make some very sharp incisions into the bread –

four or five widthwise, or one long one sideways right in the middle of the bread or rolls.

Slide the tray into the pre-heated oven immediately after making the cuts, and bake the loaves for about 25–30 minutes and the rolls for about 8–10 minutes. Remove when the bread or rolls have beautiful golden crusts. Leave to cool for a minimum of 1 hour.

VARIATION

Once you have shaped the bread, before proving, you can brush the surface with water (or spray with water). Place a generous amount of sesame seeds on a cloth and roll the dough on it so that the surface is coated with the seeds.

CHEF'S NOTES

Hold the blade of the razor flat against the surface at about a 30 degree angle. It is essential that the cuts are not too deep – they should be about 2–3 mm (¹⁄₆–¹⁄₈ in) – and not too vertical. If the angle is not sharp enough the fold will close up during the cooking and if too deep the loaf is very likely to open up during baking. Each cut should be a minimum of 3 cm (1¼ in) apart.

When baking, check the bread or rolls don't overcook; time will vary, depending on the oven.

Basic Recipes

The following are recipes referred to in the recipe sections throughout the rest of the book. To understand the science involved in many of these, read the Scientist's Notes attached to the relevant recipes, or the chapters on A Pinch of Science, Ingredients or Cooking Techniques.

Home-made Pasta

You can buy good-quality pasta anywhere, but making your own is one of the most satisfying cooking experiences, and it is so easy.

FOR 4–6 GUESTS
PREPARATION TIME: 15 minutes

RESTING TIME: 1 hour

SPECIAL EQUIPMENT: A pasta machine (optional).

INGREDIENTS
350 g (12 oz) durum wheat flour or pasta flour marked '00'
3 medium free-range eggs
2 tablespoons olive oil
salt

METHOD

1 · Making the pasta by hand
Sift the flour on to a work surface. Make a well in the centre, break the eggs in and add the olive oil and $\frac{1}{2}$ teaspoon salt. Incorporate the eggs, olive oil and salt into the flour, gradually mixing in the flour. When roughly mixed, clean the sticky dough off your hands.

Knead the dough for about 10–15 minutes, as you would bread, until you reach a very smooth and elastic texture. Flour lightly and wrap in a tea towel. Refrigerate and relax the dough for an hour.

2 · Making the pasta in a food processor
This is by far the easiest.

Place the sifted flour into the food processor bowl, add the eggs, olive oil and $\frac{1}{2}$ teaspoon salt, and mix until the dough is just coming together (30–40 seconds).

Scrape the dough out on to a lightly floured

surface and knead the dough for about 10 minutes until you have an elastic and smooth texture. Flour lightly and wrap in a tea towel. Refrigerate and relax the dough for an hour.

3 · Rolling the pasta by hand
You can roll the pasta simply with a rolling pin. First lightly flour the work surface, then cut the dough into four pieces. Flatten each piece with the rolling pin, then roll each out, turning it from time to time to prevent sticking, and stretching it occasionally. Roll until it is about 1 mm ($\frac{1}{16}$ in) thick.

4 · Rolling the pasta by machine
This is by far the easiest. You can buy a hand pasta machine – it will prove to be a very good investment.

Fix the machine on to the side of the table. Cut the dough into four pieces, and flatten each piece with a rolling pin. Roll the dough in the machine, using the thickest setting, then fold each sheet back on itself and repeat, thinning it each time on a finer setting until the pasta is about 1.5 mm ($\frac{1}{32}$ in) thick.

5 · Cutting the pasta
The pasta is now ready to be cut into any shape you wish – strips wide or narrow, for ravioli, noodles, tagliatelli, etc.

6 · Drying the pasta
If you are not going to use the pasta immediately, drape it loosely on a tray or a stick to dry, for a minimum of 6 hours. Store it in a glass storage jar in your kitchen for future use.

7 · Cooking the pasta
The pasta must be cooked in large amounts of boiling salted water. Use 15 g ($\frac{1}{2}$ oz) salt per litre ($1\frac{3}{4}$ pints) water. Cook for $3\frac{1}{2}$–4 minutes if the pasta has been dried, $1\frac{1}{2}$–2 for fresh. To prevent sticking, stir the pasta from time to time. Taste often while it is cooking so the pasta is only cooked

al dente. Drain well, and serve immediately on warmed plates with sauces or accompaniments of your choice.

VARIATIONS

The best way of learning how to use this recipe and how to vary it, is to buy Antonio Carluccio's book *Antonio Carluccio's Passion for Pasta* (BBC Books, 1993); he has devoted most of his professional life to the preparation, cooking and serving of pasta and also of wild mushrooms and truffles.

Green pasta Add 2 tablespoons Chlorophyll of Spinach (see below) to the dough before kneading.

Red pasta Add 2 tablespoons of Chlorophyll of Red Pepper (see below) to the dough before kneading.

Black pasta Add 1 tablespoon squid ink to the dough before kneading (you may need extra flour to soak up the extra fluid).

CHEF'S NOTES

Durum wheat flour is without any doubt the best. It is imported from Canada and America, and will give a firm texture to the pasta.

According to the flour you use, you may need a little more flour if the dough is too sticky, or a little water if the dough is too firm.

The kneading is essential to mix all the ingredients intimately together. This ensures a smooth dough. The dough will become elastic as the gluten of the flour has been worked, so the pasta needs to rest before rolling.

A lot of cooks put olive oil into the water when cooking pasta, hoping to prevent it sticking or boiling over. I find this totally unnecessary: the olive oil simply floats on the surface.

The more water used, the quicker it will regain its boil after the pasta is added. This also means that the amount of starch released by the pasta is minimized too.

Many people overcook pasta which ruins the texture. It should still have some firmness to it. Also, pasta is often cooked in advance, refreshed in cold water and then re-heated. The result of this is that the pasta is sticky and unpleasant, as well as overcooked.

Chlorophyll of Red Pepper

MAKES 3 TABLESPOONS

INGREDIENTS

1 medium red pepper
500 ml (17 fl oz) water

METHOD

Remove the pepper stalk, then halve, seed and discard the white ribs. Purée the pepper with the water until velvet-smooth. Strain through a fine conical sieve, then through a muslin cloth into a small saucepan. Gently bring to the boil. The rising temperature will coagulate the chlorophyll in the purée and the gentle boil will carry it to the surface where it can be scooped off with a tablespoon.

You will obtain 3 tablespoons of a red paste with a mild taste of red pepper.

Keep for one to two days in a covered container in the fridge, or for one or two weeks in the freezer.

Chlorophyll of Spinach

MAKES 2 TABLESPOONS

INGREDIENTS

250 g (9 oz) fresh spinach
    leaves
500 ml (17 fl oz) water

METHOD

Snap off the spinach stalks and wash the leaves in plenty of cold water. Liquidize with the measured water until very smooth and all the fibres have been broken down.

Process as for the Chlorophyll of Red Pepper above. Store as above as well.

White Chicken Stock

This subtle stock is used to enrich and enhance the flavours of many dishes, as well as soups. The technique in this stock illustrates the exchange of flavours of ingredients into the water.

MAKES 1 LITRE ($1^3/_4$ PINTS)
PREPARATION TIME: 20 minutes

COOKING TIME: 1 hour

PLANNING AHEAD: This stock can be made in advance and stored for a couple of days in the fridge, or up to two months in the freezer.

INGREDIENTS
2 kg ($4^1/_2$ lb) chicken wings
15 g ($^1/_2$ oz) unsalted butter or chicken fat
1 small onion, peeled and finely chopped
white of 1 small leek, finely chopped
1 small celery stalk, finely chopped
100 g (4 oz) button mushrooms, washed and finely sliced
1 garlic clove, peeled and crushed
10 white peppercorns, crushed
200 ml (7 fl oz) dry white wine (optional)
1.5 litres ($2^1/_2$ pints) cold water
1 bouquet garni (1 bay leaf, 4 sprigs fresh thyme, 6 sprigs fresh parsley, tied together)

METHOD

In a large saucepan, sweat the chicken wings in the butter over a low heat for 5 minutes without colouring. Stir occasionally.

Add the chopped vegetables, garlic and crushed peppercorns, and sweat for a further 5 minutes. Pour in the wine, if using, and boil to reduce by one-third.

Cover with the cold water, bring back to the boil and skim. Add the bouquet garni and simmer for 1 hour, skimming occasionally. Strain through a fine sieve and leave to cool, before storing in a covered container in the fridge or freezer.

CHEF'S NOTES

We use chicken wings here, but you could equally use chopped raw chicken carcasses. If you want a really rich-tasting stock, use a plump boiling fowl; it can then be served as a meal with vegetables.

The stock must boil for only a few minutes, to bring impurities up to the top. These can then be skimmed off. The stock then should simmer very gently so that it remains clear and the flavour remains pure.

Do not add salt to the stock: this can be added when you use the stock in a dish.

Brown Chicken Stock

Very often home cooks wish they could reproduce the sauces that are made in professional kitchens. Usually these stocks are very lengthy, complicated and impractical for the domestic cook. This recipe, however, has many merits: it is cheap, the yield is good, and the stock is well flavoured with good colour ... and will not take hours of your time. Of course it is not so easy as dissolving a stock cube in water, but the results are not comparable and are well worth the effort. It is the simplest way I know to add that touch of magic to your sauces!

Once the stock has been made, it can be stored in small containers in the freezer to be used as and when required.

MAKES 400 ML (14 FL OZ)
PREPARATION AND COOKING TIME: $1^1/_4$ hours

PLANNING AHEAD: The stock can be made in advance and chilled for a week or frozen for three weeks.

INGREDIENTS
100 ml ($3^1/_2$ fl oz) non-scented oil (safflower, sunflower or grapeseed)
1.5–2 kg ($3^1/_2$–$4^1/_2$ lb) chicken wings or carcases, finely chopped into 5 cm (2 in) pieces
1 medium onion, peeled and finely chopped
1 garlic clove, peeled and crushed
100 g (4 oz) mushrooms, chopped
1 tablespoon tomato purée
6 black peppercorns, crushed
$^1/_2$ bay leaf
1 sprig of fresh thyme
about 900 ml ($1^1/_2$ pints) water
2 teaspoons arrowroot or cornflour diluted in 50 ml (2 fl oz) water

METHOD
Pre-heat the oven to 230°C/450°F/Gas 8.

In a large flameproof roasting pan, heat the oil until it is smoking then, over the strongest heat, brown the chicken wings or carcases for 8–10 minutes, stirring occasionally with a wooden spoon. Add the chopped onion, garlic and mushrooms and cook for another 5 minutes until lightly coloured. Cook in the pre-heated oven for 15 minutes until the chicken wings and vegetables turn a rich brown.

Spoon out and discard the excess fat. Add the tomato purée, peppercorns, bay leaf and thyme and stir. Add 200 ml (7 fl oz) of the cold water, and scrape up all the caramelized juices from the bottom of the pan.

Transfer the bones and liquid to a large pan, cover with the remaining cold water and bring to the boil. Skim, then simmer for 20–30 minutes. Strain off the juices and skim off any fat.

Whisk the diluted arrowroot or cornflour into the stock and bring to the boil to bind the stock lightly. Cool, then chill or freeze.

VARIATIONS

A beautiful veal juice can be made in the same way with veal trimmings.

CHEF'S NOTES

I prefer to keep this stock neutral tasting so that it will not interfere with the flavour of the sauce to which it is added. If you want more depth to the taste, add a glass of white wine or dry Madeira, before adding the water.

———

You should chop the chicken bones into small pieces, about 5 cm (2 in) square, because the smaller the chicken pieces are, the less cooking time will be needed, thus producing a clearer, stronger flavour and also a better colour.

———

The degree of browning of the bones will determine the taste and quantity of the stock. If it does not have sufficient colour, add a teaspoon of soy sauce. Too much browning or cooking in the oven will have an adverse effect on the flavour; the bones and meat will dry out and impart a bitter taste to the stock.

———

There is no salt in the stock because it may have to be reduced before use, and this would concentrate the saltiness. It's best to add salt at the last minute.

Vegetable Stock

This light vegetable stock is the base for many of my sauces. It has a wonderfully concentrated aroma of the garden and is very simple to make: it is best to prepare a large quantity and keep it covered in the fridge (for one week) or in the freezer (for one month).

MAKES ABOUT 600 ML (1 PINT)
PREPARATION AND COOKING
TIME: 20 minutes

INGREDIENTS

1 onion, peeled and finely chopped
1 large courgette, trimmed and finely sliced
1 small leek, trimmed and finely chopped
1/2 fennel bulb, finely sliced (optional)
1 garlic clove, peeled and finely chopped
12 black peppercorns, crushed
about 600 ml (1 pint) cold water
2 sprigs of fresh tarragon, chopped
a tiny bunch of fresh chervil, chopped

METHOD

Place all the vegetables and the garlic and peppercorns in a medium saucepan. Cover with the cold water, bring to the boil and simmer for 15 minutes. Add the chopped herbs, and simmer for a further 5 minutes.

Using the back of a ladle, force the liquid through a fine conical sieve into a small bowl (or a suitable container for freezing).

CHEF'S NOTES

Vary the herbs according to the dish you are cooking; add them at the last moment to preserve their fragrance and colour.

Do not exceed 15 minutes' cooking time in order to preserve the freshness of flavour.

Add salt only when using the stock in a recipe.

Hollandaise Sauce

A traditional hollandaise sauce is made with 200 g (7 oz) butter per 3 egg yolks, which is a real killer. This sauce uses only 50 g (2 oz) butter; besides its improved lightness, there will be no feelings of guilt! It can be served with poached fish, broccoli, asparagus or spring greens.

FOR 4 GUESTS

PREPARATION AND COOKING TIME: 15 minutes

SPECIAL EQUIPMENT: A large, very fine and supple stainless-steel or electric whisk; a sugar thermometer; a saucepan large enough to hold a bowl (see also Cooking in a Bain-marie, p. 35)

PLANNING AHEAD: The sauce can be prepared an hour in advance and kept in a warm *bain-marie* at 50°C (122°F), covered with a butter paper to prevent a skin forming.

INGREDIENTS

3 free-range egg yolks
4 tablespoons water
50 g (2 oz) unsalted butter, melted
1 pinch of salt
1 pinch of cayenne pepper
juice of $\frac{1}{4}$ lemon

METHOD

1 · Preparing the bain-marie
Fill the saucepan two-thirds with water, and sit the bowl on the top edges of the saucepan so the base touches the water. The water should be just under simmering point.

2 · Cooking the sabayon
Place the egg yolks and water in the bowl and whisk over the gentle heat vigorously for about 10 minutes until you obtain a beautifully expanded, light and lemon-coloured foam, about six or seven times its original volume. (Use an electric whisk, unless you are a masochist like me!) Continue whisking until the foam has more texture.

3 · Incorporating the butter
Pour the melted butter into the sabayon, and whisk in briefly. Season with the salt, cayenne pepper and lemon juice. Taste, and correct seasoning if necessary.

Cover with butter paper, and keep warm in the water-bath at 50°C (122°F) for up to an hour.

VARIATIONS
This can be used as the basis for many other sauces: you can add herbs such as tarragon, basil and chives, and, if you are feeling rich, a few drops of truffle essence.

Boil a finely chopped shallot with 4 tablespoons of vinegar until you have about a teaspoon left. Add to the hollandaise sauce with some finely chopped tarragon to make a Béarnaise sauce. By adding a teaspoon of tomato purée to the Béarnaise, you have a Choron sauce. Both of these sauces go very well with meat and grilled fish.

CHEF'S NOTES

The egg yolks must be free-range, as this will give both taste and colour.

The addition of the water will increase the volume of the sabayon foam.

When cooking the sabayon, the whisking of the water and egg yolk will emulsify the egg yolks and introduce air into the mixture. Separately and simultaneously, the heat will help develop the foam and after 10 minutes you will have a large volume of lemony foam composed of millions of tiny air bubbles, surrounded by egg yolk protein.

You may be tempted to believe that the sabayon is now ready. However, at this stage it is not stable, as the egg protein around the little air bubbles has not coagulated and the air could seep out of them very quickly which would cause the sabayon to collapse. The temperature within the egg yolk is about 50°C (92°F), so more heat needs to be applied while whisking continuously, in order to partly cook the egg yolks.

It is difficult to specify exactly when the sabayon

is ready, but if you see small particles of cooked egg yolk this should alert you to imminent disaster. The best way to ensure success, until you have acquired the skill and a true understanding of what is happening, is to use a thermometer and check the temperature – it should be between 60 and 65°C (140–149°F).

———

The melted butter can be incorporated all at once, as it is such a small quantity.

———

This is a very delicate sauce, so very little salt needs to be added. Remember that you can add, but not subtract.

Lemon Butter Sauce

This classic sauce, known as *beurre blanc*, or 'white butter', is legendary. Despite its richness it still shines alongside lighter, more modern sauces. It makes a simple and delicious accompaniment to any poached or grilled fish. It is also very easy.

SERVES 4–6

PREPARATION AND COOKING
TIME: 15 minutes

INGREDIENTS
50 g (2 oz) shallots, peeled and finely chopped
2 tablespoons white wine vinegar

100 ml (3¹⁄₂ fl oz) dry white wine
1 tablespoon cold water
200 g (7 oz) unsalted butter, chilled and diced
salt and freshly ground white pepper
lemon juice

METHOD
In a small heavy-bottomed saucepan, combine the chopped shallot, vinegar and wine and boil until you have about 1 tablespoon of syrupy liquid left. Add the cold water (this extra liquid will help the emulsion) then, over a gentle heat, whisk in the cold diced butter, a little at a time, until completely amalgamated.

The finished sauce will be creamy and homogeneous, and a delicate lemon yellow. Season with a tiny amount of salt and pepper and enliven with a squeeze of lemon. Keep warm.

CHEF'S NOTES

Shallots have a tough, fibrous second layer of skin. Remove this as well as the peel, but leave the finely chopped shallots in the sauce for a pleasant, rustic flavour and texture.

———

The success of the sauce depends greatly on the quality of the butter. Use the very best unsalted butter you can find. The butter must also be cold. If too soft, it will melt too quickly and not emulsify.

———

Ideally, the temperature of the sauce should be more than 70°C (158°F) when incorporating the butter. Test with your finger from time to time – the heat should be bearable. If the sauce is too cold, the butter will cream and separate. Try to maintain an even temperature.

———

If the liquid is not sufficiently reduced, the sauce will be too sharp. (If so, add a little more butter or 2 tablespoons of whipping cream at the end.)

———

Lemon butter sauce is an emulsified sauce. The application of heat stabilizes the emulsion. Constant whisking is extremely important to produce a smooth emulsion, especially at the beginning.

———

The sauce will remain rather delicate, and should be kept for no more than 1 hour in a warm *bain-marie* at 120–150°C (248–300°F). Whisk from time to time to maintain the emulsion. If the sauce does separate, bring 2 tablespoons of whipping cream to the boil in a clean saucepan, then slowly whisk in the separated sauce.

VARIATIONS
This 'mother' sauce can produce many offspring: add julienne strips of ginger, blanched for 15 minutes; lemon or orange zests, blanched for 3–4 minutes; or scent the sauce with shredded coriander, tarragon or other herbs.

For a rosemary butter, simply infuse 2 teaspoons of chopped rosemary leaves in the butter.

Hazelnut Butter or Beurre Noisette

'Hazelnut' butter is butter which has been heated to a sufficiently high temperature for the solids contained in the butterfat to start cooking. This makes the butter foam, turns it a rich golden colour, and gives it a distinct taste of hazelnuts. Be warned, though: the stage beyond hazelnut butter is *beurre noir*, or *black* butter, which is rather nasty and pretty indigestible.

Mayonnaise

Mayonnaise is an emulsified sauce which illustrates the magical power of egg yolks. Smooth and delicious, this classic sauce is very simple to make. Use sunflower, safflower or grapeseed oil.

FOR 4 GUESTS
PREPARATION AND COOKING
TIME: 10 minutes

INGREDIENTS
2 egg yolks
1 teaspoon Dijon mustard
salt and freshly ground
    white pepper
250 ml (8 fl oz) best-quality
    non-scented oil (see
    above)
1 teaspoon white wine
    vinegar
2 teaspoons lemon juice

METHOD
In a large mixing bowl, whisk together the egg yolks, mustard, 2 pinches of salt and 3 turns of pepper. Start adding the oil in a steady trickle, whisking energetically until the oil is absorbed and the mixture turns pale yellow and thickens, usually after adding about 150 ml (5 fl oz) of oil.

Thin down or loosen the consistency with the white wine vinegar and lemon juice, then whisk in the remaining oil. Taste and correct seasoning if necessary. Store in a covered container for two to three days in the lower part of the fridge.

VARIATIONS
Mayonnaise is a mother sauce from which others can be made. Add 1 tablespoon of tomato sauce or paprika, 1 teaspoon of curry powder or $^1/_4$ teaspoon of saffron, etc.

If you make the mayonnaise with olive oil, by simply adding 2 crushed garlic cloves and a pinch each of saffron and cayenne, you have the most beautiful *rouille* for a fish dish or a fish soup.

CHEF'S NOTES

All the ingredients must be at room temperature, especially the oil. If too cold, it will be difficult to incorporate.

If you are not going to use the mayonnaise immediately, make it with grapeseed oil, which prevents it from separating in the fridge.

The most difficult stage in the mayonnaise is the start. If you add the oil too quickly it is very likely to curdle as the emulsifiers in both mustard and egg yolk will not be able to absorb it.

When the sauce is emulsified and homogeneous, it will become stable, and the rest of the oil can be added in greater quantities.

If the mayonnaise separates, add 1 teaspoon of mustard in a different container and gradually incorporate the mayonnaise until smooth.

Tartare Sauce

FOR 4 GUESTS
PREPARATION TIME: 10
minutes

INGREDIENTS
1 quantity Mayonnaise (see
    above)
30 g (1$^1/_4$ oz) gherkins,
    chopped
30 g (1$^1/_4$ oz) tiny capers,
    washed and patted dry
2 tablespoons chopped fresh
    parsley
2 tablespoons chopped fresh
    chervil
2 shallots, peeled and finely
    chopped

METHOD
Put the mayonnaise into a bowl or dish and stir in the remaining ingredients.

Mustard Vinaigrette

This is one of the most delicious dressings with lots of depth of flavour. It is the one that most French families favour.

MAKES 150 ML (5 FL OZ)
PREPARATION TIME: 5 minutes

INGREDIENTS
1 tablespoon Dijon mustard
salt and freshly ground
    white pepper
100 ml ($3^1/_2$ fl oz) groundnut
    oil, at room temperature
1 tablespoon white wine
    vinegar
50 ml ($1^3/_4$ fl oz) warm water

METHOD
Place the Dijon mustard, a pinch of salt and 2 turns of pepper in a salad bowl and slowly whisk in a quarter of the oil, doing so at a trickle, and very gradually.

Add the white wine vinegar which will thin down or loosen the mixture.

Slowly incorporate the remaining oil, and thin down with the warm water.

VARIATIONS
This recipe can be made with different oils such as olive and sunflower.

You can make the vinaigrette in much larger quantities and keep it for up to a week in your kitchen at room temperature, shaking the bottle about once a day.

CHEF'S NOTES

Mustard holds an emulsifier which will allow it to absorb quite large quantities of liquid and oil. However, this process has got to be done carefully. The mustard should be emulsified by whisking it, not with a spoon or a fork, whilst the oil is added at a trickle.

To help the emulsification, the oil should be at room temperature.

Adding warm water will help smooth the vinaigrette and thin down its richness.

Mustard and Dill Sauce

This is especially good with smoked trout.

FOR 4 GUESTS
PREPARATION TIME: 5 minutes

INGREDIENTS
1 tablespoon Dijon mustard
1 small shallot, peeled and
    very finely chopped
100 ml ($3^1/_2$ fl oz) sunflower
    oil
1 tablespoon warm water
salt and freshly ground
    white pepper
1 teaspoon finely cut fresh
    dill
30 g ($1^1/_4$ oz) small capers,
    rinsed

METHOD
Place the mustard in a bowl. Add the chopped shallot and progressively trickle in the oil, whisking all the time, until the mustard has completely absorbed it, and the sauce is velvety and emulsified.

Dilute it with the warm water, then add a little salt and pepper, the chopped dill and capers.

Non-scented Dressing

MAKES ABOUT 75 ML
($2^3/_4$ FL OZ)

INGREDIENTS
1 tablespoon white wine
    vinegar
4 tablespoons non-scented
    oil such as safflower,
    sunflower or grapeseed
    oil
salt and freshly ground
    white pepper

METHOD
Mix the oil and the vinegar together and add a large pinch of salt and 8 turns of pepper. Store in a jar with a lid. Shake well before serving.

VARIATIONS
A few freshly chopped tarragon or chervil leaves and a finely chopped shallot will give this vinaigrette a little more depth.

To make Hazelnut Oil Dressing, replace 1 tablespoon of the non-scented oil with 1–2 tablespoons of hazelnut oil.

To make Walnut Oil Dressing, replace 1 tablespoon of the non-scented oil with 1–2 tablespoons of walnut oil.

Hazelnut and Soured Cream Dressing

So many flavoured oils, direct offspring of the *nouvelle cuisine*, have been much abused and used in so many wrong ways, just for the sake of novelty. I know you will enjoy this dressing, however, as it goes particularly well with goats' cheese salad, leeks or just salad leaves.

MAKES 250 ML (8 FL OZ)
PREPARATION TIME: 5 minutes

PLANNING AHEAD: This dressing can be prepared a few hours in advance.

INGREDIENTS
1 tablespoon Dijon mustard
salt and freshly ground white pepper
100 ml (3½ fl oz) hazelnut oil
2 tablespoons white wine vinegar
100 ml (3½ fl oz) soured cream
4 tablespoons warm water

METHOD
Place the Dijon mustard, a pinch of salt and 2 turns of pepper in a salad bowl, and slowly whisk in a quarter of the oil, doing so at a trickle, and very gradually. Add the white wine vinegar which will thin down or loosen the mixture.

Slowly incorporate the remaining oil, then whisk in the soured cream. Then thin down with warm water to obtain the right texture, a thickness that will coat the back of a spoon.

CHEF'S NOTES

As both mustard and soured cream have a good thick texture, the dressing needs loosening or thinning down with a little water.

The use of the soured cream in this recipe will bring a rich texture, but primarily it will add a roundness and tone down the otherwise strong taste of the hazelnut oil.

Balsamic Vinegar and Olive Oil Dressing

MAKES ABOUT 300 ML (10 FL OZ)
PREPARATION TIME: 5 minutes

INGREDIENTS
50 ml (2 fl oz) water
200 ml (7 fl oz) olive oil
50 ml (2 fl oz) balsamic vinegar
2 tablespoons sherry vinegar
½ teaspoon freshly ground black pepper
1 level teaspoon salt
½ teaspoon caster sugar (optional)

METHOD
Whisk all the ingredients together. Taste and correct seasoning, adding the sugar if necessary.

CHEF'S NOTES

The quantity of balsamic vinegar used will depend on its maturity. If it is old and thicker, you may need to increase the quantity; if it is younger, it will be more acidic, so you may need to use a little less.

Tomato Vinaigrette

Serve this simple sauce with fish such as red mullet, scallops, etc.

MAKES ABOUT 175 G (6 OZ)
PREPARATION TIME: 10 minutes

INGREDIENTS
200 g (7 oz) ripe tomatoes
a large pinch of salt
a large pinch of caster sugar
a dash of white wine vinegar
3 tablespoons extra virgin olive oil
freshly ground white pepper

METHOD
Halve the tomatoes and remove the seeds with a teaspoon. Chop the flesh roughly and purée finely in a food processor, then force through a fine conical sieve into a mixing bowl, using a ladle. Or you can put the tomatoes through a vegetable mill to remove the skin, etc. Season with salt and sugar, add the vinegar then whisk in the olive oil until

well emulsified. The sauce should be smooth. Finally, season with 4 turns of pepper.

CHEF'S NOTES

The success of a tomato vinaigrette depends completely on the ripeness of the tomatoes. Use fat, fleshy Marmande, olive-shaped Roma or sweet cherry tomatoes.

──────────

You can whisk the oil in using the liquidizer if you wish. The dressing will lose its deep red colour, but it will still be emulsified.

──────────

This sauce can be served cold or warm. If you warm it beware of not boiling it or the proteins of the tomatoes will cook, solidify, and the sauce will be grainy and unpleasant, losing its freshness and colour.

──────────

Whilst re-heating this sauce, do so for only 30–40 seconds, and whisk it all the time to circulate the heat and to emulsify the olive oil.

Black Olive Purée

This is the olive spread/dip of Provence, known as *tapenade*.

MAKES 250 G (9 OZ)
INGREDIENTS
200 g (7 oz) black olives with
  herbs, pitted
2 garlic cloves, peeled and
  chopped

2 anchovy fillets
50 ml (2 fl oz) olive oil
2 large pinches of freshly
  ground black pepper

METHOD
Place all the ingredients in a liquidizer, and purée finely. Push the ingredients down in the bowl once or twice. Reserve in a jar in the fridge.

Oven-dried Tomatoes

What is sold under the label of sun-dried tomatoes is often misleading, as most of them are dried in a ventilated oven; in order to be absolutely safe, all the moisture of the tomatoes has to go. The result is hardly palatable as they are so dry and chewy, and often taste very unpleasant. Drying your own tomatoes will give you the most delicious and visually satisfying pleasure.

FOR 4 GUESTS
PREPARATION TIME: 5
minutes

OVEN DRYING TIME: 11–12
hours

PLANNING AHEAD: This dish can be prepared a week in advance and the tomatoes kept in a jar of olive oil in the fridge.

INGREDIENTS
8 ripe Roma tomatoes
250 ml (8 fl oz) extra virgin
  olive oil
1 teaspoon fresh thyme
  leaves
salt and freshly ground
  black pepper
1 whole stalk of fresh basil
  leaves
1 garlic clove, peeled

METHOD
Pre-heat the oven to 60°C (140°F), or to the very *lowest* it can go. The floor of a gas oven on slow is about right.

Remove the stalk or calyx of the tomatoes, then cut *into* the tomatoes at this calyx end to remove the tiny round core of flesh. Cut each tomato in quarters lengthways. Place them on a small tray, sprinkle with 50 ml (2 fl oz) of the extra virgin olive oil and the thyme, and mix together to coat the tomatoes. Sprinkle with a pinch of salt and pepper.

Arrange the tomatoes on their skin side, cut side up, and dry in the pre-heated oven for 11–12 hours until all the moisture has evaporated.

Place the tomatoes in a large jar and cover with the remaining olive oil. Add the basil and garlic, and reserve in the fridge. Keep for up to a week.

CHEF'S NOTES

The best time to prepare these tomatoes is between July and the end of September and certainly not in January, February or any of those dreary months. Then the only tomatoes available come from Holland, and are absolutely tasteless, colourless and watery, real Frankenstein monsters of genetic engineering and intensive farming. During the English tomato season, use English tomatoes, but make sure they are not too large as there would be too much moisture. Marmande are not right. Roma are perfect as they are fleshy, with very little acidity and water content.

The aim is to remove most of the moisture of the tomatoes to create different textures and flavours. The temperature is extremely important: too low and there will not be enough evaporation of the moisture and the tomato would be likely to ferment and spoil; too high a temperature would take too much moisture too quickly and the tomato would shrivel and have a very unpleasant texture and taste, very much the same as those you can buy in the shops.

It is better to place the tomato quarters on their skin side, fleshy parts up, as the drying process will be more efficient and thorough. The warm air will carry away the water molecules as they evaporate from the surface of the tomatoes.

If you wish to keep your oven-dried tomatoes for many weeks, you need to dry them for 3 more hours, for 14–15 hours in total. After that time all the moisture will have gone from the tomatoes, and they will be safe to keep, at room temperature, in jars of olive oil with some herbs.

Provençale Breadcrumbs

FOR 8 GUESTS
PREPARATION TIME: 10 minutes

PLANNING AHEAD: These savoury crumbs can be kept in a sealed container in the fridge for up to one week.

INGREDIENTS
100 g (4 oz) dried bread

1 garlic clove, peeled and crushed
1 tablespoon finely chopped fresh parsley
1 teaspoon dried thyme
3 tablespoons olive oil
salt and freshly ground white pepper

METHOD
Place all the ingredients, except for the olive oil and seasoning, in a food processor and grind until a rough, sandy texture is achieved. Transfer the crumbs to a large bowl and mix in the olive oil. Taste, then season with salt and pepper. Use immediately, or store as required.

CHEF'S NOTES

The bread must be completely dry before you grind it, or the moisture combined with the olive oil will make the mixture lumpy.

Pat the parsley dry only once, before chopping. It is common practice to press parsley in a tea towel once chopped, but this weakens its vigorous taste, and leaves you with tasteless pieces of fibre.

Vary the herbs and add more to suit your taste or the dish it accompanies: rosemary, basil, tarragon and chervil are good alternatives.

North Indian Mango Pickle

MAKES ABOUT 900 G (2 LB)
PREPARATION TIME: 10 minutes

MARINATING TIME: 4–5 days

PLANNING AHEAD: This pickle must be made at least two weeks before needed, but it can keep for up to three months in the fridge.

INGREDIENTS
4 large green mangoes

4 tablespoons fenugreek seeds, soaked in cold water and drained
4 tablespoons cumin seeds
4 tablespoons fennel seeds
2 tablespoons black peppercorns, crushed
2 tablespoons onion seeds
2 tablespoons chilli powder
3 tablespoons salt
1 tablespoon turmeric
sunflower oil

METHOD
Cut the mangoes plus their skins into bite-sized pieces, or smaller dice if you like. Place in a suitably-sized bowl or casserole. Combine all the spices and mix them into the mangoes. Stir in 4 tablespoons of oil and leave to one side for two

days, covered, at room temperature. This allows the flavours to mingle.

Heat enough oil to cover the mixture. Cool it a little before adding a further tablespoon of chilli powder if you like (it's optional, and you could use paprika instead for the extra colour), then pour it over the marinated mangoes. Stir well and leave the dish, covered, in a warm place for two to three days.

Pour the pickle into clean glass bottles or jars, seal, and leave for a further week before eating.

CHEF'S NOTES

The use of green, unripe mangoes is essential as the acidity within them is the preservative factor.

Be sure to cover the mango completely with oil, otherwise the pickle will start to ferment.

Garlic Butter

FOR 1 GUEST
INGREDIENTS
1 tablespoon unsalted
   butter, softened

½ garlic clove, peeled and
   puréed

METHOD
Simply mix the butter and garlic together and use. You can chill it for a day or two, or freeze it, well wrapped.

Croûtons

Croûtons can either be sliced from a small baguette or diced from slices of a sliced loaf of bread.

FOR 4 GUESTS
INGREDIENTS
30 g (1¼ oz) unsalted
butter

2 slices bread (about
   150 g/5 oz), diced

METHOD
Pre-heat the oven to 220°C/425°F/Gas 7.

Melt the butter, add the diced bread, and toss to cover the dice with butter. Roast in the pre-heated oven for about 5–8 minutes until they are golden. Drain on absorbent paper and re-heat gently when needed.

VARIATIONS
Olive oil croûtons can be cooked in exactly the same way as above, simply by replacing the butter with olive oil.

The croûtons can also be flavoured with garlic. Simply add 1 teaspoon of finely puréed garlic, after cooking, then mix.

Raspberry Jam

Traditionally, jam is made with 1 kg (2¼ lb) raspberries and the same quantity of sugar, which means that the jam consists of 67–70 per cent sugar. This jam is made with only 30 per cent sugar which enables it to keep its freshness and its beautiful texture.

MAKES ABOUT 1.4 KG (3 LB)
COOKING TIME: About 10 minutes

STERILIZING TIME: 20–25 minutes

SPECIAL EQUIPMENT: A sugar thermometer; sterile jars with screw-top lids.

INGREDIENTS
300 g (11 oz) caster sugar
1 kg (2¼ lb) perfectly ripe
   raspberries
100 g (4 oz) caster sugar
   mixed with 30 g (1¼ oz)
   dried pectin
juice of 1 lemon

METHOD
1 · Making the jam
Place the 300 g (11 oz) sugar in a heavy-based cast-iron pan and warm over a medium heat, stirring with a wooden spoon. Add the raspberries and mix, just breaking them up a little. Cover with the lid and boil rapidly for 5 minutes. Remove the lid and cook for a further 5 minutes until the temperature reaches 100°C (212°F). Skim off any impurities – we used to eat this when children! – then sprinkle in the mixed sugar and pectin, together with the lemon juice. Stir in and cook for a few more minutes.

2 · Testing for setting point

Check for setting point by placing a little of the jam on a cold saucer and putting in the fridge for a few minutes. If setting point has been achieved, the jam should wrinkle when pushed with a finger.

Pour the jam into the clean jars through a funnel and seal, preferably with a screw top. Leave to cool.

3 · Sterilizing the jam

Place the filled jars, with their lids still on, into a large pan of cold water, on a double layer of paper or cloth, or a wire grid. (This keeps the jars away from the direct heat on the bottom of the pan.) Bring the water to the boil gently, then simmer for 20–25 minutes from boiling point.

Remove from the water with tongs, and leave to cool.

Dry, label and store in a dark cool place. The jam keeps well, for up to a year, but once opened, it is wise to store it in the fridge.

VARIATIONS

The jam can be made with strawberries, blackberries, a mixture of fruits – but the quantity of sugar may have to vary, depending on the sweetness of the fruit.

CHEF'S NOTES

Pectin is a substance naturally present in most fruits, but in differing proportions, and it causes pulp to set. Try to find special low-sugar dried pectin: it should be available in a chemist or grocer and it is available in Waitrose.

Low-sugar jam is more difficult to make because there is less sugar to help the pectins bind to each other. This means that the jam could end up a sad, runny mess.

Proportions of pectin, sugar and acids are important in setting jam. The sugar causes a pectin chain to shed the water molecules. The acid of the juice then produces an electrical charge on the pectins, allowing them to bind to each other; as they link

up, the pectins form a three-dimensional mesh which gives the jam its wonderful thick texture.

Pastry Cream

Pastry cream – or *crème pâtissière*, as it is known in French – has many uses: as a lining for fruit tartlets, as a filling for cakes and eclairs, and as a base for sweet soufflés (see p. 45).

MAKES 600 ML (1 PINT)
PREPARATION AND COOKING
TIME: 20 minutes

PLANNING AHEAD: The cream can be made up to four days in advance and kept covered in the fridge.

INGREDIENTS
500 ml (17 fl oz) milk

1 vanilla pod, split lengthways
6 egg yolks
100 g (4 oz) caster sugar
25 g (1 oz) plain flour
20 g ($^3/_4$ oz) cornflour
1 teaspoon caster sugar for dusting

METHOD

In a large heavy-bottomed saucepan, bring the milk to the boil. Add the split vanilla pod and infuse at just below simmering point for about 5 minutes. Draw off the heat and remove the vanilla.

Cream together the egg yolks and sugar, then whisk in the flour and cornflour.

Pour 100 ml ($3^1/_2$ fl oz) of the hot milk into the egg mixture, and whisk until well blended. Bring back to the boil, whisking until smooth. Add the remaining milk and boil for 1 minute, whisking continuously.

To store, transfer to a bowl or container and sprinkle the surface with caster sugar to prevent a skin forming. Cool, seal with cling film and chill.

Vanilla Cream

As its French name – *crème anglaise* – suggests, the French have taken the idea of this cream from

England. It is the most delicious sauce which can complement and create all sorts of desserts – ice creams, bavarois mousses and so on.

FOR 6–8 GUESTS
PREPARATION TIME:
5 minutes

COOKING TIME: 10 minutes

PLANNING AHEAD: This cream can be made a day in advance, if kept chilled.

INGREDIENTS
1 vanilla pod
5 free-range egg yolks
75 g (3 oz) caster sugar
500 ml (17 fl oz) milk

METHOD

Split the vanilla pod in half lengthways and scrape out the seeds. Chop the pod finely.

In a large bowl, use a hand-held mixer to whisk together the egg yolks and caster sugar for about 30 seconds until a pale yellow colour. The mixture should trail off the whisk in ribbons.

In a medium pan, mix the vanilla seeds and chopped pod with the milk.

Bring to the boil, then simmer gently for about 5 minutes. Pour the vanilla milk through a fine sieve on to the egg yolk and sugar mixture, whisking all the time. With the back of a spoon, press the vanilla seeds and pod against the side of the bowl to extract as much flavour as possible.

Return the mixture to the pan and, over a medium heat, stir until it thickens and coats the back of the spoon. Strain the cream immediately into a bowl and continue stirring for a few more minutes. Cool and then reserve in the fridge for up to 24 hours.

VARIATIONS

Lemon cream

Remove 6 strips of lemon zest using a potato peeler, add to the milk during simmering, and proceed as above.

Orange cream

Remove 8 strips of orange zest using a potato peeler and add to the milk during simmering. For extra interest and flavour add a dash of Grand Marnier when cool.

Chocolate cream

Add 25 g (1 oz) of good-quality plain chocolate, broken into small pieces, to the milk during simmering and proceed as above.

Coffee cream

Dissolve 20 g ($^3/_4$ oz) of instant coffee granules in 50 ml (2 fl oz) of boiling water. Cool and mix into the milk during simmering. Or add 50 ml (2 fl oz) of very strong espresso coffee, or 50 ml (2 fl oz) of coffee essence.

CHEF'S NOTES

The sole purpose of whisking the egg yolks and caster sugar together is to intimately bind both, to mix the protein of the egg yolk with the sugar. The pale colour comes from the air that has been trapped into the sugar/egg yolk mixture.

When you pour the hot vanilla milk on to the egg yolks, whisking is essential to prevent the egg yolk proteins cooking, coagulating and ruining the cream. (They would 'scramble'.)

Although this recipe is simple enough, it is essential to understand what is happening. What we try to achieve is the partial cooking of the egg yolk proteins which will coagulate and give texture to the cream. If the heat is too strong the egg yolk will be overcooked and the cream will be ruined.

Stirring the cream whilst cooking is equally important, as this will distribute the heat properly. That is why it must be done on a medium heat rather than strong.

To make sure that the cream is ready, lift the spoon and trace a line with your finger on the back of it. Angle the spoon, and the cream should be thick enough not to flow back into the finger mark. Another method is to use a thermometer but this would be highly impractical ... Practice makes perfect!

Italian Meringue

PREPARATION AND COOKING TIME: 25 minutes

SPECIAL EQUIPMENT: A sugar thermometer; a straight-sided sugar pan

PLANNING AHEAD: It is always easier to make a larger quantity than a small one. This meringue, which does not require further cooking, can be made up to a day in advance and stored in an airtight container in the fridge.

INGREDIENTS
4 tablespoons water
120 g (4½ oz) caster sugar
2 egg whites
1 teaspoon lemon juice, strained

METHOD

1 · Cooking the sugar

Put the water in a straight-sided sugar pan and add the sugar. Bring to the boil over a medium heat, stirring from time to time.

When the syrup has melted and reaches 105–110°C (220–230°F), leave on the heat and start beating the egg whites.

2 · Beating the egg whites

In an electric mixer on medium speed, beat the egg whites to a soft peak, then add the lemon juice and beat until firm.

3 · Mixing the sugar syrup and egg whites

When the temperature of the sugar syrup reaches 120°C (248°F), set your mixer at its lowest speed, and gradually add the boiling syrup, pouring it in between the sides of the mixing bowl and the whisks.

Continue beating at low speed until the meringue is tepid. Cool completely, then store in an airtight container until required.

CHEF'S NOTES

Egg whites will foam better if they are three or five days old. As the egg ages there is an evaporation of water, giving more strength to the albumen and making the white less prone to separation.

Always ensure that the bowl and whisk are meticulously clean and free of fat. Any trace of fat whatsoever would diminish the bulk of the foam by up to one-third. For the same reason, when you separate egg yolk from white, ensure there is no trace of yolk in the white because of the former's fat content.

For safety reasons, when adding the boiling syrup, it is important to reduce the speed of the whisk and pour the syrup in between the whisk and the side of the bowl. The 120°C (248°F) temperature will partly cook the egg white protein and will strengthen the foam and make it stable.

You can add the syrup at 110°C (230°F), but the meringue will be less firm.

Watch the syrup temperature carefully; it must not exceed 120°C (248°F). If you have no sugar thermometer but plenty of confidence, use the following method: dip your thumb and index finger into cold water, then immediately in hot syrup and immediately back into cold water, rubbing the sugar between your fingers. If it can be shaped into a ball, it is ready. Please *do not attempt this* unless you feel really confident or have a first-aid kit! So, investing in a thermometer is a wise choice.

Stock Syrup

This stock syrup is often used to soak sponge used in 'compound' desserts (see p. 249). Use an alcohol flavouring appropriate to the dessert.

PREPARATION TIME: 5 minutes

COOKING TIME: 15 minutes

INGREDIENTS
50 ml (2 fl oz) water
50 g (2 oz) caster sugar
1 tablespoon strong alcohol such as dark rum or kirsch
a dash of lemon juice

METHOD

Place the water, then the sugar into a saucepan, and bring to the boil to dissolve the sugar. Remove from the heat and allow to cool.

Add the alcohol and lemon juice. The syrup is now ready!

CHEF'S NOTES

Too often the sugar is added first then the water. This means that the sugar does not have time to dissolve, and often burns. Simply bring the water and sugar to the boil; do not continue the cooking process or you may end up with a very sticky syrup or, even worse, a caramel.

The syrup must be cooled before the alcohol is added or it will evaporate.

The lemon juice counterbalances the sweetness of the sugar and increases the flavour.

Soups

Fresh Vegetable Soup
with Chervil (see p. 73)

Raymond Blanc

Pasta Soup with Watercress, Peas and Lettuce

SCIENTIST'S NOTES

The two basic ingredients of pasta are flour and eggs. When pasta is boiled, water is absorbed by the starch granules in the flour which swell, releasing molecules into the water. The swelling of the starch and the fusion of the granules is continuous during the cooking of the pasta and is only stabilized by the presence of the coagulating proteins in the egg yolks. It is important to keep the water boiling rapidly so that the addition of the cold pasta does not substantially reduce the water temperature. If the temperature of the water drops below 60°C (140°F), much more of the starch from the flour will drain into the water, thus damaging the texture of the pasta.

NUTRITIONIST'S NOTES

Watercress, spinach and lettuce are packed with iron, folic acid and beta-carotene. There's also a hefty serving of calcium in the dark green vegetables.

FOR 4 GUESTS

PREPARATION TIME: If you make your own pasta (see p. 52), 20 minutes; otherwise about 5 minutes.

COOKING TIME: 5–10 minutes

INGREDIENTS

1.5 litres (2½ pints) White Chicken Stock (see p. 54) or salted water
50 g (2 oz) shell pasta
50 g (2 oz) macaroni
50 g (2 oz) butterfly pasta
50 g (2 oz) smoked streaky bacon, rinded and very finely chopped

1 Little Gem lettuce, chopped in 8 lengthways, or 200 g (7 oz) iceberg lettuce, chopped
100 g (4 oz) spinach leaves, tough stalks removed
100 g (4 oz) watercress leaves, picked from the stalks
100 g (4 oz) courgettes, very thinly sliced
150 g (5 oz) podded young peas
salt and freshly ground black pepper

METHOD

Bring the chicken stock or water to the boil in a large pan, then add the pasta. Bring back to the boil, and boil until the pasta is just *al dente*: 1 minute for fresh pasta; 4 minutes for dried fresh pasta; 8–10 minutes for bought dried pasta. Add the chopped streaky bacon and cook for a further 1 minute. Finally add all the vegetables and cook for a further 2 minutes. Taste, season sparingly with salt and pepper, and pour into a large, hot soup tureen. Serve to your guests.

VARIATIONS

You can obviously use any form or shape of pasta. You can also add many other types of vegetables, such as tomatoes, French beans and so on, and replace the smoked bacon with very finely chopped ham. A generous sprinkling of freshly grated Parmesan would also be a good addition.

CHEF'S NOTES

Cooking time of dried pasta will be longer than that of fresh.

As we have cooked the smoked bacon in the chicken stock or

water, it will have released some of its saltiness into the soup, so be careful about seasoning. One little word of wisdom, if you will allow me: remember that it is always easier to add rather than subtract salt or any other seasoning.

The cooking time of this soup is very short to keep the textures and colours at their best.

SCIENTIST'S
NOTES

The cell walls of many plants are fairly strong which is why vegetables can withstand a comparatively long simmering time without disintegrating. Boiling, as opposed to simmering, could damage the vegetable, causing small particles to be separated off thereby causing the cooking water to become cloudy. If this happens, filter the stock through a very fine sieve, or clarify the stock (see p. 42). The other advantage of simmering is that the loss of aroma and flavour, as well as liquid, is also minimized.

.

The reason why it is important to add some hot liquid to the egg and soured cream mixture is because it helps to balance out the heat of the soup with the coagulating qualities of the egg. It thereby reduces the likelihood of the mixture curdling in the soup.

Bortsch

FOR 4 GUESTS

PREPARATION TIME: 20 minutes

COOKING TIME: $2\frac{1}{2}$ hours

PLANNING AHEAD: The bortsch can be made up to two days in advance and kept covered in the fridge.

INGREDIENTS
750 g (1½ lb) raw beetroots.
30 g (1¼ oz) unsalted butter
1 small onion, peeled, quartered and thinly sliced
1 medium carrot, sliced 3 mm (⅛ in) thick
1 medium leek, sliced 5 mm (¼ in) thick

2 celery sticks, sliced 5 mm (¼ in) thick
1 garlic clove, peeled and finely chopped
2 bay leaves
2 cloves
2 tablespoons blackcurrant jam
100 ml (3½ fl oz) white wine vinegar or blackcurrant vinegar
1.25 litres (2¼ pints) water
1 teaspoon salt
4 large pinches of freshly ground white pepper

TO FINISH (optional)
150 ml (5 fl oz) soured cream
2 egg yolks

METHOD

1 · Making the soup
Scrub all the earth from the beetroots, wash them in tepid water, peel and then cut into 2.5 cm (1 in) cubes.

Melt the butter in a large pan and sweat the onion, carrot, leek and celery for about 5–8 minutes until soft. Add all the remaining ingredients (but not the optional ones) and bring to the boil. Skim and cover with the lid slightly open. Simmer for $2\frac{1}{2}$ hours. Taste and correct the seasoning.

2 · Finishing the soup
Mix the soured cream and egg yolks together in a bowl. Add 6 tablespoons of the hot soup to the bowl and mix together. Pour

N U T R I T I O N I S T ' S
N O T E S

Beetroot is a great source of folic acid, one of the B vit-amins, important for healthy red blood cells and especially important for women during pregnancy. It's also high in fibre. It has a slightly higher content of natural sugars (about 7 g in a 100 g/4 oz portion) than most other veg-etables which helps to develop its distinctive flavour.

This soup is low in fat (without the addition of the soured cream!) and high in fibre.

back into the bulk of the hot soup and stir. Place the soup in a large, hot tureen and serve to your friends and family.

VARIATIONS

This soup can be served hot or cold.

By adding a 450 g (1 lb) whole piece of topside, silverside or blade of beef to the soup, you will create a much better flavour. Before serving, lift out the beef, cut it into very fine slices, then mix with the soup.

C H E F ' S N O T E S

Vegetables are sweated in butter or oil in order to remove their acidity and strong taste, especially that of the onions and leeks.

When something is being cooked for a long time, boiling would not only damage the texture but also the flavour, and the soup would be cloudy. Simmering prevents this.

With the lid on properly, there is a danger that the soup would boil over. With the lid a little open, evaporation is minimized. Without the lid, you can lose up to 600 ml (1 pint) of liquid. (When I once tried making soup without a lid, *half* the soup evaporated!)

The egg yolks are used to enrich and slightly bind the soup. If you were to put the egg yolks directly into the soup, they would coagulate and harden. Once the egg yolk and soured cream are mixed one adds a little bit of hot soup so they mix better with the liquid of the soup. It is important that the soup be hot, but not boiling, otherwise the egg yolk would cook and produce nasty bits of hard-boiled egg yolk in the soup.

Fresh Vegetable Soup with Chervil

—— ILLUSTRATED ON PAGE 68 ——

This soup is part of the essential vocabulary of family food. It is also one of the simplest, needing very little time to make. You will be able to create hundreds of variations from it.

FOR 4 GUESTS

PREPARATION TIME: 15 minutes

COOKING TIME: 15 minutes

PLANNING AHEAD: The soup can be prepared a couple of hours in advance, adding the chervil at the last moment.

INGREDIENTS

20 g (³⁄₄ oz) unsalted butter
1 shallot, peeled, halved and sliced
1 medium carrot, peeled and diced roughly into 1 cm (¹⁄₂ in) pieces
1 celery stick, trimmed and cut into 5 mm (¹⁄₄ in) slices

1 medium leek, outer leaves discarded, halved lengthways, and cut into 5 mm (¹⁄₄ in) slices
1.2 litres (2 pints) water or White Chicken Stock (see p. 54)
1 medium potato, peeled and diced
1 teaspoon salt
2 large pinches of freshly ground white pepper
2 tomatoes, hulled and each cut into 8 pieces
about 25 g (1 oz) fresh chervil, stalks removed and leaves finely chopped

METHOD

Gently melt the butter in a large pan without allowing it to brown, and sweat all the vegetables except for the potato and tomatoes over a low heat for 2 minutes until softened. Add the water or stock, the potato, salt and pepper. Bring to the boil and skim off any impurities. Reduce the heat to a simmer, and cover with the lid slightly askew. Simmer for 15 minutes. Add the tomatoes and chervil and simmer for another minute or so. Taste, correct the seasoning if you wish, and serve in a large, hot soup tureen to your friends and family.

VARIATIONS

This soup offers hundreds of variations. You can use all sorts of vegetables such as broccoli, cauliflower, turnips, parsnips, sorrel leaves and so on, and create many delicious and earthy flavours. Or you can choose to use a single vegetable such as potato, cauliflower or leek.

If you like smooth soups, you can liquidize the whole lot to a purée. Of course, you can enrich the soup with milk or cream and loads of butter – it is up to you.

C H E F ' S N O T E S

You can prepare the soup in advance and it will be just as delicious, but make sure it is covered with cling film so there is no interference from other smells.

———————

Do not cut your vegetables too far in advance, as they will lose a lot of their flavour.

———————

We sweat the vegetables in order to remove some of their acidity and to extract the sugar and taste. You must not brown them, so the sweating must be done on a low heat.

———————

Generally, a soup should be tasty and refreshing. Too much salt or pepper would endanger its freshness and delicate taste.

———————

When the water comes back to the boil, the albumen will be extracted and coagulated by the heat, and will float to the surface in the form of a whitish scum. Simply spoon this off. It will not harm you, but it is unsightly.

———————

Why simmering instead of boiling? Well, that is easy. If you boil vegetables too fast, you are likely to overcook the outside (puréeing them), and you will lose the delightful textures. (See also the Scientist's Note on p. 71.)

———————

It is better to add both chervil and tomatoes in the last few minutes. If you cook chervil too long, its flavour loses punch and freshness. As for the tomatoes, they would be grossly overcooked.

*N U T R I T I O N I S T ' S
N O T E S*

All the vegetables in this recipe provide an excellent array of vitamins – beta-carotene, vitamin C and folic acid – which are believed to have a key role in helping to protect us against cancer, heart disease and premature ageing.

It's definitely worth trying to get hold of fresh herbs, not just for their superior flavour, but also for their nutritional value. Fresh chervil is packed with iron (more than spinach and other greens) as well as many other important minerals such as potassium and magnesium.

Consommé of Peppers and Tomato

Obviously this is not a winter dish. It should be served on a glorious summer day, when the tomatoes are at their best. It should also be served cold. Served hot, the flavours would be too astringent.

FOR 4 GUESTS

PREPARATION TIME: 15 minutes

COOKING TIME: 40 minutes

PLANNING AHEAD: The consommé can be prepared a day in advance and chilled.

INGREDIENTS
1 large onion, peeled and finely chopped
100 ml (3½ fl oz) olive oil
300 g (11 oz) red peppers, seeded and finely chopped
1 kg (2¼ lb) ripe tomatoes, seeded and each chopped into 8 pieces
4 garlic cloves, peeled and sliced

4 sprigs fresh thyme
1 teaspoon black peppercorns, crushed
1 heaped teaspoon salt
1 teaspoon caster sugar
1 litre (1¾ pints) water

FOR THE CLARIFICATION
250 g (9 oz) ripe tomatoes, roughly chopped
8 fresh basil leaves
4 fresh tarragon leaves
3 egg whites

FOR THE GARNISH
4 slices Mozzarella cheese
4 fresh basil leaves, finely chopped
8 black olives, pitted
2 tomatoes, skinned, quartered and seeded

METHOD

1 · Preparing the broth base
In a large pan, sweat the onion for about 4 minutes in the olive oil over a low heat until softened. Add the chopped peppers and cook for a further 10 minutes. Increase the heat and add the tomatoes, garlic, thyme, peppercorns, salt and sugar. Cover and cook over a medium to low heat for about 15 minutes. Add the water to this broth base, bring to the boil, skim and simmer for another 5 minutes. Strain the resulting broth into another pan, pressing the pulp down with a ladle to extract all the juices. Cool and reserve. Taste and correct the seasoning.

2 · Preparing the clarification
Liquidize the tomatoes, basil, tarragon and egg whites together, and add to the cold tomato broth.

Consommé of Peppers
and Tomato (see p. 75)

(see p. 75)

3 · Clarifying the tomato broth

Whisk the clarification ingredients into the tomato broth, and bring to a gentle boil. Simmer for about 10 minutes until a layer or crust of impurities is created on the surface. Place a colander over a saucepan and line it with a wet tea towel. Delicately pour in the broth, letting it drip through, while the solidified egg white remains in the cloth. Leave the clarified broth – now a consommé – to cool.

4 · Serving

In one large bowl or four individual ones, place the Mozzarella cheese, the finely chopped basil leaves, the black olives and the tomato segments. Pour the cold consommé into the bowl or bowls, and serve to your guests.

CHEF'S NOTES

It is not necessary to use the best extra virgin olive oil when cooking, as its character will change, and much of its fragrance will be lost.

———————

This dish should be successful if you buy the very best tomatoes; it is not quite the same ripening them on your window sill.

———————

Do not use brined olives, but rather some plump and tasty black olives kept in olive oil and herbs.

———————

Sugar is a medium which brings out taste and will give a rounded flavour to the consommé.

———————

For information on clarifying, see p. 42. Using fresh tomatoes in the clarification brings back freshness to the consommé and gives it masses of flavour.

For information on clarifying, see p. 42.

NUTRITIONIST'S NOTES

This soup uses olive oil which is very high in monounsaturates, now known to be particularly good for keeping the heart and circulatory system healthy. Monounsaturates help to lower the harmful types of cholesterol in the bloodstream whilst maintaining the beneficial types of cholesterol.

The soup follows the Mediterranean tradition of using garlic as an integral part of the dish. Garlic is also beneficial for the heart and the immune system. Overall this soup is a good source of vitamin C, monounsaturates and beta-carotene.

Soup with Coconut Milk and Lime

I spent my last holiday in Thailand and I was won over by the exuberance and freshness of the tastes and aromas. These flavours may be unknown to you, but I can assure you they are certainly worth trying. You will be able to obtain all the ingredients easily, either in ethnic food shops or in supermarkets. Many large supermarkets stock coconut milk in tins or cartons.

FOR 4–6 GUESTS

PREPARATION TIME: 10 minutes

COOKING TIME: 30 minutes

PLANNING AHEAD: The soup can be prepared a day in advance.

INGREDIENTS

4 chicken legs and thighs (the latter boned), skinned
4 tablespoons sesame oil
2 garlic cloves, peeled and thinly sliced
1 teaspoon cumin seeds, crushed
1 teaspoon coriander seeds, crushed
1 heaped teaspoon curry powder
2 fresh red chillies, seeded and finely chopped
2 tablespoons soy sauce
3 lime leaves
1 teaspoon caster sugar
1 litre (1¾ pints) White Chicken Stock (see p. 54) or water
2×400 ml (14 fl oz) tins coconut milk
15 g (½ oz) fresh coriander, leaves picked from stalks and chopped
15 g (½ oz) green spring onion stalks, thinly sliced

METHOD

1 · Preparing the chicken

Using poultry shears, cut the chicken legs into three pieces (with the bone in), and cut each boned thigh into four pieces.

2 · Making the soup

Sweat the chicken pieces in the sesame oil over a low heat for 5 minutes until sealed on all sides, but without colouring. Add the garlic, cumin, coriander, curry powder and chillies and sweat for a further 5 minutes, stirring occasionally. Add the soy sauce, lime leaves, sugar, chicken stock or water, and coconut milk. Bring to the boil, skim and simmer for 20 minutes. Make sure the chicken is cooked through.

3 · Serving

At the last moment, pour into soup bowls and sprinkle with the chopped coriander and spring onion. Serve to your guests.

VARIATIONS

The addition of about 50 g (2 oz) of ground cashew nuts would add an extra nuance of flavour and texture.

The chicken can be replaced by shrimps or a firm white fish such as monkfish, about 100 g (4 oz) per person. Cook for only 10–15 minutes.

The curry powder could be replaced by some Thai green curry paste if you can find it.

CHEF'S NOTES

Technically, there is no difficulty in making this dish. The only danger is that the chicken is browned instead of being sweated. This would alter the flavour.

Spinach and Watercress Soup

FOR 4 GUESTS

PREPARATION TIME: 10 minutes

COOKING TIME: 12 minutes

PLANNING AHEAD: This soup can be prepared a day in advance, cooled down quickly over ice, and then kept covered in the fridge.

INGREDIENTS

300 g (11 oz) watercress leaves
400 g (14 oz) spinach leaves

about 1.2 litres (2 pints) water
20 g (¾ oz) unsalted butter
2 shallots, about 65 g (2½ oz), or same quantity of onion, peeled and chopped
1 teaspoon salt
4 large pinches of freshly ground white pepper
100 ml (3½ fl oz) single cream (optional)
1 teaspoon lemon juice (optional)

METHOD

1 · Preparing the watercress and spinach
The taste and pepperiness of watercress can vary enormously. Taste yours, and if it is very peppery, cut off all the stalks. If gentle in flavour, leave the stalks on. Wash and drain. Remove the stalks from the spinach and wash the leaves in plenty of water. Drain well.

2 · Making the soup
Bring 1 litre (1¾ pints) of the water to the boil in a large pan.

In a separate large pan, melt the butter and sweat the shallots or onion without colouring for 1 minute. Add the spinach, watercress and the remaining small quantity of water to the shallots, cover with a lid and cook on a fierce heat for 3 minutes, shaking the pan occasionally. Remove the lid and pour in the boiling water. Add the salt and pepper, then liquidize, in batches if necessary.

3 · Finishing the soup
Rub the soup through a sieve and add the cream and lemon juice, if using. Taste and correct the seasoning, if necessary. Serve to your guests.

CHEF'S NOTES

You will notice that we bring the bulk of the water for the soup to the boil first. This is to minimize the length of cooking so both the vivid colour and taste of the watercress and spinach leaves will be kept as fresh as possible.

A small amount of water is added to the spinach and watercress so the steam generated by this water will help the leaves to cook faster. Placing a lid on the pan will also maximize the cooking speed: 3 minutes will be enough.

Do not wait for the soup to cool down before liquidizing, otherwise the heat will alter both freshness of taste and colour. If you are preparing the soup in advance, cool it down on ice, for the same reason as above.

The cream is purely optional. Actually, I prefer it without. A dash of lemon juice can always be added to lift the taste.

NUTRITIONIST'S NOTES

This soup is a delicious way to eat spinach, which, along with the watercress, gives you iron (for healthy blood), potassium, calcium and lots of beta-carotene. In fact, you get a very impressive helping of most minerals in this dish.

The fat content of the soup is kept low as the vegetables are sautéed in only a tiny amount of butter – unless you add the optional single cream, in which case it goes up a little more.

Butter Bean Soup with Smoked Streaky Bacon

In my native Franche-Comté, the pig is as celebrated as a demi-god. This soup is a simple and delicious way to enjoy it.

NUTRITIONIST'S NOTES

Butter beans and other pulses are a much undervalued food, valuable sources of protein, B vitamins, iron and other minerals and, of course, fibre. The overall protein value of the soup is enhanced by the bacon, and also if you accompany the soup with some bread. Beans are, of course, extremely low in fat and high in complex carbohydrates.

The type of fibre in beans (soluble fibre) is good for helping to control blood cholesterol levels. It slows the digestion and absorption of carbohydrates and so helps control blood-sugar levels – thought to be important for diabetics. However, everyone can benefit from more beans in their diet.

FOR 4 GUESTS

SOAKING TIME: 12 hours

PREPARATION TIME: 10 minutes

COOKING TIME: 1 hour

INGREDIENTS

300 g (11 oz) dried butter beans
20 g (¾ oz) unsalted butter
1 medium onion, peeled, quartered and thinly sliced about 3 mm (⅛ in) thick
4 garlic cloves, peeled and sliced
4×100 g (4 oz) slices streaky bacon, rinded and cut into 3 cm (1¼ in) pieces
1 bouquet garni (2 dried bay leaves and 2 sprigs of fresh thyme, tied together)
200 ml (7 fl oz) dry white wine (optional)
1.5 litres (2½ pints) water
4 large pinches of freshly ground white pepper
½ teaspoon salt

METHOD

Soak the beans for 12 hours in plenty of cold water.

In a large, heavy-based pan, gently melt the butter – it must not brown – and sweat the onion and garlic over a medium heat for about 5 minutes, stirring occasionally, until soft. Add all the remaining ingredients except the salt and stir together. Bring the soup to the boil, skim, then reduce the heat and simmer for 50 minutes, with the lid slightly askew. Add the salt, then continue to simmer for a further 10 minutes.

Before serving, taste and correct the seasoning, if necessary. Remove and discard the bouquet garni. Pour the soup into a hot tureen and let your friends and family help themselves.

VARIATIONS

Butter beans are quite large and well textured. I like them very much in this soup but you could mix in other varieties such as broad, cannellini, borlotti, haricot or flageolet.

A good addition would be a small Savoy cabbage, chopped roughly and added for the last 20 minutes.

About 4 or 5 skinned, chopped tomatoes, added towards the

end, would be delicious. A small bunch of parsley leaves, blanched for 2 minutes then chopped, could be added towards the end. And, of course, if you like cream, please indulge in it.

Diced carrots and courgettes give a nice texture to the soup. Add them 10 minutes before the end of the cooking time.

CHEF'S NOTES

If you use fresh bay leaves, double the quantity. The flavour of the leaves is strengthened and concentrated during drying.

The onion must not brown while sweating as this would alter the flavour and colour of the dish. So make sure the heat is not too strong, and stir from time to time. The heat will partly cook the onion, will soften its strong character and bring out all the sugars.

For skimming, see the Chef's Note on p. 74.

The soup needs an hour to cook, so the heat must be gentle. If it is too strong, the beans will break up and release too much starch and the bacon will shrivel and harden. For reasons for leaving the lid askew see the Chef's Note on p. 72.

Chicken in a Vegetable and Herb Broth

FOR 4 GUESTS

PREPARATION TIME: 20 minutes

COOKING TIME: 30–40 minutes

PLANNING AHEAD: The chicken can be cooked a couple of hours ahead and re-heated at the last moment.

INGREDIENTS

1×1.5 kg (3–3½ lb) free-range chicken
12 shallots, or 24 baby onions, peeled
8 small carrots, peeled
2 large leeks, trimmed and cut in half lengthways
2 medium turnips, peeled and each cut into 8 segments
1 bouquet garni (2 sprigs of fresh thyme, 6 sprigs of fresh parsley and 1 small sprig of fresh tarragon)
4 garlic cloves, peeled
2 tablespoons of chopped fresh mixed chervil and tarragon

NUTRITIONIST'S
NOTES

This is one of the healthiest ways of cooking and serving chicken. It involves no additional fats or oils and the chicken is simmered in a tasty broth with lots of vegetables. The final fat content of the dish is, therefore, very low and the vitamin and fibre content high. Since the cooking liquid is retained and served with the chicken, there is practically no loss of vitamins. The carrots and leeks provide beta-carotene and potassium. The green part of the leeks contain the most vitamins so cut off as little as possible.

METHOD

1 · Preparing the chicken

Make sure that all the giblets, if any, have been removed from the chicken. If necessary, singe the bird with a lit candle or over a gas flame to remove any feather stubs. Rinse the inside with water to remove traces of blood. Dry thoroughly, inside and out.

2 · Cooking the chicken

Place the chicken into a cast-iron dish just large enough to hold it plus the vegetables. Surround it with the vegetables and aromatics (the bouquet garni and garlic) and cover with cold water. Bring to the boil, skim, cover with a lid and then simmer *very gently* for between 30 and 40 minutes, according to the size of the chicken. Pierce the thigh with a skewer or thin sharp knife; if the liquid is still pink, simmer on for a few more minutes.

This dish benefits from resting off the heat for 20–30 minutes after it has finished cooking, to allow the flavours to infuse.

About 5 minutes before serving, add the chopped chervil and tarragon to the chicken juices.

3 · Serving

Lift the chicken on to a cutting board and cut off the legs at the joint above the thigh, then slice off the breasts. Divide the legs and breasts into two, for eight pieces altogether. Place the chicken pieces back in the liquid in the casserole. Serve in a soup bowl as a fragrant broth containing chicken and vegetables.

VARIATIONS

The chicken can be replaced by guinea fowl. The chicken liver could be pan-fried, puréed with garlic and parsley, and served on toasted bread. Use different vegetables and herbs.

C H E F ' S   N O T E S

If you use fully matured summer tarragon, blanch it for about 10 seconds in boiling salted water and refresh under cold water before chopping to ensure the scent of the tarragon is not too overpowering. Young tarragon leaves can be used as they are.

Bringing the water to the boil will coagulate the proteins and carry them to the surface of the liquid where they can be collected. The dish should then be simmered very, very gently so that the heat permeates the chicken very slowly and the flesh remains moist and tender.

Starters

Duck Ham Salad
(see p. 86)

Duck Ham Salad

—— ILLUSTRATED ON PAGE 84 ——

Curing meat with salt, which renders it more digestible, more palatable and less prone to decay without boiling, has been practised for thousands of years. Basically, salt dissolves in water, so if salt or a salt solution is placed in contact with some material containing pure or less salty water, the salt will draw this water out.

If crisp cucumber slices, for instance, are sprinkled with salt they quickly release water and become limp. Meat too contains water, so when salt is sprinkled on meat, a concentrated solution will form on the surface which will draw the water in the meat out. Some salt (and spices too, if used) will conversely penetrate *into* the meat tissue, giving it taste, but the cells and, more importantly, the micro-organisms will still become dry (and the latter will die). The surface layers of the meat thus become relatively sterile, free of bacteria, so that the second stage, the drying, can now continue by evaporation in a dry atmosphere.

FOR 4 GUESTS

PREPARATION TIME: 30 minutes

CURING TIME: 24 hours, and 6–7 days' drying time

PLANNING AHEAD: The duck ham can be prepared and ready some days in advance of serving.

INGREDIENTS

2 large *magret* duck breasts (see Chef's Notes below) or 4 medium duck breasts
100 g (4 oz) coarse salt
2 teaspoons black peppercorns, crushed

4 sprigs of fresh thyme
salt and freshly ground black pepper

FOR THE SALAD
4 handfuls of mixed salad leaves such as batavia, frisée, chicory, etc.
4 tablespoons Walnut Oil Dressing (see Non-scented Dressing, p. 59)
duck skin from the *magrets*
1 tablespoon hazelnuts, crushed
1 tablespoon flaked almonds, lightly toasted

METHOD

1 · Preparing the duck breasts
Place the duck breasts, flesh side down, on your work surface. With a very sharp knife, slice off the skin, leaving about 3 mm (⅛ in) of fat adhering to the meat. Roll the skin up, wrap in cling film, tie and freeze.

2 · Curing the duck breasts
Place the duck breasts in a small container, and sprinkle the coarse salt, crushed peppercorns and thyme over them. Mix together well. Cover with cling film, place in the bottom of the fridge, and leave to cure for 24 hours, turning after 12 hours.

3 · Drying the duck breasts
Remove the duck breasts from the fridge. Brush off the salt and spices, and tie each breast separately in a muslin cloth. Hang the breasts up in a draught-free room at about 18°C (64°F) temperature for 6–7 days.

4 · Finishing the dish and serving
Pre-heat the grill. Remove the duck skin from the freezer and remove the cling film. Chop the skin into fine slivers, then place under the pre-heated grill until crispy and golden. Season lightly and reserve.

Remove the muslin cloths from the duck hams. The breasts may have over-dried slightly on the flesh side. Cut off these pieces. Then slice the duck hams across in very thin slices. Arrange the slices in a rosette shape around the individual plates.

Mix the salad leaves with the dressing and arrange them in a mound in the middle of each plate. Sprinkle with crushed hazelnuts, almonds and crispy duck skin. Serve to your guests.

Duck is very high in fat but nearly all of this lies below the skin so you can control the amount of fat you eat by not eating the skin, as in this recipe. Duck provides a reasonable amount of iron and zinc and good amounts of the B vitamins.

The salad leaves add extra vitamins to the dish and the walnut dressing and nuts are high in healthy mono-unsaturates. The overall fat content of this dish is high so follow with a lower-fat main course.

C H E F ' S   N O T E S

The *magret* comes from ducks which have been fattened to produce *foie gras*. It is a large breast, about 250–300 g (9–11 oz) in weight. It is ideal for this dish as the flesh will stay moist. If you cannot find *magrets*, use as large duck breasts as possible.

It is essential to leave a layer of fat of the specified thickness as this will protect the duck ham and also give it flavour. The duck hams must also be cut thinly, as this allows the moisture and taste to come through. Slice too thickly, and the meat will be too firm, almost chewy.

The duck ham is prepared using two very distinct techniques – first the curing (see p. 41) and then the drying.

Leeks with Hazelnut and Soured Cream Dressing

The leek is often regarded as a poor relation of asparagus. In fact in France we call it 'asparagus of the poor'. I can assure you it is as delicious as asparagus itself when served luke warm.

FOR 4 GUESTS

PREPARATION TIME: 5 minutes

COOKING TIME: 20–25 minutes, according to the size of the leeks.

PLANNING AHEAD: This dish can be prepared half a day in advance.

INGREDIENTS
16 medium leeks
3 litres (5¼ pints) water
65 g (2½ oz) salt
200 ml (7 fl oz) Hazelnut and Soured Cream Dressing (see p. 60).

METHOD

1 · Preparing the leeks
First be very careful about choosing the leeks, as some may have

NUTRITIONIST'S
NOTES

Leeks contain practically no sodium and lots of potassium which is a very healthy balance indeed. If you suffer from water retention all vegetables help to relieve the symptoms, but leeks are an especially good choice. Do not discard more of the green part than you have to as the green leaves are rich in minerals and vitamins. Leeks in general are a good source of iron and the vitamin beta-carotene.

a woody core which is absolutely inedible and tasteless. Trim the base of the leek without cutting into the leek itself. Remove some of the coarser green leaves at the top. Remove the first two layers of outer leaves as these still remain stringy after cooking (they can be used for stock). Split the leek in half, running down to about 10 cm (4 in) from the base, and wash under running tepid water. This will ensure the earth is removed more easily. Tie the leeks in three bundles with string.

2 · Cooking the leeks

Bring the water to the boil with the salt and throw in the leeks, ensuring that they are well covered with water. When the water comes back to the boil, reduce the temperature to a gentle boil and cook for 20–25 minutes.

To test whether the leeks are properly cooked, slide the point of a knife right through the base of the leek. You should not be able to feel the layers. Remove the leeks from the water, and cool on a tray lined with a tea towel.

3 · Serving

Cut off the string and arrange the leeks on a serving dish. Offer the hazelnut and soured cream dressing separately.

VARIATIONS

About 20 g ($^3/_4$ oz) of freshly sliced hazelnuts sprinkled over the top of the leeks provide a nice contrast in taste as well as adding flavour and texture.

You can also serve the leeks with mustard vinaigrette (see p. 59).

CHEF'S NOTES

You will notice that there is quite a large amount of salt. This amount is necessary as there is a lot of water, but it will season the leeks perfectly.

If the leek cooking water were at too fast a boil, this would overcook the outside of the leek. The direct effect would be a slimy feel and unpleasant texture.

Leeks are members of the onion family and like onions or shallots they must be very well cooked in order to have the best flavour (see the Scientist's Note on p. 75). Undercook the leeks and they would have an unpleasant texture and taste.

Leeks with Hazelnut and
Soured Cream Dressing
(see p. 87)

Garden Salads with Herbs and Deep-fried Vegetables

Salads can create the most versatile and delicious starters.

If preparing the salad in the summer, use red butterhead lettuce, rocket, purslane and radicchio, but not, *please not*, those tasteless designer salads such as lollo rosso or oak leaves. They look pretty, but that is all. If preparing the salad in the winter, use frisée, endive, batavia or radicchio.

FOR 4 GUESTS

PREPARATION TIME: 15 minutes

COOKING TIME: 20 minutes

PLANNING AHEAD: The dressing and the deep-fried herbs and vegetables can be prepared a day in advance. Keep the latter in a dry place so they do not absorb any humidity.

INGREDIENTS

4 large handfuls of salad leaves
1 shallot, peeled and finely chopped
100 ml (3½ fl oz) Balsamic Vinegar and Olive Oil Dressing (see p. 60)
1 pinch of fresh thyme leaves, finely chopped
4 fresh rosemary leaves, finely chopped
2 fresh tarragon leaves, finely chopped
2 sprigs of fresh chervil, finely chopped
6 fresh peppermint leaves, finely chopped
freshly ground black pepper

FOR THE DEEP-FRIED HERB AND VEGETABLE GARNISHES

12 fine shavings each of celeriac (or turnip or swede), beetroot, carrot and courgette
1 litre (1¾ pints) vegetable oil for deep-frying
4 small sprigs of fresh tarragon or tarragon leaves
8 sprigs of fresh parsley, stalks on
4 fresh basil leaves
salt

METHOD

1 · Deep-frying the herbs and vegetables

To make the 'shavings' of vegetable, use a potato peeler or a mandoline. The shape is not important but they must be very thin.

Pre-heat the oil to 160°C (325°F). Deep-fry the herbs for 1 minute, and the vegetables for about 5 minutes, until crisp and lightly golden. Watch carefully so that they don't overcook. Place on kitchen paper, season with a tiny amount of salt and reserve.

Salad leaves such as lettuce, radicchio and frisée are highly nutritious. They are excellent sources of potassium and vitamins such as vitamin C, folic acid and beta-carotene. The greener the leaves the better, as they are richer in nutrients. So make sure you don't throw away the outer green leaves as they can contain up to 50 times more beta-carotene than the inner white ones.

The dressing and the deep-frying increase the oil content of the dish quite substantially, but at least the oil in the dressing is the healthy mono-unsaturated type which is usually lacking in the average British diet. Follow with a lower-fat main course.

2 · *Preparing the salad*

If you are going to serve the salad in a large bowl, mix together in it the shallot and the balsamic dressing and arrange the drained salad leaves (see Chef's Notes below) and fresh herbs over them. Give a few turns of freshly ground black pepper and toss just as you serve. Serve the deep-fried herbs and vegetables separately so the guests can help themselves.

Alternatively, you can mix the dressing, fresh herbs, shallot and salad leaves together and arrange in the middle of each individual plate, surrounding the salad leaves with the deep-fried vegetables and herbs.

VARIATIONS

Of course, you can forget the deep-fried vegetables – although this is a shame, as their texture and flavour add a lot to the dish. But it would certainly be simpler.

You could also cut very fine julienne sticks of leek (one leek per person), deep-fry them and arrange them on the top of the salad. This looks stunning, and adds another texture and flavour.

You could also add pan-fried scallops and baby squid.

CHEF'S NOTES

Most salad leaves are delicate and need to be handled with care. Never tear salad leaves with your hands, as this would bruise them. Always cut them with a small, sharp knife. Soak salad leaves in plenty of water for about 3–4 minutes. This amount of time will refresh them, beyond that it will drown them. Lift carefully and place in a salad drainer. The majority of this soaking water should be removed as it would dilute the sharpness and taste of the dressing. If not using straightaway, wrap in a cloth or plastic bag and refrigerate.

———

A dressing should always be mixed with salad leaves at the very last moment as the acidity of the vinegar will attack the fragile leaves.

———

It is amazing how the flavour of some herbs is markedly strengthened through the deep-frying process, while others, just as strong when fresh, can *lose* their flavour.

Parsley, sage, chives and tarragon retain, even increase, their flavour after deep-frying.

Poached Quails' Eggs in a Deep-fried Nest of Vegetables

FOR 4 GUESTS

PREPARATION TIME: 40 minutes

COOKING TIME: 10 minutes

SPECIAL EQUIPMENT: 7–8 cm (3–3¼ in) bird-nest frying moulds (or see Variations); a cooking thermometer; and a deep frying pan or deep-fryer.

PLANNING AHEAD: The dish can be pre-prepared up to step 2. The quails' eggs can be cracked open ready to be poached.

INGREDIENTS

50 g (2 oz) smoked bacon, cut into thin strips, blanched and refreshed
1 handful of rocket or mâche leaves
1 handful of salad leaves
1 tablespoon Mustard Vinaigrette (see p. 59)
salt and freshly ground black pepper

FOR THE NESTS
65 g (2½ oz) courgette
65 g (2½ oz) leek
100 g (4 oz) potatoes
1 litre (1¾ pints) vegetable oil for deep-frying

FOR THE EGGS
150 ml (5 fl oz) white wine vinegar
1 tablespoon salt
24 quails' eggs, very fresh
2 tablespoons flour
1 egg, beaten
50 g (2 oz) fine breadcrumbs

METHOD

1 · Preparing the deep-fried nests
Cut the courgette, leek and potatoes into very fine julienne sticks about 1 mm (¹⁄₁₆ in) thick and 8 cm (3¼ in) long. Wash the courgette and leek and pat dry. Pat dry the potatoes but do *not* wash. Place the julienne sticks of vegetables in a bowl, and add 1 tablespoon of the oil. Divide them into 4 portions.

2 · Deep-frying the nests
Pre-heat the oil to 160°C (325°F).
   The frying moulds are composed of two different-sized cup-shaped spheres, which lock into each other. Flatten the base of the top one by pushing it in. This will stop the julienne of vegetables being so compressed. With a brush, lightly oil the netting of the spheres. Open them and arrange one portion of the julienne of vegetables on the bottom one, so it has the shape

Poached Quails' Eggs in a
Deep-fried Nest of Vegetables

SCIENTIST'S NOTES

The albumen in egg white coagulates more rapidly in boiling water containing vinegar than in pure water. The reason is as follows. The proteins of the egg white are like coiled chains when raw, but they will uncoil and separate when heated. In pure water these chains of proteins are electrically charged so that they repel each other, and further heating is necessary to make them come together or coagulate. By adding an acid – vinegar in this case – hydrogen ions are introduced: these weaken the electrical repulsion, making it easier for the egg white proteins to bond and coagulate, i.e. to change from a transparent jelly-like substance to a white opaque mass.

of a nest. Lock in the top basket and deep-fry in the heated cooking oil for about 2 minutes.

Delicately remove the deep-fried nest from the frying moulds. (They can stick.) Reserve in a warm place on kitchen paper while you fry the remaining nests.

3 · Poaching the quails' eggs

In a low-sided saucepan, bring to simmering point about 1 litre (1¾ pints) of water with the white wine vinegar and salt. With a small knife, make an incision in the middle of each egg, carefully crack it open and slide it into the pan of barely simmering liquid. Do the same with another 4 or so eggs and cook for 30 seconds. Remove using a slotted spoon and drain on kitchen paper. Repeat for the remaining quails' eggs.

4 · Deep-frying the quails' eggs

Roll the eggs in the flour, then in the beaten egg, then finally, in the breadcrumbs. Deep fry for 30 seconds at 160°C (325°F).

5 · Serving

Warm the bacon strips in a frying pan. Mix the salad leaves with the vinaigrette. Place a few salad leaves on the middle of each plate. Arrange the deep-fried nests in the middle. Place the remaining salad leaves in the middle of each deep-fried nest, add the warm quails' eggs, season with salt and pepper and scatter the warm bacon over the top. Serve to your guests.

VARIATIONS

You can pan-fry the quails' eggs instead of poaching them.

If you cannot find the special bird-nest moulds, simply pile up the deep-fried vegetables into little nest shapes, and arrange the poached eggs on top.

You could use ordinary hens' eggs (1 per person) instead of the quails' eggs. The dish won't look quite the same, though! Adjust the poaching time accordingly.

You could add pan-fried baby squid to the leaves in the basket, and perhaps some scallops too. Garnish with a few streaks of tomato coulis, some pesto, and a wonderful 30-year-old balsamic vinegar, so rich it's more like a sauce. Decorate with peppery rocket flowers.

C H E F ' S   N O T E S

A vegetable oil such as groundnut is best for deep-frying as it is practically odourless and the temperature it can reach without breaking down is high.

NUTRITIONIST'S
NOTES

*The vegetables in this recipe
provide lots of vitamins, minerals and fibre. Deep-frying in
hot oil is a good way of preserving the vitamins and stopping them being leached
away. Make sure the oil is at
the right temperature, though.
It's best not to save and re-use
oil too many times because
repeated heating can cause
changes in the chemical structure of the oil molecules.*

*The overall fat content of
this dish is fairly high because
it is deep-fried.*

The little nests will hold and stick together principally because of the starch of the potatoes which will act as 'glue'. That is the reason why we do not wash the potatoes.

———

The temperature of the deep-frying oil is crucial, so you need to use a thermometer. Over 160°C (325°F), the vegetables are likely to burn and not cook thoroughly; under that temperature the vegetables will soak up the oil and be unappetizing.

———

The deep-frying nest moulds are oiled to prevent the starch sticking to the wires.

———

The timing of the deep-frying will vary slightly according to how thinly you have cut the julienne sticks.

———

The quails' eggs must be extremely fresh. If they are old, the egg white will be very loose around the egg yolk.

Tartare of Scallops with Coriander

FOR 4 GUESTS

MARINATING TIME: 10 minutes

PREPARATION TIME: 20 minutes

SPECIAL EQUIPMENT: A round cutter 2.5–3 cm (1–1¼ in) in diameter; 4×5 cm (2 in) stainless steel or plastic rings.

PLANNING AHEAD: The dish can be prepared a few hours in advance.

INGREDIENTS
8 large, very fresh scallops, shelled, trimmed and washed
25 ml (1 fl oz) lime juice

1 lime leaf (optional), finely chopped
1 tablespoon finely chopped fresh coriander leaves
extra virgin olive oil
salt and freshly ground white pepper
2 large ripe tomatoes, skinned, seeded and diced
1 drop of white wine vinegar

FOR THE DRESSING
2 very ripe tomatoes
2 tablespoons olive oil
pinch of caster sugar

METHOD
1 · Preparing the scallops
With the small cutter, cut out 4×3 cm (1¼ in) cylinders from 4

Tartare of Scallops with
Coriander (see p. 95)

of the scallops. Cut these cylinders into 6 fine slices. Reserve the
trimmings.

Separate the scallop slices, place on a shallow tray, and
sprinkle them with 1 tablespoon of the lime juice and the
chopped lime leaf if using. Cover with cling film and leave to
marinate for 20 minutes.

Chop the trimmings and the other 4 scallops into 5 mm ($^1/_4$ in)
thick pieces. Mix in the chopped coriander with 1 teaspoon of
extra virgin olive oil and add the remaining lime juice. Season
lightly with salt and pepper.

2 · *Dressing the tomatoes*

Place the tomato dice in a small bowl, and add $^1/_2$ tablespoon of extra virgin olive oil and the drop of wine vinegar. Season with salt and pepper.

3 · Building the tartares

On a small tray, place the steel or plastic rings, and fill up two-thirds of their height with scallop dice. Top each ring with some of the tomato dice and press a little bit with a teaspoon so all the ingredients adhere well. Arrange 5 or 6 marinated scallop slices in a rosette shape on each tartare.

4 · Preparing the dressing

Cut the tomatoes in half and remove the seeds with a teaspoon. Chop and purée the flesh in a liquidizer, adding the olive oil. Season with salt and pepper and a pinch of sugar. Strain into a small container.

5 · Serving

Brush the top of the scallop tartares with extra virgin olive oil, and a half turn of pepper.

Slide a palette knife under each ring and lift on to the middle of the plate. Lift the ring off to free the tartare. Sprinkle a little bit of extra virgin olive oil around the tartare and spoon the tomato dressing around it as well. Do the same with the other plates. Serve to your guests.

VARIATIONS

The scallops can be replaced by very fine slices of salmon. The coriander can be replaced by Japanese *shiso* leaves (from the beefsteak plant, and available fresh in some Asian stores) or fresh basil leaves.

C H E F ' S N O T E S

The scallops must be the freshest possible as they are not actually *heat* cooked, but served raw, lightly marinated.

The marinating time is very short, and the citric acid from the lime will just have time to impart flavour rather than cure.

Season lightly – this dish is very delicate and needs very little salt.

The tomatoes must be at room temperature so when puréed they will absorb the olive oil more easily. The sauce can be easily warmed up and served with a piece of pan-fried fish.

Terrine of Sardines and Potatoes

A classic combination with a twist, turning two everyday ingredients into an attractive, easily prepared and delicious starter for all seasons.

NUTRITIONIST'S
NOTES

Sardines, like other oily fish, are rich in a special group of unsaturated fatty acids which help reduce the stickiness of the blood and so reduce the chances of blood clotting (thrombosis) and heart attacks. The dish contains a fairly large amount of oil which results in a high calorie and fat content but this can be balanced with low fat dishes in the rest of the meal.

Potatoes contain reasonable amounts of vitamin C and B vitamins and also provide some fibre to the dish – peel thinly to retain more vitamins.

MAKES 10 PORTIONS

PREPARATION TIME: 30 minutes

COOKING TIME: $1^3/_4$ hours

RESTING TIME: 12 hours

SPECIAL EQUIPMENT: A terrine mould 25×8 cm (10×3$^1/_4$ in); greaseproof paper to line the mould.

PLANNING AHEAD: The terrine *must* be made in advance, as it needs to rest and set for at least 12 hours before cutting and serving.

INGREDIENTS
the fillets from 6 small sardines
5 large potatoes (use the terrine size as a guide)
4 small shallots
1 large bunch of fresh thyme
salt and freshly ground black pepper
freshly grated nutmeg

100 ml (3½ fl oz) olive oil, plus extra for greasing the terrine

FOR THE VINAIGRETTE
⅓ teaspoon freshly ground white pepper
65 ml (2½ fl oz) white wine vinegar
225 ml (7½ fl oz) groundnut oil
20 capers, finely chopped, plus a little of their juice
3 shallots, peeled and very finely chopped
a small bunch of fresh parsley, chopped

FOR THE CREAM GARNISH
1×150 ml (5 fl oz) pot soured cream
2 teaspoons water
freshly ground white pepper and cayenne pepper
juice of ½ lemon

METHOD

1 · Preparing the vinaigrette
Dissolve 1½ teaspoons salt and the white pepper in the white wine vinegar, then whisk in the groundnut oil. Add the capers and reserve. Stir in the shallots and parsley just before serving.

2 · Preparing the cream garnish
Place the soured cream in a small bowl and dilute with the water. It should just cover the back of a spoon. Season with salt, white pepper, cayenne and lemon juice.

3 · Preparing the terrine mould
Brush the inside of the terrine mould with olive oil. Cut a piece of greaseproof paper to the size of the bottom of the terrine and put in place.

Raw potatoes – as well as apples, avocadoes, bananas, pears etc – turn brown when they are cut and the flesh is exposed to the air. This browning is due to an enzyme which reacts with oxygen and turns compounds in the fruit or vegetable tissue brown or grey – not too dissimilar to the oxidation of metal which causes rust. Chilling can slow the enzyme's action down, as can immersing the food in cold water (thus cutting off the oxygen supply to the enzyme). The citric acid in lemon and other citrus juice makes the enzyme work very slowly. The method employed to counteract oxidation must depend on the particular food involved – water immersion for potatoes, lemon juice for fruit. As the potatoes here need their starch content, they cannot be placed in water, so must be sliced at the very last minute to prevent oxidation.

Pre-heat the oven to 190°C/375°F/Gas 5. Prepare a bain-marie or water bath with enough water to come three-quarters of the way up the sides of the terrine.

4 · Preparing the terrine ingredients

Sardines   The fishmonger will have taken off the bigger bones, leaving smaller ones along the centre of the fillets. You can remove these if you like, but they will all but dissolve during the final cooking of the terrine. Reserve the fillets on a tray in the fridge.

Potatoes   Wash and then peel the potatoes. Wash again. Using the width of your terrine as a guide, cut the potatoes into rectangles; the trimmings will thicken your soup that night. Slice the potatoes approximately 5 mm (¼ in) thick and reserve (do not wash).

Shallots and thyme   Peel and finely chop the shallots. Remove the thyme leaves from their woody stalks, then bruise the leaves lightly with the side of a large knife. Mix the shallots and thyme together, and reserve.

5 · Assembling the terrine

Start by sprinkling an even layer of salt, black pepper and nutmeg over the bottom of the terrine. Arrange an even layer of about a quarter of the potato slices on top and season again, this time adding about a quarter of the thyme and shallot mixture and half the oil. Cover with two fillets of sardine, skin-side down, and top to tail, then add a third fillet cut in two lengthways. Season again, using a heavier hand this time, then sprinkle again with shallot and thyme, and oil.

Continue layering the terrine in this fashion, finishing with a final layer of potato.

6 · Cooking and pressing the terrine

Cover the terrine with aluminium foil, and place in the simmering water bath. Ensure that the water reaches three-quarters up the sides of the mould, then carefully place the water bath in the pre-heated oven.

Cook for 1¾ hours. Test to see if the terrine is cooked by sliding the thin blade of a knife into the centre; if it slides in very easily, remove the terrine mould from the water bath and leave to cool in a tray of cold water.

Take a piece of cardboard, cut to the size of the top of your terrine mould, and wrap it in aluminium foil. Press it down on

the top layer of potatoes in the mould, and top this with evenly distributed weights. Leave for 12 hours to cool, settle and set. Store in the fridge.

7 · Unmoulding and serving the terrine

Remove the weights and cardboard. Run the blade of a knife down the sides of the terrine, turn out and remove the greaseproof paper.

Wrap the terrine three times in cling film before slicing.

Cut the terrine into slices of about 1 cm (½ in) thick and place in the middle of a large plate. Remove the cling film. Add the shallots and parsley to the vinaigrette then spoon it over and around. Garnish with a little of the flavoured soured cream. Serve to your guests.

VARIATIONS

Mackerel or herrings can be used instead of sardines. The garnish sauce can be changed to taste.

C H E F ' S   N O T E S

The sardines should be the freshest possible. You should use fish of similar sizes to make for even cooking.

Choose large young potatoes for their starch content (see the Scientist's Note on p. 232): this plays a vital part in holding the terrine together, so *don't* wash the slices. Make sure you cut these only when everything else is ready or they will blacken.

Do not be tempted to serve the terrine before it has been pressed for 12 hours. It will not have the same beautiful clear layers, and it will be impossible to cut.

Terrine of Sardines and
Potatoes (see p. 98)

Deep-fried Aubergine Slices with Aubergine Purée

A very attractive and delicious summer starter, this is more dinner-party fare than everyday cooking.

FOR 4 GUESTS

PREPARATION TIME: 15 minutes

COOKING TIME: 40 minutes

SPECIAL EQUIPMENT: An oil thermometer.

PLANNING AHEAD: The purée, deep-fried slices of aubergine, and tomato vinaigrette can be prepared well in advance. The dish must be brought together at the last moment, though, as the moisture in the purée would soften the crisp aubergine slices.

INGREDIENTS

1 litre (1¾ pints) vegetable oil for deep-frying
2 aubergines, 350–400 g (12–14 oz) each

FOR THE AUBERGINE PURÉE

¼ lemon
150 ml (5 fl oz) olive oil
salt and freshly ground black pepper
1 teaspoon caster sugar
2 tiny sprigs of fresh rosemary
1 garlic clove, peeled
2 anchovies, washed briefly and patted dry

TO FINISH

100 ml (3½ fl oz) Tomato Vinaigrette (see p. 60)
4 tablespoons extra virgin olive oil
12 quarters Oven-dried Tomatoes (see p. 61) (optional)

METHOD

1 · Deep-frying the aubergine slices
Pre-heat the deep-frying oil to 160°C (325°F).

With a very sharp knife cut about 28 very fine aubergine slices, about 1 mm (¹⁄₁₆ in) thick. Do this *width*ways. (You need 24, but allow for mistakes.) You will be left with one and one-third aubergines. Cut both of these in half, horizontally. Reserve.

Deep-fry the slices of aubergine in batches of 8 or so at a time, for about 6 minutes, until crisp and golden. Remove from the hot oil and drain on kitchen paper. Leave to cool. Season lightly.

2 · Preparing the aubergine purée
Pre-heat the oven to 200°C/400°F/Gas 6.

Criss-cross cut 3 cm (⅛ in) deep with the blade of a knife into the flesh side of the aubergine pieces. This helps the heat to penetrate the flesh. Place the aubergine pieces on a large sheet of kitchen foil. Rub the pulp of the lemon quarter over the aubergine flesh (to minimize discolouring), brush with 50 ml (2 fl oz) of the olive oil, season with salt and pepper and sprinkle with sugar (this will sharpen the taste). Place a few rosemary leaves on each piece of aubergine. Bring the foil round and fold the edges together to make a secure parcel.

Bake in the pre-heated oven for 40 minutes until soft. Open the foil parcel and scoop the aubergine flesh from the skins into a liquidizer. Squeeze in the remaining lemon juice from the lemon quarter, and add the garlic and anchovies. Blend for about 5 minutes to a fine purée, pouring in the remaining olive oil progressively. Taste and correct the seasoning. Reserve the purée in a small container.

3 · Layering and finishing the dish
You will need two triple-decker aubergine 'sandwiches' per person; each one made up of three slices of aubergine sandwiched together with aubergine purée.

Place eight slices of deep-fried aubergine on a tray. Cover each with a large spoonful of aubergine purée, then another aubergine slice. Add another layer of purée and top with an aubergine slice. Reserve.

4 · Serving
Spoon the raw tomato vinaigrette on to each plate in an attractive manner, sprinkle with a little olive oil and arrange two triple-deckers per plate. Garnish with oven-dried tomatoes if you like. Serve to your guests.

VARIATIONS
The variations are endless: you could include diced tomatoes and courgettes in the purée; you could add basil to it; garnish the dish with Braised Fennel with Cardamom (see p. 234); add Parmesan shavings on the top, and so on.

C H E F ' S   N O T E S

A good ripe, fresh aubergine should be heavy, an attractive deep purple colour, and firm.

The temperature of the oil is terribly important as, if it is too hot, it will brown the outside of the aubergine slice without cooking the inside, and the aubergine slice will become very

Deep-fried Aubergine
slices with Aubergine
purée (see p. 102)

limp after a few minutes. On the other hand, if the oil is at too low a temperature − 275–300°F (140–150°C), say − it is likely to soak into the aubergine giving a very oily and heavy result.

You will need only 24 aubergine slices (three per triple-decker construction), but it is far safer to do a few more.

Cooking can be a very inexact science and, according to the thickness of the slices and the ripeness of the aubergine, the deep-frying time may vary minimally. The aubergine slices will be ready when there are no bubbles on the surface of the oil, which means all the moisture has gone.

According to the ripeness of the aubergine, you may need a little more sugar or lemon juice, so taste the purée to see.

Marinated Red Mullet Fillets with Carrots, Orange, Coriander and Basil

FOR 4 GUESTS

PREPARATION TIME: 15 minutes

MARINATING TIME: 24 hours

PLANNING AHEAD: The dish can be prepared one or two days in advance, covered and kept in the fridge.

INGREDIENTS
4×80–100 g (3–4 oz) red mullet fillets, prepared
2 tablespoons extra virgin olive oil

FOR THE MARINADE
65 ml (2½ fl oz) extra virgin olive oil
100 ml (3½ fl oz) freshly squeezed orange juice
juice of 1 lime
1 teaspoon caster sugar
6 fresh basil leaves, chopped
1 tablespoon chopped fresh coriander leaves
2 sprigs of fresh thyme (lemon thyme if possible)
2 medium carrots, *very* thinly sliced
4 shallots, peeled and very thinly sliced
½ teaspoon salt
4 large pinches of freshly ground white pepper

Each of the two main ingredients of the marinade, namely olive oil and citrus juice (the lime and orange), has its own distinct function. The olive oil not only imparts its own flavour to the fish, but also acts as a 'pathway' for the flavours and fragrance of the herbs, vegetables and spices to reach the fish. Oil also provides some protection from oxidation by the air.

The main function of the fruit juice is a 'cooking' effect on the fish proteins. Acids such as citric acid (in lemon juice) or acetic acid (in vinegar) are characterized by the presence of hydrogen atoms which attach themselves to protein molecules of meat or fish. These protein molecules, no longer repelling each other because of the influence of the hydrogen, can now join together, bond or coagulate – in other words 'cook' (see also the effect of vinegar in egg poaching water, p. 94).

Marinating is a slow rather than fast process, since it depends on a liquid penetrating into a fairly dense material (see Cooking Techniques, p. 42).

METHOD

1 · Preparing the red mullet fillets

Your fishmonger should fillet the fish for you. However, he is unlikely to remove the small bones along the middle of the fillet unless he is of a very good disposition. So, run your finger along the middle of the fillet to locate the small bones and then remove them, using a pair of small pliers or tweezers. Pull gently so as not to damage the fillet. Score the skin lightly, with a very sharp knife about 2 mm ($\frac{1}{16}$ in) thick so that the marinade can penetrate the flesh.

2 · Searing the red mullet fillets

In a large non-stick pan, heat the olive oil and sear both skin and flesh sides of the fillets for 5 seconds. Place the fillets on a small tray, flesh side up. Handle gently; the fillets are very delicate.

3 · Marinating the fish

Mix together all the marinade ingredients and pour over the fillets. Seal with cling film and marinate for 24 hours in the bottom of your fridge.

4 · Serving

Arrange the fillets of red mullet and vegetables attractively on an oval dish, and serve to your guests.

VARIATIONS

Scallops, sardines, herrings, fine slices of sea bream or tuna can all be marinated in the same way. The cooking and marinating times will vary accordingly.

A few leaves of finely chopped lemon verbena would also be delicious added to the marinade.

CHEF'S NOTES

It is essential that the red mullet fillets are as fresh as possible.

Scoring the skin of the fillets will allow the heat to penetrate the fish, and prevent it curling. It will also allow the marinade to permeate the flesh better.

When searing, the objective is to cook the fish rare. This should be done very fast in hot olive oil, then the fish should be placed immediately in the marinating container.

I stipulate 24 hours for the marination, but it can be extended to 48 hours (but no longer). For the marinade to act, it is best not to place the fish in too cold a place, which is why we choose the bottom of the fridge.

Summer Plate

A happy little summer plate: a wonderful reminder of summer when the sun refuses to shine.

FOR 4 GUESTS

PREPARATION TIME: 10 minutes

COOKING TIME: 15 minutes

SPECIAL EQUIPMENT: A cooking thermometer

PLANNING AHEAD: This dish can be prepared a day in advance.

INGREDIENTS
100 ml (3½ fl oz) olive oil
4 aubergine slices, 2 cm (¾ in) thick
salt and freshly ground black pepper
1 pinch of caster sugar
1 tablespoon white wine vinegar
1 tablespoon water
1 large courgette, about 150 g (5 oz), or 2 small ones

100 g (4 oz) Parma ham, very thinly sliced and cut into slivers
1 litre (1¾ pints) vegetable oil for deep-frying
24 onion rings
8 fresh tarragon leaves
8 fresh parsley heads with stalks
4 fresh basil leaves (optional), finely chopped
16 quarters Oven-dried Tomatoes (see p. 61)
50 g (2 oz) shavings of mature Parmesan cheese

FOR THE SAUCE
100 ml (3½ fl oz) raw Tomato Vinaigrette (see p. 60)
50 ml (2 fl oz) extra virgin olive oil

METHOD
Pre-heat the oven to 200°C/400°F/Gas 6.

1 · Cooking the aubergines and courgettes
Heat half the oil in a frying pan and colour one side of the aubergine slices. Turn them over, season with salt, pepper and sugar, and place in a dish. Cook in the oven for 15 minutes, then add the wine vinegar and water. Reserve.

Slice the courgette lengthways about 3 mm (⅛ in) thick. Heat

1 tablespoon of olive oil and colour the courgette for 30 seconds on one side only. Season with salt and pepper and reserve.

2 · *Pan-frying the Parma ham*
Heat the remaining oil in a non-stick frying pan and pan-fry the Parma ham for 5 seconds. Do not add salt.

3 · *Deep-frying the onion rings and herbs*
Pre-heat the deep-frying oil to 160°C (325°F).

Deep-fry the onion rings for about 6 minutes until crispy and brown. Deep-fry the tarragon leaves for 30–40 seconds. Deep-fry the parsley heads for 50–60 seconds. Reserve all of the above on kitchen paper.

4 · *Serving*
Arrange the courgettes on individual plates, folded into two or three, so little parcels are formed. Sprinkle over the basil leaves, if using. Arrange one slice of aubergine per plate and 4 quarters of oven-dried tomatoes. Spoon some raw Tomato Vinaigrette on to each plate and sprinkle with olive oil. Scatter over the shavings of Parmesan, the Parma ham, and the deep-fried onion rings, parsley and tarragon.

VARIATIONS

This dish can be a blueprint for many other ideas – roasted peppers, French beans, artichokes, or marinated red mullet (see p. 105).

CHEF'S NOTES

Try to find a mature Parmesan, as it will be so much more tasty and have a beautiful texture.

For pan-frying, you do not need to use an extra virgin olive oil. A good quality olive oil will do.

The courgettes should be barely cooked, only slightly brown on one side. In no way should they be overcooked.

The cooking time for the Parma ham should be very short, just to sear it, not to cook it. If overcooked, the concentration of salt would be too high, and the texture too fibrous.

Summer Plate (see p. 107)

Fillets of Herring with a Potato Salad

FOR 4 GUESTS

MARINATING TIME: 48 hours

PREPARATION TIME: 30 minutes

PLANNING AHEAD: The dish can be prepared two days in advance, covered and kept in the fridge.

INGREDIENTS
8×50 g (2 oz) herring fillets
salt and freshly ground
  white pepper

FOR THE MARINADE
200 ml (7 fl oz) water
85 ml (3 fl oz) white wine
  vinegar
½ garlic clove, peeled
caster sugar
10 button onions, peeled and
  thinly sliced in small
  rings, blanched in boiling
  water for 10 seconds

1 sprig of fresh thyme
½ bay leaf
1 teaspoon salt
4 large pinches of freshly
  ground white pepper

FOR THE POTATO SALAD
400 g (14 oz) new potatoes
  (the best are Pink Fir
  Apple, Ratte or Jersey
  Royal), washed and not
  peeled
40 g (1½ oz) shallots, peeled
  and finely chopped
100 ml (3½ fl oz) dry white
  wine
50 ml (2 fl oz) white wine
  vinegar
50 ml (2 fl oz) groundnut oil
1 teaspoon of chopped fresh
  parsley

METHOD

1 · Marinating the herring
Score the herring fillets on the skin side about 2 mm ($^1/_{16}$ in) deep, and place in a small container, flesh side down.

Mix together the marinade ingredients. Warm slightly in a small pan, then pour over the herring fillets. Seal with cling film and leave to marinate for 48 hours in the bottom of your fridge, turning occasionally.

2 · Preparing the potato salad
Cook the potatoes in simmering salted water for about 8–10 minutes according to size. Make sure they are not overcooked. Strain and leave to cool until warm. Cut into 5 mm ($^1/_4$ in) slices with the skin on.

In a pan, mix the chopped shallots, wine and wine vinegar. Bring to the boil for 30 seconds, then add the sliced, warm

The oil in herrings contains a special class of fatty acids called the omega-3 fatty acids, which play a vital role in our bodies. They can be converted into hormone-like substances called prosta-glandins, some of which reduce the risk of heart attacks caused by thrombosis, some of which help control inflammatory conditions like arthritis. Large scientific studies have shown that people who eat oily fish regularly are significantly less likely to die from heart disease, thus many scientists now recommend that we should include oily fish (such as herring and sardines) in our diet two or three times a week.

Herrings have other benefits too: they are high in protein, packed with vitamins and minerals, especially the B vitamins, vitamins A and D.

potatoes. Cover and cook for 1 minute over a low heat. Stir, then add the oil. Taste, season with ¼ teaspoon of salt and 4 large pinches of pepper, then cool and add the parsley.

3 · Serving
Simply place a small mound of potatoes in the middle of each plate and arrange the herring fillets on top. Spoon some of the marinating juices over with the onion rings. Serve to your guests.

VARIATIONS
Fresh sardines could easily replace the herrings.

Very finely chopped leeks and carrots could be added on the top, to give both texture and flavour.

CHEF'S NOTES

The herring fillets should come from small herrings, when the bones do not need to be removed. If you use large fillets, ask your fishmonger to remove the bones for you. It is essential that the fish are fresh.

By scoring the skin of the fillets you allow the flavour of the marinade to come through and the acetic acids to act and 'cure' the fish.

In this particular marinade it is the *vinegar* which permeates and 'cooks' the fish fillets. The marinade is added warm to activate the curing process.

The potatoes for the salad must be slightly on the firm side as there is a short secondary cooking in the vinegar and white wine. The potatoes must still be warm when you add the vinegar and white wine as this will ease the exchange of flavours. Whilst cooking the potatoes in the vinegar and white wine the dish is covered. This is to complete the cooking of the potatoes; the acidic vapours will also give them taste.

The parsley is added only at the last moment, as the combination of acidity and warmth would not only discolour it but also spoil its flavour.

Salad 'Façon Maman Blanc'

FOR 4 GUESTS

PREPARATION TIME: 15 minutes

PLANNING AHEAD: Prepare the
ingredients in advance and mix at
the last moment.

INGREDIENTS

**100 ml (3½ fl oz) Hazelnut
Oil Dressing (see Non-
scented Dressing p. 59)**
**100 g (4 oz) Gruyère or
Emmenthal, cut into
matchsticks**

**4 handfuls of mixed salad
leaves such as chicory and
batavia, prepared (see
p. 91)**
**100 g (4 oz) firm, very fresh
button mushrooms, finely
chopped**
**100 g (4 oz) ham, cut into
julienne sticks**
**30 g (1¼ oz) hazelnuts,
toasted then crushed or
sliced**
freshly ground black pepper

METHOD

Pour the hazelnut dressing into a large bowl. Add the salad
leaves and scatter over the cheese, mushrooms, ham and, lastly,
the hazelnuts. Grind a little pepper over the salad. Toss the
salad in front of your guests, and serve immediately.

Assiette Albert

A small tribute to my former head gardener.

FOR 4 GUESTS

PREPARATION TIME: 20 minutes

COOKING TIME: 15 minutes

PLANNING AHEAD: The asparagus can
be cooked an hour beforehand, then
refreshed under cold water. The
hollandaise sauce can be prepared
half an hour in advance and kept in
a bain-marie.

INGREDIENTS

**400 g (14 oz) small English
asparagus spears, peeled**

40g (1½ oz) salt
freshly ground white pepper
20 g (¾ oz) unsalted butter
**4 fresh peppermint leaves,
finely chopped**
**1 tablespoon finely chopped
fresh chervil**
100 ml (3½ fl oz) water
120 g (4½ oz) very young peas
16 young lettuce leaves
**a handful of rocket leaves
(optional)**
**1 quantity Hollandaise
Sauce (see p. 56)**

METHOD

1 · Cooking the asparagus

Bring to a brisk boil in a large saucepan about 2 litres (3½ pints) of water. Add 40 g (1½ oz) salt, then throw in the asparagus. Cover with a lid until it comes back to the boil. Remove the lid, and cook for a further 5–6 minutes, according to the size of the spears.

With a slotted spoon, lift the asparagus out and refresh in cold water. Drain well, then cut each spear in half.

2 · Cooking the remaining vegetables

Mix the butter, chopped mint and chervil with the measured water in a large pan. Season with salt and pepper, then bring to the boil. Throw in all the remaining vegetables – the peas, lettuce leaves and rocket if using – cover and cook for 2 minutes. Add the asparagus and re-heat for 30 seconds.

3 · Serving the dish

Place all the vegetables, plus their juices, on to a serving dish, and serve to your guests. Offer the hollandaise sauce separately.

CHEF'S NOTES

Of course, for this dish to be successful all the ingredients must be the very freshest and youngest. They should encapsulate spring.

———

Thinner, green asparagus is more popular in Britain and the USA than on the Continent, where plump white stalks are the norm. Green asparagus stems have been allowed to grow out of and above the ground to acquire their colour; white asparagus has been blanched or kept out of the light (by earthing up or covering).

———

A common mistake is to cook a large quantity of vegetables in a small amount of water, so that it takes ages for the water to come back to the boil and the vegetables become very tired and grey. A large amount of boiling water will regain its boil very quickly, cook the vegetables perfectly, and ensure they keep their colour and all their nutrients (see also the Scientist's Notes on pp. 33 and 226).

The 40 g (1½ oz) of salt may seem a large amount but it has a dual role. As the cooking time of the asparagus is only 5–6 minutes the salt will not have time to permeate the asparagus, so this larger quantity will season it perfectly during that limited cooking time.

———————

As the cooking time for the vegetables is so short, we place a lid on so that the steam can cook the vegetables.

Scallop Mousse with a Mussel and Saffron Juice

———————

NUTRITIONIST'S NOTES

Scallop meat forms the basis of this unusual mousse and is, in itself, a rich source of many minerals and protein. Scallops are very low in fat but, combined with the cream, the overall fat content of the dish becomes quite high. Mussels also provide good amounts of iron, magnesium and vitamin B_{12}. The fibre content of the dish is low with only small amounts coming from the mushrooms and spinach.

FOR 4 GUESTS

PREPARATION TIME: 20 minutes

COOKING TIME: 25 minutes

SPECIAL EQUIPMENT: 4 ramekins, Apilco size 2

PLANNING AHEAD: The mousse can be made and moulded half a day in advance and cooked at the last moment. The sauce can be prepared a day in advance.

INGREDIENTS
150 g (5 oz) fresh scallops
1 teaspoon salt
a pinch of cayenne pepper
1 free-range egg yolk
200–250 ml (7–8 fl oz) whipping cream

TO WRAP THE MOUSSE
8 large spinach leaves, tough stalks removed
1 teaspoon unsalted butter

FOR THE MUSSEL AND SAFFRON JUICE
1 small shallot, peeled and finely chopped
25 g (1 oz) unsalted butter
60 g (2¼ oz) button mushrooms, finely chopped
50 ml (2 fl oz) dry white wine
50 ml (2 fl oz) water
a tiny pinch of saffron strands
8 Bouchot mussels, scraped and cleaned (see p. 118)

FOR THE GARNISH
20 Bouchot mussels, scraped and cleaned
1 tomato, skinned, seeded and diced
1 teaspoon whipping cream
4 sprigs of fresh chervil
1 teaspoon finely snipped fresh chives

METHOD

1 · Preparing the mousse (see Mousse-making, p. 43)
Pre-heat the oven to 120–140°C/250–275°F/Gas ½–1.
Purée the scallops in a food processor for about 2–3 minutes.

Add the salt and cayenne pepper, then the egg yolk. Trickle in 200 ml (7 fl oz) of the cream. Taste and correct seasoning. Spoon a small amount into a ramekin and cook in a bain-marie in the pre-heated oven for 10 minutes. Taste for texture and seasoning. If needed, add more cream, then chill until ready to cook.

2 · Lining and filling the ramekins

Blanch the spinach leaves in plenty of boiling salted water for 30 seconds. Lift out and refresh in cold water. Drain on a tea towel, pressing lightly.

Butter the inside of the ramekins and line each with two spinach leaves so there is some overlap. Spoon or pipe the mousse into the ramekins, right up to the top. Fold the overlapping spinach over and reserve.

3 · Making the juice

Sweat the shallot in 2 teaspoons of the butter for 1 minute, without colouring. Add the button mushrooms, and sweat for a further minute. Add the white wine, then the water and saffron, and bring to the boil for 10 seconds.

Add the mussels, cover and cook for 1 minute until the shells open. Strain the juices into a small casserole, pressing with a spoon to extract as much juice as possible. Reserve the juice and keep the mussels for another dish or add to the garnish.

4 · Cooking the mousse

Place the ramekins in a low-sided casserole or a small roasting pan and pour in enough boiling water to come two-thirds up the sides of the ramekins. Bring to boiling point, then cover loosely with perforated aluminium foil. Carefully place into the pre-heated oven and cook for 25 minutes. Check the consistency by pressing the middle of the mousse.

5 · Finishing and serving

Re-heat the juice and whisk in the remaining butter. Taste and correct the seasoning.

Cook the mussels with 2 tablespoons of water in a covered casserole for $\frac{1}{2}$–1 minute, until they open.

Warm the tomato dice with the cream for 30 seconds.

Turn the ramekins out on to the middle of each plate. Place a little mound of diced tomatoes on the top of each mousse, garnish with a sprig of chervil and sprinkle with chives. Surround each mousse with five mussels and the re-heated mussel and saffron juice.

VARIATIONS

This mousse can also be made with fish such as turbot, sole and brill, but if so, the mousse mixture will need to be sieved. The quantity of cream will vary accordingly.

If you feel rich, the diced tomato can be replaced by caviar or salmon eggs.

The sauce could be replaced by hollandaise (see p. 56).

If you want to simplify the dish, omit the spinach casing.

C H E F ' S   N O T E S

Try to find the freshest scallops and ask your fishmonger to open them for you. The larger they are, the tastier they are.

The egg yolk here is to enrich rather than bind.

Choose button mushrooms which are firm and white. Older ones will discolour the sauce.

Bouchot mussels are very small, plump and juicy, and are available in most shops.

No salt is needed in this recipe as the mussels will provide it.

Use whipping cream as it is much lighter than double cream. Food can be a very inexact science and the amount of cream will depend on the freshness of the scallops. So only add a proportion, then test as described.

The blanching of the spinach should be very, very short, barely enough to cook it. Prepare the cold water beforehand, so you can refresh it immediately and prevent it from losing its colour.

Under no circumstances should the shallots brown. Sweating removes the strong taste of the shallots, and brings out their sweetness.

As we use a very small quantity of white wine (any table wine will do), 10 seconds will be enough to reduce the alcohol content and some of its acidity. The wine is used as part of the build-up of flavour.

Scallop Mousse with a
Mussel and Saffron Juice
(see p. 114)

Risotto with Mussels

FOR 4 GUESTS

PREPARATION TIME: 15 minutes

COOKING TIME: 40 minutes

PLANNING AHEAD: The dish must be made at the last moment.

INGREDIENTS

450 g (1 lb) arborio or other risotto rice

100 ml (3½ fl oz) dry white wine

1.25 litres (2¼ pints) White Chicken Stock (see p. 54)

80 g (3¼ oz) onion, peeled and finely chopped

40 g (1½ oz) unsalted butter
salt and freshly ground white pepper

FOR THE MUSSELS

1.5 kg (3½ lb) mussels

50 g (2 oz) onion, peeled and finely chopped

2 garlic cloves, peeled and roughly chopped

1 teaspoon unsalted butter

100 ml (3½ fl oz) dry white wine

4 sprigs of fresh thyme

1 bay leaf

NUTRITIONIST'S NOTES

Rice is rich in complex carbo-hydrates which give us energy. Most of us get too little of our total energy from complex carbohydrates, too much from fats. So, we need to base more of our meals on foods such as rice, pasta and potatoes.

Mussels are very low in fat but rich in minerals such as iron, zinc and iodine. So they make an ideal, nutritious accompaniment to the rice.

METHOD

1 · Preparing and cooking the mussels

Place the mussels in a sink of cold water and pick over, discarding any that do not close when tapped with the blade of a knife. If they continue to gape, they are dead. Scrape off any barnacles, using the blade of a small sharp knife, and pull away the black threads or beards. Wash thoroughly, then drain.

In a large cast-iron pan, sweat the chopped onion and garlic over a low heat in the butter for a few minutes until soft but not brown. Add the wine, thyme and bay leaf, and boil for 10 seconds over a high heat. Add the mussels, cover and cook, shaking the pan, for 1 minute until the mussels are just opened. Discard any that remain closed.

Drain the juices from the mussels into a small saucepan through a fine sieve or cloth. Pick the mussels out of their shells and keep them in their cooking juices.

2 · Cooking the risotto

Do not wash the rice. Bring the wine to the boil for 5 seconds. Reserve. Bring the stock to a simmer in a saucepan.

Sweat the chopped onion in the butter for 1 minute, then add the rice and stir. Add the wine and a ladleful of hot chicken stock. On a medium heat, bring the rice to near simmering point and cook until the rice has absorbed most of the chicken stock. Stir from time to time. Then add another ladle of chicken stock, stirring delicately.

The rice will gradually cook as the stock is gradually added. Keep the temperature low, as on no account must the risotto boil. This process will take about 30 minutes, stirring whilst adding the hot chicken stock. The risotto should be creamy in consistency, the grains plump and moist, not dry.

3 · Serving

Mix the mussels and their juices into the risotto. Stir and cook on a medium heat for a further minute, season to taste, then serve to your guests.

VARIATIONS

You can reserve 20 of the mussels, cook them at the last moment in their shells and arrange them in their shells around the dish.

The risotto can also be made with other ingredients such as vegetables – ceps, asparagus or courgettes for example – and seafood such as prawns or pieces of fish.

C H E F ' S   N O T E S

Discard any mussels that remain open before cooking, or remain shut after cooking. They are probably dead, and could be a health hazard. When buying mussels, the freshest ones usually feel heavy with sea water.

For both the rice and the mussels, we boil the white wine to reduce its alcohol content, but we shall still have the taste. Do not overcook the mussels (3–4 minutes will be enough), to ensure they are juicy and tender.

There are many different types of rice which all need to be cooked in different ways, as they have different powers of absorption. Long- and medium-grain rices will absorb up to three times their weight in liquid. Arborio and other risotto rices have medium to long grains, and are used for risottos because no other rice grain can absorb so much liquid without becoming too soft. Arborio rice also has a hard core which is what produces the characteristic texture of risottos – the grains creamy on the outside while still slightly *al dente* in the middle.

Stilton Soufflé

This recipe was kindly given to me by Mr Peter Kromberg, Executive Chef of Le Soufflé restaurant at the Inter-Continental Hotel, London.

FOR 4 GUESTS

PREPARATION TIME: 20 minutes

COOKING TIME: 13–15 minutes

SPECIAL EQUIPMENT: 4 small soufflé dishes, about 10 cm (4 in) in diameter and 5 cm (2 in) in height.

PLANNING AHEAD: The milk mixture and the breadcrumbs can be prepared well in advance but the soufflé must be baked at the last moment.

INGREDIENTS

45 g (1¾ oz) plain flour
45 g (1¾ oz) unsalted butter
250 ml (8 fl oz) full-fat milk

90 g (3½ oz) Gruyère cheese, grated
4 free-range egg yolks
salt and cayenne pepper
7 free-range egg whites
juice of ¼ lemon
90 g (3½ oz) Stilton cheese, crumbled

TO LINE THE SOUFFLE DISHES

1 tablespoon unsalted butter, softened
25 g (1 oz) dry breadcrumbs
20 g (¾ oz) walnuts and hazelnuts, very finely chopped
10 g (¼ oz) Parmesan cheese, finely grated

METHOD

1 · Lining the soufflé dishes
Pre-heat the oven to 190°C/375°F/Gas 5, and place in it a baking sheet.

Generously butter the insides of the four soufflé dishes. Mix the breadcrumbs, chopped nuts and Parmesan together and divide between the buttered dishes. Shake them and turn to line them completely. Tip out any excess and chill until needed.

2 · Preparing the soufflé mixture
Mix the flour and butter together until smooth. Separately boil the milk. Add the flour and butter mixture to the milk and bring it back to the boil, whisking all the time, so you obtain a very smooth texture. (Or you could make the béchamel soufflé base in the more traditional way – stirring the flour into the melted butter, then adding the milk gradually, stirring constantly.)

Remove from the heat, cool a little, then add the grated Gruyère and the egg yolks. Whisk into the mixture. Add a pinch

each of salt and pepper, then taste. Correct the seasoning if necessary.

Whip the egg whites until very soft peaks are formed, then add the lemon juice. Continue whisking until you have firm peaks, then whisk in a little salt and fold in most of the crumbled Stilton.

Whisk a quarter to a third of the egg white into the Gruyère base mixture to lighten it a little, then fold in the remainder carefully.

3 · Cooking the soufflés
The oven must be well pre-heated by now.

Fill the four soufflé dishes with enough soufflé mixture to come half-way up, add the remaining Stilton, and fill to the top with the remaining mixture. Smooth with a palette knife. Run your thumb along the sides of the dishes to push the mixture slightly away from the sides.

Place the dishes on the hot baking sheet (this helps provide an instant lift), and bake in the pre-heated oven for about 13–15 minutes until well risen and golden. Serve immediately to your guests.

VARIATIONS
You could replace the Stilton with another blue cheese, such as Roquefort. The Gruyère could be replaced by Parmesan.

CHEF'S NOTES

All the technical points within this recipe are explained in the soufflé section, so please consult this before starting (see p. 45).

The amount of salt used should be quite small as the cheeses are already salted. According to which cheese you use, you may need a little more or less.

The béchamel sauce used as the soufflé base must cool a little before the egg yolks are added. If they were stirred into a hot sauce (higher than 60°C/140°F), they would scramble.

Potato Gnocchi with Macaroni, Parma Ham and Parmesan

FOR 4 GUESTS

PREPARATION TIME: 30 minutes

COOKING TIME: 10 minutes

PLANNING AHEAD: The gnocchi can
be prepared and made a day in
advance.

INGREDIENTS

**80 g (3¼ oz) bought
  macaroni, 1 cm (½ in) in
  diameter**
**salt and freshly ground
  white pepper**
2 teaspoons butter
**4 handfuls of spinach leaves,
  stalks removed**

**150 ml (5 fl oz) whipping
  cream**
**100 g (4 oz) Parma ham, cut
  into fine slivers**
**60 g (2¼ oz) Parmesan
  cheese freshly grated**

FOR THE GNOCCHI

**500 g (18 oz) potatoes
  (Estima, Wilja, Maris
  Piper or Cara), scrubbed**
125 g (4½ oz) plain flour
2 egg yolks
**4 pinches of freshly grated
  nutmeg**

METHOD

1 · Making the gnocchi

Place the potatoes, unpeeled, in a pan of water to cover, at least
1 litre (1¾ pints). Add 1 tablespoon of salt and cook at a gentle
simmer for about 30 minutes. Drain well.

Peel the potatoes and purée them whilst still warm in a
vegetable mill. Place in a bowl.

Add the flour, egg yolks, 1 teaspoon salt, 2 large pinches of
pepper and the nutmeg. Mix the ingredients together well with
a wooden spoon, then shape into a ball. If sticky, add a little
more flour, but not too much or the gnocchi will be heavy.

Cut the ball in quarters and roll each quarter into small
cylinders about 1 cm (½ in) thick on a lightly floured surface.
Cut these cylinders into 2 cm (¾ in) gnocchi. Make an indent-
ation with the back of a fork (or your thumb) on each of the
gnocchi to give an interesting shape. Practice makes perfect
when making gnocchi!

2 · Cooking the macaroni and gnocchi

Cook the macaroni in plenty of boiling salted water for about
7–8 minutes. Drain, using a slotted spoon, then keep warm.

In the same water, cook the gnocchi at simmering point for 3–4 minutes, or until they rise to the top of the pan. Drain well and keep warm.

3 · Cooking the spinach

In a pan, melt the butter, add the spinach and season with salt and pepper. Cook, covered, for 2–3 minutes until just wilted.

4 · Finishing and serving

Pre-heat the grill to hot.

Whip the cream to a soft consistency, not too firm.

Divide the cooked spinach between four flameproof plates or dishes. Arrange on them the gnocchi, macaroni and the slivers of Parma ham. Spoon over the whipped cream, sprinkle with Parmesan and brown under the hot grill. Serve to your guests.

CHEF'S NOTES

The simmering time will vary according to the size and variety of potato.

Lamb Sweetbreads
with Lettuce and Peas

FOR 4 GUESTS

PREPARATION TIME: 15 minutes

COOKING TIME: 10 minutes

PLANNING AHEAD: Allow time for soaking the sweetbreads in cold water overnight.

INGREDIENTS

8 large lamb sweetbreads (from the heart)
80 g (3¼ oz) unsalted butter

salt and freshly ground white pepper
150 ml (5 fl oz) water
8 fresh tarragon leaves, finely chopped
1 teaspoon finely chopped fresh parsley
200 g (7 oz) very young peas
2 Little Gem lettuces
4 tomatoes, skinned, seeded and diced
a dash of lemon juice

METHOD

1 · Preparing and cooking the sweetbreads

Soak the sweetbreads in cold water overnight. Drain.

Blanch the sweetbreads in boiling water for 10 seconds. With

Potato Gnocchi with Macaroni, Parma Ham and Parmesan (see p. 123)

a slotted spoon, remove and refresh them in cold water. Drain them, pat them dry and with a small knife, peel off the membranes and cartilage.

In a non-stick pan, melt 50 g (2 oz) of the butter until it foams and becomes a rich golden brown in colour. Add the sweetbreads and colour them for 3–4 minutes on each side. Season with salt and pepper. Spoon out and discard the butter, then reserve the sweetbreads, covered to keep warm.

2 · Preparing the peas and lettuce

Mix the water and 2 teaspoons of the butter in a pan. Add the chopped tarragon and parsley, and bring to the boil. Add the peas and lettuce together, cover and cook for 3 minutes.

3 · Serving

With a slotted spoon, lift out the vegetables and divide them between four soup plates.

Whisk the remaining butter into the cooking juices, then add the diced tomatoes. Taste, season with salt and pepper, and lift with a dash of lemon juice.

Arrange two sweetbreads in the middle of each plate, and spoon over them some of their own juices. Spoon the tomato dice and juice around, then serve to your guests.

VARIATIONS

Young spinach leaves or asparagus spears could be added.

CHEF'S NOTES

The best time to make this dish is in the spring and summer, when the lambs are still young. Sweetbreads come from the thymus gland of young animals. One of this gland's functions is to produce growth hormones, and it diminishes in size as the animal grows. The gland comes in two parts, one part near the heart, one nearer the neck. The former are the fattest and nicest; the latter are very stringy and unappetizing.

The sweetbreads are blanched for a few seconds in boiling water to solidify the membranes surrounding them. This can now easily be removed. The sweetbreads are then plunged into cold water which immediately stops the cooking.

The diced tomatoes are added right at the end so they are just warm and to give a nice refreshing acidity to the dish.

Puff Pastry Tartlet with Monkfish

SCIENTIST'S
NOTES

With puff pastry the idea is to create many near-perfect layers of fat between layers of dough. When the dough is baked in a very hot oven, the air and water vapour expand and push the layers of dough apart. Any imperfection in the fat layers will allow the dough layers to stick together.

Puff pastry desserts (and croissants) are popular because of their texture and mouth-feel — ideally puff pastry should melt at mouth temperature. Some inferior puff-pastry leaves the mouth coated in solid fat, which feels unpleasant, although the original product may have looked appealing.

.

If the pastry has been worked too hard during its making (not a problem here, with bought pastry), the proteins in the gluten might have become stretched beyond their natural length. Resting the pastry before rolling allows the proteins to resume their initial conformation. At the same time, the starch granules of the flour will be able to absorb all the water used in making the pastry. The pastry is also rested after rolling and cutting for the same reasons. Chilling is actually of secondary importance to resting if making puff pastry from scratch.

Starters

FOR 4 GUESTS

PREPARATION TIME: 30 minutes

COOKING TIME: 10 minutes

SPECIAL EQUIPMENT: 1 baking sheet; 4 circles of silicone paper, 18 cm (7 in) in diameter; a round pastry cutter, 14 cm (5½ in) in diameter.

PLANNING AHEAD: The tartlet cases can be prepared a few days in advance and kept frozen. The tartlets plus filling can be baked an hour before serving.

INGREDIENTS
250 g (9 oz) high-quality bought puff pastry

FOR THE FILLING
120 g (4½ oz) red peppers, seeded and finely diced

4 tablespoons olive oil
120 g (4½ oz) tomatoes, skinned, seeded and diced
salt and freshly ground white pepper
a dash of white wine vinegar
2×175 g (6 oz) monkfish fillets, boned and skinned (net weight)
2 tablespoons extra virgin olive oil
12 fresh basil leaves or 24 fresh coriander leaves

TO FINISH
½ teaspoon Dijon mustard
2 tablespoons extra virgin olive oil

METHOD

1 · Preparing the puff pastry tartlets
Lightly flour the work surface. Cut the puff pastry dough into quarters. Roll each quarter into circles of about 18 cm (7 in) in diameter, and about 3 mm (⅛ in) thickness. Place these on a lightly floured tray and chill for 8–10 minutes.

With the pastry cutter, stamp out four slightly smaller circles and place each of them on to the circles of silicone paper. With the pastry trimmings, prepare thin strips about 3 mm (⅛ in) in height and 5 mm (¼ in) wide. With water and a brush moisten the outside of the circles, then curl and stick on the thin strips to make the sides of the tartlets. Chill or freeze.

2 · Cooking the filling
Sear the pepper dice in half the olive oil, then cook at a lower temperature for 3 minutes. Do not colour them, as we want the texture to be very crisp. Add the diced tomatoes and cook for a further minute. Taste and season with salt and pepper. Add the dash of wine vinegar. Cool and reserve.

Heat the remaining oil in a frying pan and sear the monkfish fillets for about 2 minutes, turning from time to time. Season with salt and pepper and leave to cool.

Cut the fillets into very fine slices. Place them in a bowl, and add the extra virgin olive oil and some salt and pepper. Chop the basil or coriander leaves and mix them with the monkfish. Reserve.

3 · Filling the tartlets
Remove the tartlets from the freezer or fridge. Still on their silicone paper, place them on the baking sheet.

Divide the pepper and tomato mixture between the centre of the tartlets and spread out evenly. Cover this base with the slices of monkfish, making sure they overlap. Leave the sides free of filling. Season with salt and pepper.

4 · Cooking and serving
Pre-heat the oven to 200°C/400°F/Gas 6. Place the baking sheet in the oven, and bake the tartlets for 10 minutes.

Roughly mix the Dijon mustard and olive oil together and brush over the tops and sides of each cooked tartlet. Serve to your guests.

VARIATIONS
These tartlets can also be made with scallops or fresh tuna. Or, for a vegetarian alternative, you can replace the monkfish with slices of good tomatoes or courgettes with basil or chervil.

You can also, of course, use the pastry to line four 14 cm (5½ in) tins. This is marginally easier.

C H E F ' S   N O T E S

Always buy the best puff pastry you can find (such as Waitrose's). Puff pastry made with unsalted butter is the best. *Never* buy anything made with margarine.

The thickness of the pastry is terribly important. The finer the better, as it will cook to a crisp. Too thick, and it is likely to be soggy.

The pastry has to be rested before baking (see Scientist's Notes). It is chilled in order to make the fat in the pastry as solid as possible, which reduces the danger of it liquifying and being absorbed into the dough.

N U T R I T I O N I S T ' S
N O T E S

All pastry dishes tend to be high in fat and the puff pastry here contains a high proportion of fat to flour which inevitably increases the overall fat percentage. The filling is monkfish, a good low-fat source of protein, combined with red peppers and tomatoes which are both rich in vitamin C. The recipe uses a fair amount of olive oil, good for keeping blood cholesterol levels in check but still high in calories.

Puff Pastry Tartlet with
Monkfish (see p. 127)

When searing the monkfish fillets you will notice that the fibres shrink or retract a little. We sear the fillet before cooking in the tart in order to prevent further retraction, but it will also heighten the taste. We only want to cook it rare, though.

Smoked Haddock Fritters

FOR 4 GUESTS

PREPARATION TIME: 20 minutes, plus 2–2½ hours' resting

COOKING TIME: 3 minutes

SPECIAL EQUIPMENT: A deep-fryer or a deep frying pan; an oil thermometer.

PLANNING AHEAD: The batter must be prepared 2 hours in advance.

INGREDIENTS
8 small spring onions, trimmed
2 tablespoons sesame oil
salt and freshly ground white pepper
vegetable oil for deep-frying
4×60 g (2¼ oz) pieces of smoked haddock

1 quantity Tartare Sauce (see p. 58)

FOR THE BATTER
10 g (¼ oz) fresh yeast
100 ml (3½ fl oz) dark beer (a stout, for instance; Guinness for the best results)
150 ml (5 fl oz) water
2 egg yolks
cayenne pepper
200 g (7 oz) plain flour
40 g (1½ oz) unsalted butter, melted
3 egg whites
juice of ¼ lemon
2 tablespoons chopped fresh coriander

METHOD

1 · Making the batter
Crumble the yeast into a bowl or jug, and dissolve in the beer and water. Whisk in the egg yolks, then season with 2 pinches of cayenne pepper.

Place the flour in a large bowl and mix in the yeast mixture. Whisk for a perfect mix, then stir in the melted butter. Allow to prove at room temperature for 2–2½ hours, or leave overnight to prove in your fridge.

2 · Preparing the spring onion garnish
Chop the spring onions very finely. Fry them for 1 minute maximum in the hot sesame oil, stirring constantly. Do not allow them to brown, and do not overcook. They should be *al dente*. Season with salt and pepper and reserve.

3 · *Finishing the batter*

Just before using the batter, whisk the egg whites to a delicate foam. Add the lemon juice and whisk to firm peaks. Fold in the egg whites, scant ½ teaspoon of salt and chopped coriander.

4 · *Deep-frying the haddock*

Pre-heat the deep-fryer to 180°C (350°F).

Dip the haddock pieces into the batter and deep-fry them in the hot fat for 2–2½ minutes until golden brown. Drain well.

5 · *Serving*

Divide the stir-fried spring onions between the plates, and place a hot haddock fritter on top. Serve to your guests, with the Tartare Sauce offered separately.

VARIATIONS

Lots of other fish can be used instead of the smoked haddock – cod, salt cod, herring, skate etc. You could also use other herbs such as mint, parsley or lemon thyme.

CHEF'S NOTES

Salt must never come in direct contact with yeast as it will cancel its effect. And only a very small quantity of salt is needed anyway, as the smoked haddock is quite salty already.

———

To protect the haddock from the high temperature of the deep-frying oil, it is first coated with a batter. A thin batter would cook to a light crispness, but it would run off the fish and not adhere very easily; a thick batter would adhere much more effectively, but would be stodgier in texture when cooked. The medium-thick batter here, therefore, contains yeast which, during the 2–2½ hours' proving aerates the batter with carbon dioxide making it much lighter. The yeast also adds flavour.

———

If you want a short proving for the yeast batter, the temperature has got to be between 22 and 26°C (72–79°F); this will take about 2½ hours. You can prove for a longer time in the fridge; the yeast cells will continue to multiply but more slowly.

———

The lemon juice added to the egg white will help the binding or coagulation of the egg whites (see also the Scientist's Note on p. 94), and will prevent them becoming grainy. It will also enhance the taste.

Bread Rolls Filled with Wild Mushrooms

FOR 4 GUESTS

PREPARATION AND COOKING TIME: 20 minutes

INGREDIENTS

4 round, good-quality white bread rolls
2 large garlic cloves, peeled and halved
50 ml (2 fl oz) olive oil

FOR THE FILLING
200 g (7 oz) wild mushrooms, prepared (see p. 205)
25 g (1 oz) unsalted butter

50 ml (2 fl oz) water mixed with 1½ teaspoons lemon juice
salt and freshly ground black pepper
1 teaspoon chopped fresh chervil
a few tarragon leaves, blanched in boiling water for 10 seconds, then chopped
1 teaspoon chopped fresh parsley
50 ml (2 fl oz) whipping cream, whipped

METHOD

1 · Preparing the bread rolls
Pre-heat the oven to 180°C/350°F/Gas 4.

Take each bread roll and slice off the top about one-third of the way down. Scoop out the soft insides. Rub the inside of the hollow and the top inside of the 'lid' with garlic, then brush the olive oil over the same surfaces. Place in the pre-heated oven to dry out and crisp for 10 minutes.

2 · Preparing the mushroom filling
Sauté the wild mushrooms in the butter for 1 minute. Add the water and lemon juice and cook for a further minute with the lid on. Taste, and season with salt and pepper, then reserve.

3 · Serving
Add the chopped herbs to the whipped cream, then taste and season with salt and pepper. Just before serving whisk the whipped cream into the mushrooms and their juices.

Divide the mushrooms between the hollows in each bread roll, and spoon the sauce on and around. Top with the 'lids' and serve to your guests.

Open Lasagne of Spring Vegetables and Wild Mushrooms

FOR 4 GUESTS

PREPARATION TIME: 20 minutes

COOKING TIME: 10 minutes

PLANNING AHEAD: The dish can be prepared up to and including stage 2 in advance. The purée and the pasta *must* be prepared in advance.

INGREDIENTS
250 g (9 oz) Home-made Pasta (see p. 52)
24 sprigs of fresh chervil
salt and freshly ground white pepper

FOR THE LASAGNE FILLING
1 handful of shelled small peas
1 handful of shelled broad beans
1 handful of mangetout peas, topped and tailed

8 thin green asparagus stalks
200 ml (7 fl oz) water
1 heaped teaspoon unsalted butter
1 handful of wild mushrooms, prepared (see p. 205)
4 tablespoons Spinach and Watercress Purée (see p. 223)

TO FINISH THE SAUCE
30 g (1¼ oz) cold unsalted butter, diced
1 tablespoon finely chopped fresh chervil
1 tablespoon finely snipped fresh chives
10 fresh basil leaves, finely chopped
a dash of lemon juice

METHOD

1 · Preparing the pasta sheets
Roll the pasta out into two sheets with a rolling pin or pasta machine. It should be about 1 mm thick.

Scatter the chervil leaves on one of the pasta sheets and place the other sheet over it. Roll again with a rolling pin or pasta machine back to 1 mm thickness. The chervil leaves will be trapped within the pasta and will make it look wonderful.

Cut the pasta into sixteen 6 cm (6½ in) squares. Reserve on a floured tray in the refrigerator, covered with cling film.

2 · Preparing the vegetable filling
Peas and broad beans Set aside to be cooked at the last moment.
Mangetout peas Cook in plenty of boiling salted water for 2 minutes. Lift out with a slotted spoon, refresh in cold water, drain and reserve. Keep the cooking water.

Asparagus   Cut off the base of the asparagus stalk, then cut each stalk in half along its length. Cook in the same water as used for the sugar snap peas for 2 minutes. Refresh in cold water, drain and reserve.

3 · Cooking the vegetable filling

Place the water and butter in a saucepan, season and bring to the boil. Add the peas and broad beans and cook for 1 minute. Add the mangetout peas, asparagus and wild mushrooms and cook on for a further minute.

4 · Finishing the filling and sauce

Whisk the cold diced butter into the hot vegetables, then add the chervil, chives and chopped basil leaves. Taste and correct seasoning, and add a dash of lemon juice to lift the flavour. Reserve.

   Re-heat the Spinach and Watercress Purée.

5 · Cooking the lasagne

Cook the lasagne squares for 1 minute in plenty of boiling salted water. Drain well.

6 · Serving

Place one square of lasagne in the middle of each plate. Spread 1 tablespoon of watercress and spinach purée on each and scatter with vegetables. Place another layer of lasagne on top. Repeat this process until you have three layers of vegetables. Top with a final, fourth layer of lasagne. Scatter the remaining vegetables and juice over and around. Serve to your guests.

CHEF'S NOTES

When broad beans are tiny, the outer skin does not need to be removed. But if they are mature, the skin will be tough, so blanch the beans in plenty of boiling salted water for 1 minute (this will soften the skin), then the beans can be easily squeezed out. Make an incision in the skin and squeeze gently.

———

The basil must be chopped at the very last moment as it will discolour and lose most of its taste and scent.

———

The cooking time is very short, which will ensure that taste, texture and colour will be at their best. Increase the cooking time by a minute if the vegetables are slightly older.

Fish

Fillet of Plaice with Spring Vegetables 138

Fresh Home-made Pasta with Squid, Scallops, Almonds and Cashew Nuts 140

Poached Slivers of Monkfish and Scallops in a Vegetable Broth 142

Salmon Steak Poached in an Aromatic Vegetable Stock on a Bed of Watercress and Spinach with Hollandaise Sauce 145

Roast Fillets of Sea Bream on a Bouillabaisse Sauce with Fondue of Tomatoes 147

Pan-fried Cod Fillet on a Purée of Potatoes with a Caper Sauce 150

Wing of Skate with Potatoes in White Wine, Caper and Gherkin Sauce 152

Pan-fried Fillet of John Dory with Aubergine Tagliatelle and Tomato Vinaigrette 154

Fillet of Monkfish with a Herb Crust and Red Pepper Sauce 156

Baby Turbot Roasted on a Bed of Fennel with Rosemary Butter Sauce 159

Fillet of Salmon in a Herb and Sorrel Juice 161

Fillets of Red Mullet with Braised Fennel and a Fennel Sauce 162

A Deep-fried Parcel of Crab and Seaweed 164

Tempura of Soused Herring and Vegetables 166

Baby Turbot Roasted on
a Bed of Fennel with
Rosemary Butter Sauce
(see p. 159)

Fillet of Plaice with Spring Vegetables

FOR 4 GUESTS

PREPARATION TIME: 20 minutes

COOKING TIME: 7 minutes

PLANNING AHEAD: The vegetables can be prepared 6–12 hours in advance.

INGREDIENTS
4×150 g (5 oz) plaice fillets
salt and freshly ground white pepper
2 shallots, peeled and sliced
30 g (1¼ oz) unsalted butter
75 g (3 oz) button mushrooms, sliced
100 ml (3½ fl oz) dry white wine or Noilly Prat
50 ml (2 fl oz) water

TO FINISH THE SAUCE
1 teaspoon cream
15 g (½ oz) cold, unsalted butter, diced
lemon juice
½ tablespoon chopped fresh chives
½ tablespoon chopped fresh chervil

FOR THE VEGETABLE GARNISH
75 g (3 oz) shelled broad beans
75 g (3 oz) shelled young peas
1 medium courgette
75 g (3 oz) French beans, topped and tailed
8 lettuce leaves

METHOD

1 · Preparing the plaice fillets
Score the plaice fillets on the outer skin side in a criss-cross pattern. Season with salt and pepper. Fold the fillets in half, skin side outwards, and reserve.

2 · Preparing and cooking the vegetable garnish
Broad beans   Cook the beans in boiling salted water for 2 minutes only. Lift out with a slotted spoon, refresh under cold water and drain. Keep the water for cooking the other vegetables. If the beans are large, peel off the skins; if they are small, leave the skin on. Reserve.
Peas   Boil in the same water for 1 minute, lift out with a slotted spoon, refresh in cold water and reserve.
Courgette   Trim at ends and slice about 3 mm (⅛ in) thick. Cook in the bean and pea water for 2 minutes. Lift out with a slotted spoon, refresh in cold water and reserve. Sieve the water.
French beans   Boil in the same water for 3–4 minutes. Lift out with a slotted spoon, refresh in cold water and reserve.

Lettuce leaves Boil in the same water for 30 seconds, lift out with a slotted spoon, refresh in cold water and reserve.

3 · *Cooking the plaice fillets*

Pre-heat the oven to 200°C/400°F/Gas 6.

In a sauté pan large enough to hold the fillets in one layer, sweat the shallots in the butter for 2 minutes. Add the sliced mushrooms and sweat for a further minute. Add the wine or Noilly Prat and boil for about 1 minute before adding the water.

Add the folded plaice fillets, bring the liquid to boiling point, and cover with a lid. Cook in the pre-heated oven for about 5 minutes. Remove from the oven and reserve in a warm place for 3–5 minutes.

4 · *Finishing the sauce and serving*

Lift the plaice fillets on to a large buttered serving dish and keep warm.

Strain the juices into a medium pan, pressing on the shallots and mushrooms to extract as much liquid as possible. Add the cream and whisk in the butter. Taste, correct seasoning and add a little lemon juice to lift the sauce.

Add the chervil and chives and all the vegetables. Bring to the boil for 30 seconds, pour over the fillets of plaice and serve.

VARIATIONS

This dish offers many variations: tomatoes, mustard, basil and leek could also be used.

Fillets of sole, lemon sole, turbot, brill, etc. can be used instead.

C H E F ' S   N O T E S

The butter is going to be incorporated in the sauce, and must be cold. If it is too soft it would melt too quickly and the sauce would not emulsify.

The butter needs to be whisked vigorously in order to disperse it and emulsify it within the juices to create a homogeneous sauce. Since it contains much less emulsifier than, for instance, hollandaise sauce, it is less stable. However, by vigorous whisking, thereby creating very small fat globules, it can be made to last for 20 minutes or more. Whisk again if it separates.

The skin side of the fillets contains many fibres. The fillets are scored in order to diminish shrinkage whilst cooking. Folding the fillets in half, exposing and 'opening out' the incisions, will allow the heat to penetrate.

For sweating of the shallots, see Cooking Techniques, p. 36.

The wine is boiled in order to remove some of the alcohol content and to reduce the acidity. The aim is to leave enough acidity to give depth of flavour; if reduced too much, the sauce is likely to be very flat.

Once the fish has been taken out of the oven, it is rested for 3 minutes. This will allow the residual heat to finish cooking the fish perfectly, and also some of the juices to escape. This will be used to enrich the sauce.

Fresh Home-made Pasta with Squid, Scallops, Almonds and Cashew Nuts

---

FOR 4 GUESTS

PREPARATION TIME: 10 minutes

COOKING TIME: 10 minutes

PLANNING AHEAD: The pasta can be prepared in advance.

INGREDIENTS

½ **quantity Home-made Pasta (see p. 52), cut into fine noodles**

salt and freshly ground black pepper
4 large scallops, prepared
50 ml (2 fl oz) olive oil
juice of ¼ lemon
20 baby squid, prepared
50 ml (2 fl oz) water
20 g (¾ oz) cashew nuts
20 g (¾ oz) pine kernels

METHOD

1 · Cooking the pasta
Cook the pasta in about 2 litres (3½ pints) of boiling water with 1 tablespoon of salt, until *al dente*. If the pasta is fresh, cook for about 3–4 minutes; if dried, about 6–7 minutes. Drain the pasta well and keep it warm.

2 · *Cooking the garnishes*

Whilst cooking the pasta, pre-heat the grill or the oven to 220°C/425°F/Gas 7.

Pan-fry the scallops in 1 tablespoon of the olive oil for 2 minutes on each side until a good colour. Season with salt and pepper and a dash of lemon juice. Reserve on a small tray.

In the same pan, and in a little more very hot oil, pan-fry the baby squid for 1 minute. Season with salt, pepper and a squeeze of lemon juice. Reserve them with the scallops.

Add the measured water to the cooking pan, and bring to the boil whilst scraping the pan. Reserve these juices.

Colour the cashew nuts and pine kernels lightly, tossing gently, under the grill or in the pre-heated oven, for about 5 minutes. Be careful not to burn them. (You could also 'dry-roast' them in a pan.) Reserve.

3 · *Finishing the dish and serving*

Place the remaining olive oil, the cashew nuts and pine kernels in a pan and mix in the pasta. Taste and correct the seasoning with salt and pepper. Transfer the pasta to a serving dish or to individual plates. Scatter the cooked squid and scallops over the pasta and pour on the reserved cooking juices. Serve.

VARIATIONS

All sorts of variations are possible with this dish – you could add diced tomato, fresh basil or diced monkfish, for example. Shellfish such as clams or cockles would also be delicious.

You could also make the pasta with squid ink (see p. 53).

CHEF'S NOTES

When cooking the pasta, it is important that the water should be at a full boil so that once the pasta is added, the water will regain its boil quicker and the cooking can be more accurate. (See also the Scientist's Note on p. 70.)

Give a good colour to the scallops, both for taste and presentation. Those 2 minutes will be enough to cook them.

For the scallop coral: poach for 5 minutes in simmering salted water, drain, cut in fine slivers and pan-fry with the squid.

Cooking the squid for more than 1 minute will make them tough.

Poached Slivers of Monkfish and Scallops in a Vegetable Broth

Both monkfish and scallops are low in fat and high in minerals such as iodine and phosphorus. The accompanying vegetables add lots of vitamins and extra fibre. Carrots are one of the best vegetable sources of beta-carotene which helps fight harmful free radicals in the body. Courgettes and cucumbers are good sources of potassium and tend to have a mild diuretic effect. Overall this dish is low in fat and high in protein.

FOR 4 GUESTS

PREPARATION TIME: 15 minutes

COOKING TIME: 10 minutes

PLANNING AHEAD: If you use the vegetable stock, you can prepare it at least a day or two in advance.

INGREDIENTS
**300 g (11 oz) monkfish fillet, thinly cut into 3 mm × 3 cm ($\frac{1}{8}$ × $1\frac{1}{4}$ in) slices
8 large scallops, cut into 5 mm ($\frac{1}{4}$ in) slices
salt and freshly ground white pepper**

FOR THE VEGETABLES
**100 g (4 oz) carrots, peeled and cut into sticks 5 mm ($\frac{1}{4}$ in) thick
10 g ($\frac{1}{4}$ oz) unsalted butter
50 ml (2 fl oz) water**

**1×100 g (4 oz) courgette, cut into sticks 5 mm ($\frac{1}{4}$ in) thick
100 g (4 oz) cucumber, unpeeled, halved, seeded and cut into sticks 5 mm × 3 cm ($\frac{1}{4}$ × $1\frac{1}{4}$ in) thick**

FOR THE STOCK
**$\frac{1}{2}$ teaspoon curry powder
1 teaspoon unsalted butter
50 ml (2 fl oz) coconut milk
juice of $\frac{1}{2}$ lime
$\frac{1}{2}$ lemongrass stalk, finely chopped (optional)
250 ml (8 fl oz) water or Vegetable Stock (see p. 55)**

TO FINISH
**2 tablespoons chopped fresh coriander
20 g ($\frac{3}{4}$ oz) cold unsalted butter, diced**

METHOD

1 · Cooking the vegetables
Carrots Place the carrots in a small casserole with the butter and water, and season with salt and pepper. Cover and cook for 5 minutes. Reserve.
Courgette and cucumber Bring a litre ($1\frac{3}{4}$ pints) of water to a galloping boil, and cook the courgette and cucumber sticks for about 2–3 minutes. Refresh in cold water, drain and reserve.

2 · Preparing the stock
On a medium heat, sweat the curry powder in the butter for 1 minute. Dilute with coconut milk, then add the lime juice, finely chopped lemongrass, if using, and water or stock. Season with salt and pepper, and bring to the boil. Turn off the heat and

leave to infuse for about 20 minutes. Strain into a larger casserole.

3 · Cooking the monkfish and scallops
Season both with salt and pepper, keeping them separate.

Bring the stock to the boil in the large casserole and slide in the monkfish slivers. Reduce the heat immediately and cook for 1 minute at just under simmering point. Add the vegetable sticks and scallops and cook all together gently for just 2 minutes more.

4 · Serving
Strain the stock into a pan, add the chopped coriander, and whisk in the cold diced butter.

In a large serving bowl, mix all the vegetables, stock, monkfish and scallops. Serve to your guests.

VARIATIONS
There are many possible variations as the monkfish slivers can be replaced by any fish. The vegetable permutations are endless as well. The flavouring herbs could also be changed: you could use lime leaves, basil, mint, chives, etc.

CHEF'S NOTES

Of course, the vegetable stock will give a much deeper flavour than water but if you are in a hurry use water.

When sweating the curry powder, it must not be heated too high or it will simply burn.

Lemongrass is easily available in your local supermarket or ethnic shop. It is finely chopped so it releases its flavour very quickly.

The fish must not be allowed to boil, or its texture will be impaired.

Salmon Steak Poached in an Aromatic Vegetable Stock on a Bed of Watercress and Spinach with Hollandaise Sauce

FOR 4 GUESTS

PREPARATION TIME: 45 minutes

COOKING TIME: 7 minutes

PLANNING AHEAD: The stock can be prepared well in advance. The purée can be prepared an hour in advance, and kept warm in a bain-marie at 50°C (122°F), covered with a butter paper to prevent a skin forming.

INGREDIENTS
4×175 g (6 oz) steaks of wild salmon

FOR THE AROMATIC VEGETABLE STOCK
80 g (3¼ oz) each of carrot, onion, celery and leek

1 strip of lemon zest
1 bouquet garni (2 sprigs of fresh thyme, 1 sprig of parsley and 2 fresh bay leaves or 1 dried, tied together)
1 garlic clove, peeled
1 tablespoon salt
1 teaspoon black peppercorns
1.3 litres (2¼ pints) water
200 ml (7 fl oz) white wine

TO SERVE
300 ml (10 fl oz) Hollandaise Sauce (see p. 56)
400 g (14 oz) Spinach and Watercress Purée (see p. 223)

METHOD

1 · Preparing the aromatic vegetable stock
Peel and slice the carrot and onion. Dice the celery and slice the leek.

Mix these and all the remaining stock ingredients together in a large pan, and bring to the boil. Skim, then turn the heat down and simmer for 40 minutes.

2 · Preparing the sauce and purée
Prepare the hollandaise sauce, and keep in a warm bain-marie. Prepare the spinach and watercress purée, and keep warm.

3 · Cooking the fish
Slide the salmon steaks into the barely simmering stock. Turn the heat up a little bit (but there should still be no boiling whatsoever), and cook for 5 minutes. Turn off the heat and

Salmon steaks are high in easily digested protein. They contain slightly more calories and fat than white fish, but the oil in fish is mostly unsaturated. This is a very healthy type of oil, believed to be beneficial in reducing heart disease risk and protecting against further heart attacks in those people with existing heart disease. It may also be useful for reducing high blood pressure and stickiness of the blood (enabling it to move more freely around the body and thus reducing clotting). Eating oily fish regularly may also help rheumatoid arthritis and psoriasis.

leave the salmon steaks for a further 2–3 minutes according to thickness.

4 · Serving

Spoon the spinach and watercress purée into a serving dish. Do the same with the hollandaise.

Place the steaks on a tray and, with the help of a fork or knife, dig into the middle bones and lift them out carefully.

Arrange the salmon steaks in a shallow dish and pour some of the stock over them. Serve to your guests, with the hollandaise sauce and spinach and watercress purée offered separately.

VARIATIONS

The salmon could be replaced by turbot, brill or halibut, etc.

Fillets of fish can be poached this way as well, but there is much more retraction of the meat which can also be a bit dry.

C H E F ' S N O T E S

The best salmon is wild, but you can also buy some very good organically farmed salmon. When poaching, I like to have the fish on the bone as it keeps its shape well, and the bone and skin protect the flesh, preserving both taste and texture.

The principle in the making of this stock is to add flavour via the vegetables and herbs, and acidity with the white wine. For these flavours to develop, a minimum of 40 minutes' very slow simmering is essential. After the initial 20 seconds' boiling, the stock should just barely simmer, otherwise the vegetables will be overcooked and the flavours will be less clear.

Poaching fish in a liquid containing wine not only helps with the flavour, but the acidity of the wine helps 'set' the protein in the flesh without the need for too much heat.

The stock should be at just under simmering point to gradually and gently cook the fish. If it boils, the texture will change and the flesh will become flaky and dry.

After 5 minutes, when the heat is turned off, the fish is cooked medium rare. The residual heat in the stock will cook the fish perfectly to medium, leaving the flesh moist and well textured.

Roast Fillets of Sea Bream on a Bouillabaisse Sauce with Fondue of Tomatoes

The technique for making the sauce is interesting from a scientific point of view too. Sauces containing oil and water must also include an *emulsifier* which will allow the two components to mix properly. In this case the emulsifier molecules are provided by the vegetable purée. One way to spot the presence of emulsifiers (sometimes called surface active molecules) is if bubbles or foam are produced when the mixture is vigorously stirred or liquidized. A simple test with a liquidizer will show that olive oil and water can be made to form a reasonable emulsion without any other ingredients (because good olive oil is not 'refined' or 'pure' and therefore contains other ingredients which can act as emulsifiers).

FOR 4 GUESTS

PREPARATION TIME: 15 minutes

COOKING TIME: 45 minutes

PLANNING AHEAD: The sauce, the tomato fondue and the deep-fried herb sprigs can be prepared and made the day before.

INGREDIENTS

4×150 g (5 oz) fillets of sea bream
2 tablespoons olive oil
salt and freshly ground black pepper
lemon juice

FOR THE BOUILLABAISSE SAUCE
80 g (3¼ oz) onions, peeled and finely chopped
160 g (5½ oz) fennel, finely chopped
40 g (1½ oz) celery, finely chopped

80 g (3¼ oz) tomatoes, finely chopped
1 garlic clove, peeled and chopped
1 sprig of fresh thyme
¼ bay leaf
150 ml (5 fl oz) olive oil
chopped bones and heads from the sea bream
¼ packet or 1 pinch of saffron strands
200 ml (7 fl oz) white wine
300 ml (10 fl oz) water
100 ml (3½ fl oz) extra virgin olive oil

FOR THE GARNISHES
200 g (7 oz) Tomato Fondue (see p. 238)
vegetable oil for deep-frying
8 sprigs of fresh basil
8 sprigs of fresh parsley
12 black olives (optional)

METHOD

1 · Preparing the fish

Get your fishmonger to scale and fillet the fish for you. Ask him to keep and chop the bones and heads, having first removed and discarded the eyes and gills.

2 · Making the sauce

First, sweat the onions, fennel, celery, tomatoes, garlic, thyme and bay leaf in 100 ml (3½ fl oz) of the olive oil. Cover with a lid and stew gently for 20 minutes on top of the stove.

Meanwhile, in a separate pan, sweat the bones and heads of the sea bream in the remaining olive oil without colouring, for about 4–5 minutes. Add the saffron at the last minute. Add the

N U T R I T I O N I S T ' S
N O T E S

The sea bream is served with a vegetable-based sauce which is made with a fairly large quantity of olive oil, making the total fat content of the dish high. However, olive oil has many beneficial properties as it contains mostly monounsaturated fats which are believed to be protective against heart disease.

There is a good variety of vitamins and minerals in this dish: all the vegetables are high in potassium, and tomatoes are an especially good source of vitamin C and beta-carotene. Balance this dish with a lower fat dessert.

Roast Fillets of Sea Bream
on a Bouillabaisse Sauce
with Fondue of Tomatoes
(see p. 147)

white wine, then the water. Bring to the boil, skim and then simmer for 15 minutes. Strain on to the stewed vegetables.

Purée in a liquidizer, and enrich with the extra virgin olive oil, adding it little by little. Taste, and season with salt and pepper.

3 · Cooking the fish
Pre-heat the oven to 180°C/350°F/Gas 4.

Lightly score the skin side of each fillet three times. Sear in the oil, flesh side first, for approximately 2 minutes, then cook on the skin side for 2 minutes. Place in the pre-heated oven for 1 minute.

4 · Preparing the garnishes
Warm through the tomato fondue. Heat the vegetable oil and deep-fry the herb sprigs for no more than 30 seconds (see also p. 243). Drain very well on kitchen paper.

5 · Serving
Place some warmed tomato fondue in the centre of each plate. Place a sea bream fillet on top and brush with the cooking juices from the pan. Season with salt and pepper and some lemon juice. Surround with a little sauce. Scatter the olives and deep-fried herbs over the fish, then serve to your guests.

C H E F ' S   N O T E S

For cooking do not use best-quality extra virgin oil – plain olive will do.

The saffron is added at the end because it is so fragile: if it is not heated for too long, its flavour will be retained.

This is an interesting way to make a sauce. The vegetables are stewed for a long time, then broken down in the liquidizer which will allow them to absorb the olive oil and give texture. The vegetables must also be totally broken down to a pulp in order to extract maximum flavour.

The fish is scored to prevent the skin tightening up on cooking. It is very important not to penetrate the flesh.

Pan-fried Cod Fillet on a Purée of Potatoes with a Caper Sauce

FOR 4 GUESTS

PREPARATION AND COOKING TIME:
About 1 hour

PLANNING AHEAD: All the garnishes can be prepared in advance and re-heated.

INGREDIENTS
50 g (2 oz) unsalted butter
4×175 g (6 oz) cod fillets, skinned and boned
salt and freshly ground black pepper
2 teaspoons lemon juice

FOR THE SAUCE
200 ml (7 fl oz) Brown Chicken Stock (see p. 54)

1 sprig of fresh rosemary
4 teaspoons small capers, washed and drained
1 teaspoon lemon juice

FOR THE GARNISHES
400 g (14 oz) Purée of Potatoes (see p. 227)
100 g (4 oz) Baton Carrots (optional, see p. 231)
100 g (4 oz) Baby Onions (optional, see p. 239)
20 large Deep-fried Parsley (optional, see p. 243)
50 g (2 oz) Garlic Croûtons (optional, see p. 63)

SCIENTIST'S NOTES

Butter, unlike pure fats and oils, is an emulsion – a stable mixture of fats and water. It contains some of the proteins from milk which act a bit like soap and allow fats and water to mix well. So butter will aid the making of the sauce.

METHOD

1 · Cooking the cod

Pre-heat the oven to 190°C/375°F/Gas 5. In a non-stick oven-proof pan on medium heat, melt the butter and cook until a light golden brown colour and foaming. Pan-fry the cod in this to sear on each side, for 2–3 minutes, until a rich golden brown. Season with salt, pepper and a little of the lemon juice.

Cook for a further 5–7 minutes in the pre-heated oven.

Use a wide spatula to remove the fish from the pan, then cover with butter paper and leave to rest in a warm place. Leave the remaining cooking juices and butter in the pan.

2 · Making the sauce

Add the brown chicken stock to the juices in the pan, and boil until the sauce reaches a good consistency. Add the rosemary, simmer for 1 minute, then strain and discard the herb.

Add the capers, then correct the seasoning with salt and pepper. Lift the taste with the lemon juice.

3 · Serving

Place one portion of potato purée in the centre of each plate.

Gently place the fish on top, and sprinkle with a turn of black pepper. Arrange the vegetable, parsley and croûton garnishes, if using, around the plate, and spoon the sauce around. Serve to your guests.

VARIATIONS

This dish can be made with other fish such as turbot, brill, plaice, etc. Obviously the cooking times will alter.

CHEF'S NOTES

Ask your fishmonger for a nice thick fillet of cod. It has to be very, very fresh.

The cod is cooked in a golden brown or hazelnut butter (see p. 58). Because we are using the butter in the sauce, it is essential that it is not burnt as this is very indigestible. Neither, if it were burnt, would the butter emulsify with the sauce. To keep the butter a golden 'noisette' colour, make sure the heat you apply is gentle enough not to burn, yet strong enough to sear the cod fillets.

According to the thickness of the portion from the fillet the cooking time may change a little.

The colour of the butter and the fish will determine the taste and the aesthetics of the dish. Beige is a horrible colour, belonging to British cuisine of the 1960s and 1970s, not now. You want a very rich brown colour. The taste will be sublime, and the appeal dramatic.

The resting time will allow the fish to cook right through. The residual heat will penetrate to the centre, cooking the fish perfectly.

The seasoning is added in two stages after the searing. Whilst the fish is cooking in the oven the seasoning added after the searing will seep out and not penetrate the flesh of the fish. For this reason, it needs to be seasoned again when removed from the oven.

The essential oils in fresh rosemary are very strong. If the rosemary were infused too long in the sauce, it would be overpowering.

The reason why fish spoils on the whole faster than meat is that fish tend to live in water that is about the same temperature as your fridge (about 4–5°C). So, unlike warm-blooded animals, their enzymes continue to work well at these low temperatures, and the firm texture of the fish is rapidly destroyed as it 'digests' itself. An added risk in the case of skate and other flat fish is that the stomach, being less protected than that in a round fish, can be ruptured and its contents can diffuse throughout the flesh.

Potatoes are a much underrated vegetable. They are not fattening (that is an old myth), in fact they are a valuable source of complex carbohydrates which give us energy and which we should eat more of in order to meet our nutritional goals. Potatoes also contain minerals such as potassium and reasonable amounts of vitamin C. Cook them in boiling water and drain immediately in order to preserve as much of the vitamin content as possible.

Wing of Skate with Potatoes in White Wine, Caper and Gherkin Sauce

FOR 4 GUESTS

PREPARATION TIME: 10 minutes

COOKING TIME: 40 minutes

SPECIAL EQUIPMENT: A lidded casserole or roasting pan large enough to hold the skate wings in one layer.

PLANNING AHEAD: The skate wings are first poached then pan-fried. They can be poached an hour beforehand, and the potatoes can also be cooked an hour in advance.

INGREDIENTS

4 fresh skate wings, 175–200 g (6–7 oz) on the bone
salt and freshly ground white pepper

FOR THE POACHING STOCK

1.5 litres (2½ pints) water
12 black peppercorns, crushed
1 bouquet garni (2 bay leaves, 2 sprigs of thyme and 1 small bunch parsley stalks, tied together)
100 ml (3½ fl oz) white wine vinegar

1 tablespoon salt

FOR THE GARNISH

500 g (18 oz) King Edward or Desirée potatoes, peeled and cut into 1 cm (½ in) dice
2 shallots, peeled and finely chopped
20 g (¾ oz) unsalted butter
2 tablespoons white wine vinegar
50 ml (2 fl oz) dry white wine
2 tablespoons chopped fresh parsley

FOR THE SAUCE

80 g (3¼ oz) unsalted butter
4 tablespoons pan-frying juices from a roast, or Brown Chicken Stock (optional, see p. 54)
20 g (¾ oz) small capers, rinsed in cold water
2 gherkins, about 30 g (1¼ oz), diced
2 tablespoons chopped fresh parsley
50 ml (2 fl oz) water
1 tablespoon lemon juice

METHOD

1 · Preparing and poaching the skate
Bring together all the poaching stock ingredients in the large pan, bring to the boil then simmer for 5 minutes.

Trim the fins on the skate wings, then wash and pat dry. Place the skate wings in the stock, cover, and poach for about 6–7 minutes. Lift the skate wings on to a tray, and reserve.

2 · Preparing the garnish

Whilst the skate wings are poaching, boil the potato dice in about 1 litre (1¾ pints) of water plus 1 tablespoon of salt for about 7–8 minutes. Drain the potato and reserve.

Sweat the shallots gently in the butter for 1 minute, then add the white wine vinegar, and boil for 30 seconds. Add the white wine and boil for 30 seconds. Add the potato dice and parsley, and mix in. Taste and correct the seasoning.

3 · Pan-frying the skate wings

In a large non-stick pan, heat the sauce butter until rich gold in colour and foaming. Add the skate wings and colour for 4–5 minutes on each side. Season with salt and pepper.

4 · Making the sauce and serving

Arrange a large mound of potato dice in the centre of a large warm serving dish. Arrange the skate wings around this.

Add the pan-frying juices or brown chicken stock to the butter in the pan, then add the capers, gherkins, parsley, water and lemon juice. Stir for a second or two. Pour over the skate wings, and serve to your guests.

C H E F ' S   N O T E S

It is essential that the skate is very fresh – it should be odourless. When skate is not fresh there is an unpleasant smell of ammonia.

The poaching must be done at just under simmering point (see Cooking Techniques, p. 35). If the liquid is nearer boiling point, the flesh of the skate wings will be very stringy and dry. The timing of the fish poaching will depend on how thick the fillets are, so check.

The same principle applies to cooking the potato dice. Too strong a heat would overcook the outer layers of the potatoes and the dice would become mushy.

If you wish, the skate wings can be boned. Simply insert a knife in at the top of the wing and run it down, lifting the flesh as you go along. This must be done very delicately. Cook thereafter for a shorter time.

Pan-fried Fillet of John Dory with Aubergine Tagliatelle and Tomato Vinaigrette

SCIENTIST'S NOTES

Vinegar consists mainly of water and between 5 and 9 per cent of acetic acid. Since acetic acid has a higher boiling point ($119°C/246°F$) than water, one would expect the water to boil away leaving the liquid more acid. There is actually only a very small change when a water/acetic acid mixture is boiled, but because of the presence of other compounds, there is a very slight reduction in acidity. Boiling reduces the acidity not because the acid alone is boiled off, but because the vinegar (acid *plus* water) is removed.

FOR 4 GUESTS

PREPARATION TIME: 20 minutes

COOKING TIME: 10 minutes

PLANNING AHEAD: The tomato vinaigrette and aubergine tagliatelle can be prepared one day in advance.

INGREDIENTS

4×150 g (5 oz) John Dory fillets
2 tablespoons olive oil
salt and freshly ground black pepper
lemon juice

FOR THE AUBERGINE TAGLIATELLE

2 firm and ripe aubergines
50 ml (2 fl oz) olive oil
2 pinches of caster sugar
1 garlic clove, peeled and halved
1 sprig of fresh thyme
2 tablespoons white wine vinegar
2 tablespoons water

TO FINISH

1 quantity Tomato Vinaigrette (see p. 60)
4 tablespoons extra virgin olive oil

METHOD

1 · Preparing the aubergine tagliatelle

Slice both ends off the aubergines. Cut them into four lengthways. Slice the flesh off the skin, leaving about 3 mm (¹⁄₈ in) thickness of flesh on the skin. Cut each of these skin quarters of aubergine into strips 3 mm (¹⁄₈ in) wide to make 'tagliatelle'.

Heat the olive oil in a large casserole, and throw in the aubergine tagliatelle. Season with salt and pepper and add the sugar, garlic and thyme. Stir then cook over a medium heat, covered, for about 3 minutes. Add the white wine vinegar, and boil for 30 seconds. Add the water, and reserve.

2 · Cooking the John Dory fillets

Pre-heat the oven to $180°C/350°F/$Gas 4.

In a non-stick pan, pan-fry the John Dory in the hot olive oil for about 30 seconds on each side. Season with salt and pepper then cook the fish for a further 5 minutes in the pre-heated oven.

Remove from the oven and rest the fish for 2–3 minutes. Add a squeeze of lemon juice to each fillet.

3 · Serving

Re-heat the tomato vinaigrette very briefly, whisking all the time.

Re-heat the aubergine tagliatelle, divide them and arrange over each plate. Arrange the John Dory fillets on top. Spoon the tomato vinaigrette and 1 tablespoon of the extra virgin oil around each plate.

VARIATIONS

John Dory can be replaced by any flat white fish. Red mullet could also be used.

CHEF'S NOTES

We use a medium heat for frying the aubergine tagliatelle because, if the oil is too hot, it will dry off the skin of the aubergine and give it a very fibrous texture. The oil must not reach smoking point, and you must also stir often to distribute the heat. For the last remaining 3 minutes the heat should be lowered so the aubergine strips barely simmer.

To reduce the acidity of the vinegar, some of the vinegar must be boiled off.

Fillet of Monkfish with a Herb Crust and Red Pepper Sauce

FOR 4 GUESTS

PREPARATION TIME: 15 minutes

COOKING TIME: 40 minutes

PLANNING AHEAD: Prepare the Provençale breadcrumbs up to two or three days in advance; keep in a sealed container. The sauce can be prepared up to two days in advance.

INGREDIENTS
2 tablespoons olive oil
1×500 g (18 oz) monkfish fillet, cut into 4 medallions
salt and freshly ground black pepper
1 teaspoon Dijon mustard
½ quantity Provençale Breadcrumbs (see p. 62)

FOR THE RED PEPPER SAUCE
3 red peppers
150 ml (5 fl oz) olive oil
50 g (2 oz) onions, peeled and chopped
2 garlic cloves, left whole with skin
1 teaspoon white wine vinegar
100 ml (3½ fl oz) water

METHOD

1 · Preparing the red pepper sauce
Pre-heat the oven to 180°C/350°F/Gas 4.

Cut the peppers in half lengthways and remove the seeds, stems and white parts.

In an ovenproof sauté pan or casserole, gently heat 50 ml (2 fl oz) of the olive oil and sweat the onion for a couple of minutes. Add the peppers and garlic, season with salt and pepper, cover and cook in the pre-heated oven for 40 minutes.

Remove the pan from the oven, add the wine vinegar and boil on top of the stove for 10 seconds. Liquidize the peppers until you have a very fine purée, then trickle in the remaining olive oil. Strain the purée through a fine sieve into a small casserole. Thin down with some of the water until you get the correct texture. Taste, correct the seasoning and reserve.

2 · Cooking the monkfish medallions
Pre-heat the grill.

In a non-stick pan, heat the olive oil until it has reached smoking point. Sear the monkfish medallions for a few seconds on each side, then season with salt and pepper. Transfer to a small casserole, cover with foil, and cook in the pre-heated oven for 7 minutes.

Fillet of Monkfish with a Herb Crust and Red Pepper Sauce

Remove the medallions from the oven and rest in a warm place for about 5 minutes. Season again with salt and pepper if necessary.

Spread mustard over the top of each fillet and spoon the Provençale breadcrumbs on top. Heat and crisp under the hot grill for 1 minute.

3 · Serving

Spoon the red pepper sauce into the middle of each plate and arrange a monkfish medallion on top. Serve to your guests.

VARIATIONS

Fillet of turbot, sea bream or brill could be used instead of the monkfish.

A good vegetable accompaniment would be Grilled Summer Vegetables (see p. 241), and black olives.

C H E F ' S   N O T E S

You may need less or more water for the sauce, depending on a number of factors – the texture of the puréed peppers, the type of pan used, the degree of evaporation or the temperature used.

The olive oil for the sauce must not be too hot or it would colour both onions and peppers and would affect both taste and appearance.

It is essential to purée the peppers very finely so the olive oil can easily be absorbed later on.

The monkfish has a very firm texture. The resting time will allow the residual heat to travel right to the centre of each medallion and the flesh will loosen up, becoming very tender.

NUTRITIONIST'S
NOTES

Monkfish is a good source of protein and minerals. It is complemented by the red pepper sauce which is packed with vitamins and minerals. Red peppers are one of the richest sources of beta-carotene and vitamin C, both important anti-oxidant nutrients that help protect the body against cancer and heart disease. One red pepper contains more vitamin C than three oranges.

Baby Turbot Roasted on a Bed of Fennel with Rosemary Butter Sauce

—— ILLUSTRATED ON PAGE 136 ——

Cooking fish on the bone gives the very best results in both taste and texture. This recipe has wonderful heady flavours from Provence, and makes a magnificent dish to serve to your friends. Do not be daunted by the carving; it is easy enough as the bones are well structured and run flat on each side of the fish.

FOR 4 GUESTS

PREPARATION TIME: 15 minutes

COOKING TIME: 1 hour

SPECIAL EQUIPMENT: A 30×40 cm (12×16 in) roasting pan; a large ridged, cast-iron grilling pan (optional).

PLANNING AHEAD: Order the baby turbot from your fishmonger well in advance. The rosemary butter can be prepared an hour in advance. The dried fennel can be purchased in good delicatessens.

INGREDIENTS
1×2 lb (900 g) baby turbot, prepared
olive oil

20 dried fennel sticks
4 dried orange and lemon peel strips
6 sprigs of fresh thyme
2 star anise
salt and freshly ground white pepper

FOR THE ROSEMARY BUTTER SAUCE (see also p. 57)
2 shallots, peeled and finely chopped
50 ml (2 fl oz) white wine vinegar
50 ml (2 fl oz) dry white wine
150 g (5 oz) cold unsalted butter
1 sprig of fresh rosemary, very finely chopped

METHOD

1 · Preparing the rosemary butter sauce
Follow the basic recipe (for lemon butter sauce on p. 57) exactly, but infuse the finely chopped rosemary in the sauce for 20 minutes. Strain. Keep warm in a bain-marie (at about 50°C/122°F).

2 · Preparing the turbot
Ask your fishmonger to cut off the side fins and to trim off the tail. Wash the fish well to remove any slime and pat dry.

   The next step is optional. If you have a large ridged, cast-iron grilling pan, brush olive oil on to the surface and heat until very hot. With a towel, dry the fish skin on the white side thoroughly, and brush with olive oil. Place the white skin side on to the hot pan for 40 seconds. Very carefully, lift the turbot and place at a different angle on the pan so that you have a criss-cross marking on the skin.

3 · Roasting the turbot

Pre-heat the oven to 180°C/350°F/Gas 4.

Line the roasting pan with a bed of the dried fennel sticks, strips of orange and lemon peel, thyme and star anise. Lay the fish, criss-cross skin side up, into the roasting pan on the bed of dried fennel, and pour 100 ml (3½ fl oz) of oil all over. Season with salt and pepper.

Roast the baby turbot in the pre-heated oven for about 20–25 minutes, basting frequently. Remove from the oven, cover with foil and rest for 7–8 minutes.

4 · Serving

Present the baby turbot as it is to your guests and, if you feel confident enough, fillet in front of your guests. Serve to your guests, with the rosemary butter sauce. You could also offer a wedge of lemon with this dish.

VARIATIONS

Baby brill, John Dory or sea bream could be used instead.

CHEF'S NOTES

The criss-cross marking of the fish is optional but it will give a better presentation, and the grilling prior to roasting will give extra flavour. The white side of the baby turbot must be dried completely; if there is too much moisture it will stick to the grill. The grill must also be very hot.

The length of time for roasting the fish may vary according to the weight and freshness of the fish. Do not be tempted to roast at a higher temperature as the delicate flesh will shrink and flake. It is important to baste the fish frequently; this moistens it, and reinforces it with the flavours of the oils, herbs and spices.

The resting time is also extremely important. At this stage residual heat will gently complete the cooking, leaving the flesh still moist and firm.

Turbot is one of the easiest fish to fillet after cooking. Make an incision down the central bone, round the gills and down the sides of the fish so you have a triangle shape. Loosen the fillets from the central bone sliding the knife down beneath the fillet and lift on to a serving plate.

Fillet of Salmon in a Herb and Sorrel Juice

NUTRITIONIST'S
NOTES

Salmon is rich in the omega-3 fatty acids which can help prevent heart attacks; just two servings of oily fish (such as salmon) per week has been shown to cut the risk by 50 per cent. The herb juice is highly nutritious, rich in iron, vitamin C and folic acid. Spinach and watercress are also high in calcium. This recipe is an excellent way of using sorrel leaves which are packed with vitamins and iron.

FOR 4 GUESTS

PREPARATION TIME: 10 minutes

COOKING TIME: 5 minutes

INGREDIENTS
20 g (¾ oz) unsalted butter
4×150 g (5 oz) salmon escalopes
salt and freshly ground white pepper
lemon juice

FOR THE HERB JUICE
200 ml (7 fl oz) water or Vegetable Stock (see p. 55)
1 whole lime leaf (optional)

1 teaspoon chopped fresh chervil
1 teaspoon chopped fresh parsley
4 fresh tarragon leaves, chopped
1 bunch watercress, stalks removed, leaves chopped
100 g (4 oz) baby spinach leaves, tough stalks removed, chopped
50 g (2 oz) sorrel leaves, tough stalks removed, chopped
20 g (¾ oz) cold unsalted butter, diced
a squeeze of lemon juice

METHOD

1 · Preparing the herb juice
Bring the water or vegetable stock to the boil and, if using, infuse the lime leaf in it for 5 minutes. Remove the lime leaf.

Add to this stock all the chopped leaves. Season with salt and pepper and boil for 1 minute.

Whisk in the diced unsalted butter, taste and correct the seasoning, then add a squeeze of lemon juice to lift. Reserve.

2 · Pan-frying the salmon escalopes
Pre-heat the grill.

Melt the butter in a non-stick pan until golden brown. Sear the escalopes in this for 30 seconds on each side. Season with salt and pepper, add a squeeze of lemon juice to each escalope and place under the pre-heated grill for about 1 minute, depending on the thickness of the escalopes.

3 · Serving

Spoon the herb juice on to each plate, and arrange the salmon escalopes on top. Serve to your guests.

VARIATIONS

Spring vegetables could be added to the juice – young peas, mangetout, French beans, young broccoli or asparagus spears. Diced tomatoes would also be a tasty addition.

C H E F ' S   N O T E S

Lime leaves will give an unusual flavour to the stock. These can be purchased at any ethnic shop.

The cooking time is very short as we want to keep the flavours of the herbs very lively and the texture firm.

Too often salmon is overcooked and becomes very dry and unpleasant, so 30 seconds on each side and the 1 minute under the grill will cook it perfectly and keep the texture moist.

Fillets of Red Mullet with Braised Fennel and a Fennel Sauce

FOR 4 GUESTS

PREPARATION TIME: 10 minutes

COOKING TIME: 2 hours

PLANNING AHEAD: The braised fennel and sauce can be cooked one or two days in advance and kept in the refrigerator.

INGREDIENTS

1 quantity Braised Fennel with Cardamom (see p. 234)

extra virgin olive oil
salt and freshly ground black pepper
8 red mullet fillets, carefully boned
lemon juice

FOR THE OPTIONAL GARNISH

1 courgette, cut into 3–5 mm (1/8–1/4 in) dice
2 tomatoes, skinned, seeded and diced
4 fresh basil leaves
8 black olives, stoned

METHOD

1 · Preparing the fennel sauce and garnish
Prepare the braised fennel as on p. 234, cooking for 2 hours.

Reserve 12 of the fennel bulbs in some of the cooking juices for the garnish. In a food processor or blender, purée very finely the remaining fennel bulbs with 100 ml (3½ fl oz) of the cooking juices. Trickle in 100 ml (3½ fl oz) extra virgin olive oil. Taste and correct the seasoning. Strain through a fine sieve and reserve in a small casserole.

2 · Preparing the optional garnish
Boil the courgette dice in salted water for 1 minute. Refresh in cold water, then drain. In a small casserole mix them with the diced tomato, basil and 2 tablespoons extra virgin olive oil. Season with salt and pepper and reserve.

3 · Cooking the red mullet fillets
Pre-heat the grill.

In a large non-stick pan heat 2 tablespoons of olive oil and pan-fry the fillets on the skin side for 5 seconds. Delicately, turn them on to the flesh side and cook for 30 seconds. Season.

Add a few drops of lemon juice to each fillet, and place the flesh side under the hot grill for a further minute.

4 · Serving
Re-heat the fennel sauce, and the courgette and tomato garnish. Heat up the olives and the reserved fennel bulbs separately.

Spoon some fennel sauce on to each plate and arrange the red mullet fillets, skin side up, on top. Divide the vegetable garnish – the fennel bulbs and the courgette-tomato mixture – and the black olives around. Serve to your guests.

VARIATIONS
This dish can be made using sea bream, monkfish or John Dory.

C H E F ' S   N O T E S

The long cooking time of the fennel is needed for the proper exchange of flavours and to break down all the fibres as some of it is going to be puréed for the sauce.

The cooking time for the mullet is obviously dependent on how thick the fillets are, so check. It is better for red mullet to be slightly undercooked, rather than overcooked.

A Deep-fried Parcel of Crab and Seaweed

FOR 4 GUESTS

PREPARATION TIME: 20 minutes

MARINATING TIME: 24 hours

COOKING TIME: 3 minutes

PLANNING AHEAD: The crab parcels can be prepared half a day in advance, but they must be deep-fried at the last moment. The vegetable garnish must be prepared and marinated 24 hours in advance.

INGREDIENTS
200 g (7 oz) white crab meat
30 g (1¼ oz) brown crab meat, finely chopped
1 teaspoon lemon juice
8 fresh coriander leaves, finely chopped
2 tablespoons water
salt and cayenne pepper
vegetable oil for deep-frying

FOR WRAPPING THE CRAB MEAT
4×19 cm (7½ in) square dried sheets of nori seaweed
50 ml (2 fl oz) sake
4 long chives or fine long strips of leek

FOR THE VEGETABLE GARNISH
15 g (½ oz) fresh ginger, peeled and diced
5 g (⅛ oz) dried seaweed
40 g (1½ oz) carrots, cut into 3 mm (⅛ in) dice
40 g (1½ oz) courgettes, cut into 3 mm (⅛ in) dice
20 g (¾ oz) skinned red pepper, cut into 3 mm (⅛ in) dice
2 tablespoons sake
1 tablespoon Takura fish sauce
1 tablespoon rice vinegar
salt and freshly ground black pepper

NUTRITIONIST'S NOTES

The seaweed used to make the parcels is a very rich source of many minerals such as potassium, iron and calcium. It also contains lots of beta-carotene, a powerful anti-oxidant, and is relatively rich in protein too. Crab meat is also a good source of protein, low in fat and high in minerals.

As the parcels are deep-fried, the fat content of the dish is moderately high, but this is mostly the healthy unsaturated type of fat.

METHOD

1 · Marinating the garnish vegetables
Blanch the ginger in plenty of boiling water for 15 minutes. Drain well.

Soak the dried seaweed in 1 tablespoon of water for 1 hour, then drain well and chop finely.

Mix all the remaining vegetable garnish ingredients together with the seaweed and ginger. Cover with cling film and marinate in the fridge for 24 hours.

2 · Making the crab and seaweed parcels
Mix together the crab meats, lemon juice, coriander and water. Season with salt and cayenne.

Lay the four sheets of seaweed on your work surface. To make them pliable brush each sheet with sake. Arrange some of

the crab mixture in the middle of each sheet. Bring the four corners together and tie the ends with chive or leek 'ribbon'.

3 · Deep-frying the crab parcels
Pre-heat the vegetable oil to 190°C (375°F) and deep-fry the parcels for 3 minutes, ensuring that the seaweed is crisp. Drain.

4 · Serving
In the middle of each plate, arrange the vegetables in a small mound. Place a deep-fried crab parcel on the top and serve.

CHEF'S NOTES

Your fishmonger should be able to extract the white and brown crab meat. I like to add brown crab meat as it lends a more definite crab flavour. Ask him to give you the shells for a soup.

The seaweed laver is known as nori in Japan, where it is used a great deal. It is first dried, then powdered and compressed together into fine sheets. You can obtain them from any oriental shop or delicatessen. Laver is available fresh in Wales.

Ginger has a particularly powerful and aggressive taste. It is essential to blanch it for 15 minutes to make it more 'mellow'.

The tops of the crab parcels must be secured very tightly, otherwise the oil will penetrate the filling.

The deep-frying temperature is very high, but this is necessary in order to crisp the seaweed parcel and to ensure the temperature in the middle will be just warm.

Tempura of Soused Herring and Vegetables

FOR 4 GUESTS

PREPARATION TIME: 10 minutes

MARINATION TIME: 24 hours

COOKING TIME: 7 minutes

INGREDIENTS
4 small herrings, filleted
salt and freshly ground
white pepper

FOR THE SOUSING MARINADE
50 ml (2 fl oz) fresh lime
juice
50 ml (2 fl oz) water
1 teaspoon caster sugar
1 shallot, peeled and finely
sliced
1 small carrot, finely sliced
1 small bunch of fresh
coriander, leaves finely
sliced

FOR THE TEMPURA BATTER
2 egg yolks
100 g (4 oz) plain flour
75 g (3 oz) cornflour
juice of 1 lime
350 ml (12 fl oz) cold water

FOR THE VEGETABLE GARNISH
12 asparagus spears
(optional)
4 baby fennel bulbs, or
1 medium fennel bulb,
quartered
8 small broccoli florets
4 shiitake mushrooms
plain flour for coating

TO COOK AND SERVE
1 litre (1¾ pints) vegetable
oil for deep-frying
1 quantity Lemon Butter
Sauce (see p. 57)

METHOD

1 · Marinating the herring fillets

Mix all the ingredients of the marinade together in a small bowl. Add ½ teaspoon salt and 2 large pinches of pepper. Lay the herring fillets, flesh side up, in a shallow flat dish and pour the marinade over them. Cover with cling film and leave to marinate in the bottom of the fridge for 24 hours (a minimum of 12).

Turn the fillets over twice during the marinating process. Then lift the herring fillets out, pat dry thoroughly, and reserve.

2 · Preparing the tempura batter

With a whisk, mix all the ingredients together, adding the water little by little. Season with salt and pepper.

3 · Cooking the tempura

Pre-heat the deep-frying oil to 160°C (320°F).

Dip all the vegetables into plain flour. Shake off the excess, then dip them in the batter and deep-fry until golden and crisp, about 4 minutes only. Fry in batches if necessary. Drain well on kitchen paper and keep warm.

Repeat this method – the flouring and battering, frying and draining – for the herring.

4 · Serving

Arrange the fish and vegetable tempura attractively on a dish and serve to your guests, with the lemon butter sauce offered separately.

VARIATIONS

The herring can be replaced by filleted sardines or slices of salmon or sea bream.

CHEF'S NOTES

The 24 hours will be ample time for the herring fillets to absorb all the flavours of the marinade. It is important to turn the fillets over so that they can absorb evenly and thoroughly.

Do not try to achieve a totally homogeneous mix when whisking the tempura batter. The texture will be better if it is not too smooth.

The vegetables and herrings are first dipped into flour, so the batter can easily coat the ingredients.

Poultry

Coq au Vin 170

Roasted Guinea Fowl Served on a Bed of Lentils 174

Duck Breast with Apple, Cherry and Cinnamon Sauce 177

Fricassee of Chicken with Dry Sherry, Morels and Wild Mushrooms 179

Pan-fried Breast of Wild Pigeon with Stewed Red Cabbage and Blackcurrants 180

Breast of Chicken with Green Curry, Mango, Lime and Coconut 183

Roast Breast of Mallard with Blackcurrant 185

Sauté of Chicken with Ginger and Sesame Seeds 186

Fricassee of Chicken
with Dry Sherry, Morels
and Wild Mushrooms
(see p. 179)

Coq au Vin

NUTRITIONIST'S
NOTES

This is an excellent way of preparing poultry and vegetables – all the juices are saved so there is no waste of vitamins. Chicken is, of course, high in protein and reasonably low in fat. In this recipe, much of the fat released during cooking is discarded, so the overall fat content of the dish is low.

The vegetables add extra vitamins, minerals and fibre as well as flavour and texture. Red wine used in the marinade may actually be good for us. More and more studies in recent years have concluded that red wine drunk in moderation can actually protect against heart disease. It's not simply the alcohol content but, according to researchers, other components in the red wine may be very beneficial to our health.

FOR 4 GUESTS

PREPARATION TIME: 15 minutes

MARINATING TIME: 12 hours

COOKING TIME: 15 minutes for searing, plus 40–50 minutes for stewing.

SPECIAL EQUIPMENT: A cast-iron saucepan or casserole with lid, about 26 cm (10½ in) in diameter.

PLANNING AHEAD: The dish can be prepared a day or so in advance, and kept in the fridge.

INGREDIENTS

1×1.5 kg (3–3½ lb) free-range chicken
50 ml (2 fl oz) corn oil
1 heaped tablespoon arrowroot or cornflour
salt and freshly ground black pepper

FOR THE MARINADE
1×750 ml (1¼ pint) bottle red wine

1 medium carrot, peeled and chopped into large sticks
1 small leek, chopped into 1 cm (½ in) thick slices
2 celery sticks, cut into 1 cm (½ in) thick slices
1 small onion, peeled, halved and cut into 3 mm (⅛ in) slices
2 garlic cloves, peeled
1 bouquet garni (3 sprigs of fresh thyme, 2 bay leaves, 1 fresh sage leaf, tied together)

FOR THE GARNISH (optional)
100 g (4 oz) smoked bacon, cut into long strips, blanched and refreshed
40 tiny onions or small shallots, cooked (see p. 239)
150 g (5 oz) button mushrooms

METHOD

1 · Preparing the chicken

If necessary, singe the bird with a lit candle or over a gas flame to remove any feather stubs. Cut the chicken into 12 pieces: 2 wings, the 2 breasts each cut in half; the 2 legs cut into drumsticks, thighs and lower part of the backbone (the latter holds delicious meat). Ask your kind butcher to do this for you. (The remainder of the chicken carcase can be used for a stock or soup.)

2 · Marinating the chicken

Pour the wine into a pan, and boil for 2 minutes. Cool a little.

Mix the marinade vegetables, garlic, bouquet garni and chicken pieces in a large bowl, then pour over the lukewarm wine. Cover with cling film and leave to marinate for 12 hours in the fridge.

3 · Cooking the chicken

Pre-heat the oven to 140°C/275°F/Gas 1.

Drain the chicken pieces, vegetables and herbs in a colander over a bowl for about 30 minutes, then pat dry in a cloth. Separate the vegetables from the chicken pieces. Pick out the garlic cloves and the bouquet garni.

Sear the chicken pieces in the oil over strong heat in the cast-iron saucepan, colouring both sides, for about 3–4 minutes on each side. Remove the chicken and keep warm.

In the same pan, sweat and lightly colour the vegetables (but not the garlic) in the chicken fat in the pan, for about 5 minutes. Spoon out and reserve the fat, then return the chicken to the pan with the vegetables. Add the marinating wine, bouquet garni and garlic, and add a little water to cover, if necessary. Bring to the boil, skim and cover with a lid. Cook in the oven for 40–60 minutes. Check that the chicken is cooked, as timing will vary according to size.

4 · Finishing the dish and serving

Skim off and discard most of the fat released by the chicken. Dilute the arrowroot or cornflour with 2 tablespoons of water and mix it into the chicken juices. Bring to the boil so that it binds the juices. Taste and correct the seasoning.

Re-heat the bacon strips and onions, pan-frying in a little reserved chicken fat to caramelize. Pan-fry the mushrooms as well in the chicken fat for 3 minutes. Season with salt and pepper. Mix the bacon, onions and mushrooms with the chicken. Serve to your guests in the cast-iron dish.

VARIATIONS

This dish could also be prepared using guinea fowl or beef (*joue de boeuf*). Add 20 g (³/₄ oz) finely sliced fresh ginger, blanched for 1 minute, to the latter during the cooking. In this case complete the dish with 1 teaspoon of Chinese five-spice powder.

C H E F ' S   N O T E S

Try to find free-range corn- or maize-fed chickens which are now available in good butchers' and supermarkets. The price difference will be worthwhile.

SCIENTIST'S
NOTES

The two essential steps in addition to marination (see Cooking Techniques, p. 42) in the preparation of meat stews like coq au vin or boeuf bourguignonne are: frying or searing to produce the Maillard reactions (see p. 19); and slow cooking in plenty of liquid (see Cooking Techniques, p. 34).

.

The more saturated a fat, the harder it is. Chicken fat is soft (as is duck fat, which sometimes does not even set when chilled), because it contains a higher proportion of unsaturated fatty acids.

Some years ago, you might have been asked to use a great red wine in cooking the chicken. Quite apart from the ludicrous cost, this was nonsense as well, because the wine will alter so much in the cooking; delicate aromas in the uncooked wine will simply dissipate. What you need is a strong, full-bodied table wine (from the Rhône Valley) or a Cabernet Sauvignon from Bulgaria, Romania or California, all of which can be obtained at a very reasonable price in good supermarket chains.

———

Once dried, bay leaves and thyme are at least twice the strength of fresh ones, so if you use fresh, double the amount.

———

The tiny little white onions used in the garnish are quite time-consuming to peel, so if you are short of time, half a large onion chopped in large dice will be fine.

———

Choose very small and firm button mushrooms and wash very briefly (for 10 seconds only) in water lightly acidulated with lemon juice. This will prevent oxidation (see also p. 99). Do not leave them to soak in the water as they will absorb it. Pat them dry before use.

———

Cornflour and arrowroot are both natural starches. Normally, a roux (a mixture of flour and butter, cooked before cooking the chicken) would be used in this dish, resulting in a heavy, sometimes punishing experience: the flour would absorb most of the fat and leave you ready to fall off your chair after a lovely meal with all the concomitant guilt. Food should never be associated with punishment. So, I favour binding the stock with arrowroot or cornflour once the fat has been skimmed off.

———

If you are short of time, you can forget about marinating the chicken, but the dish will lose some of its character. In this recipe I have boiled the wine first to reduce the alcohol and some of its acidity, which I find creates a much nicer sauce all round. If you pour the wine while tepid over the chicken the exchange of flavours will be much greater. If you feel rich use two bottles of wine instead of one, and reduce the whole quantity by half. This will create the most intense and deep-coloured sauce.

The marinated chicken pieces will have absorbed some of the red wine, so it is important not only to drain them for some time, for about half an hour, but also to pat them dry very thoroughly.

———————

The coloration of the chicken is important in that it will help both appearance and taste. Correct searing will also remove a great deal of the fat contained in the skin.

———————

By bringing the red wine to the boil, lots of albumen and proteins contained in both vegetables and chicken will escape, solidify and be brought to the surface of the stock. Simply skim them off.

———————

After skimming, the chicken must cook very slowly, otherwise the meat would be tough and dry, the vegetables overcooked and the sauce cloudy and unappetizing. The cooking time will be determined by the quality of chicken, and can vary from 40–60 minutes.

Roasted Guinea Fowl Served on a Bed of Lentils

It is well worth looking for a free-range guinea fowl, and you should ask to have it hung for a week.

FOR 4 GUESTS

PREPARATION TIME: 10 minutes

COOKING TIME: About 40 minutes

RESTING TIME: At least 10 minutes

PLANNING AHEAD: The guinea fowl, the juice and the lentils can be prepared a day in advance. The guinea fowl can be cooked an hour in advance and kept warm by wrapping it in aluminium foil.

INGREDIENTS
2 guinea fowl, each weighing 700 g (1 lb, 6 oz), trimmed weight
20 g ($\frac{3}{4}$ oz) clarified butter
1 tablespoon sunflower oil
salt and freshly ground black pepper

FOR THE LENTILS
14 baby onions, peeled

100 g (4 oz) carrots, cut into 4×1 cm ($1\frac{1}{2}$×$\frac{1}{2}$ in) batons
100 g (4 oz) smoked streaky bacon, chopped into fine strips
20 g ($\frac{3}{4}$ oz) unsalted butter
400 g (14 oz) green or brown lentils, picked over, washed and drained
a pinch of ground cloves, or 2 cloves, ground
1 bouquet garni (4 sprigs of fresh thyme and 2 bay leaf, tied together)
1 garlic clove, peeled and finely chopped

FOR THE JUICE
200 ml (7 fl oz) Brown Chicken Stock (see p. 54) or water
2 sprigs of thyme

METHOD

1 · Preparing the guinea fowl
Remove the wishbone and winglets from the birds, chop finely and reserve for the juice. Singe the guinea fowl over a flame to remove the feather stubs then truss the birds. Reserve.

2 · Cooking the lentils
Sweat the baby onions, carrot batons and bacon strips in the butter for 3 or 4 minutes without colouring. Add all the other ingredients, season with some pepper, cover and simmer for about 35 minutes. Taste for texture and flavour, then drain, reserving juices and lentils in separate pans.
    Pre-heat the oven to 220°C/425°F/Gas 7.

3 · *Roasting the guinea fowl*

In a roasting pan, sear and brown the guinea fowl in the clarified butter and oil for about 5 minutes on each thigh and $2\frac{1}{2}$ minutes on each breast. Add the winglets, and add seasoning.

Cook in the pre-heated oven for 8 minutes on each thigh. Remove the birds from the oven to a serving dish, wrap in aluminium foil, and reserve for a minimum of 10 minutes.

4 · *Making the juice*

Spoon the fat from the roasting tray, then add the stock or water, the reserved lentil liquid and the thyme to the winglets. Bring to the boil, then simmer for 10 minutes or so. Strain, season if necessary, and keep warm.

5 · *Serving*

Pre-heat the grill.

Re-heat the lentils and place them on a large heatproof serving dish. Keep warm.

Carve the guinea fowl and arrange the pieces on top of the lentils. Flash under the hot grill. Serve to your guests, with the juice offered separately.

VARIATIONS

This dish can be made with chicken. As a garnish, spring onions and more bacon could be added.

C H E F ' S   N O T E S

It is essential to have good-quality guinea fowl. Look for corn- or maize-fed, they will be worth the difference in price.

The best lentils are the French *lentilles de Puy*, which you can buy in delicatessens and large supermarkets. Simply wash them briefly before cooking.

The lentils must not boil otherwise the texture will be very soft and mushy. Taste to check when they are ready.

The searing of the guinea fowl is essential as it adds flavour and texture to the skin. It will also remove most of the fat.

Resting the guinea fowl in foil allows the residual heat to go on cooking the flesh slowly, making it more tender.

Duck Breast with Apple, Cherry and Cinnamon Sauce

FOR 4 GUESTS

PREPARATION TIME: 20 minutes

COOKING TIME: About 30 minutes

PLANNING AHEAD: In this dish we will only need the breasts on the bone, which might make you a little unpopular if you asked for this from your butcher. So order the whole duck and use the remainder for a confit or other recipe. The sauce can be prepared a day in advance. The bones of the duck can be used for a sauce or a soup.

INGREDIENTS
2 whole ducks (Barbary or Challans if possible)
2 tablespoons oil or duck fat

FOR THE SAUCE
2 teaspoons unsalted butter
2 teaspoons caster sugar
1 Granny Smith apple, peeled, cored and chopped in 1 cm (½ in) square pieces

100 ml (3½ fl oz) full-bodied red wine
250 g (9 oz) cherries, fresh or frozen, stoned
100 ml (3½ fl oz) water
1×2 cm (¾ in) piece of cinnamon stick, finely ground, or a large pinch of ground cinnamon
2 cloves, ground, or a pinch of ground cloves
5 black peppercorns, crushed
a pinch of freshly grated nutmeg

FOR THE GARNISH
12 whole cherries, fresh or frozen, stoned
50 ml (2 fl oz) full-bodied red wine
2 teaspoons unsalted butter
1 teaspoon caster sugar
salt and freshly ground black pepper

METHOD

1 · Preparing the sauce

Melt the butter and sugar together in a pan, and caramelize the diced apple for a few minutes. Add the red wine, and boil for 2 minutes. Add all the other ingredients, bring to the boil, then simmer for 10 minutes.

Liquidize until smooth, then strain through a sieve. Taste, correct seasoning, and reserve.

Duck Breast with Apple,
Cherry and Cinnamon
Sauce

NUTRITIONIST'S NOTES

Duck is only very fatty if the skin is included in the dish, since most of the fat is found just below the skin. The breasts used in this recipe are much lower in fat. The accompanying fruit sauce is packed with lots of vitamins, especially vitamin C, as well as the mineral potassium. Cherries provide natural sweetness due to their high content of fruit sugar, and this goes well with the slight acidity of the Granny Smith apple.

2 · Preparing and cooking the duck

Pre-heat the oven to 200–220°C/400–425°F/Gas 6–7.

Chop the neck and winglets, then remove the wishbone. Remove the thighs and legs and the backbones, leaving the breasts on the bone. Score the duck breasts lightly with a sharp knife and then colour them, skin side down, in the oil or fat in a hot frying pan for 3–4 minutes.

Roast the breasts for 8 minutes in the pre-heated oven. Allow to rest for 5 minutes.

3 · Preparing the garnish

Place all the ingredients together in a suitable casserole and simmer for 4 minutes.

4 · Serving

Remove the duck breasts from the bone. Season them on the flesh side and place each breast on a warmed plate. Spoon the sauce around and garnish with the spiced cherries.

CHEF'S NOTES

The searing of the duck breasts will achieve two things: it will remove some of the fat, and will give taste and an appetizing colour.

Fricassee of Chicken with Dry Sherry, Morels and Wild Mushrooms

— ILLUSTRATED ON PAGE 168 —

FOR 4 GUESTS

PREPARATION TIME: 15 minutes

COOKING TIME: 30 minutes

PLANNING AHEAD: The fricassee can be cooked a few hours in advance and re-heated.

INGREDIENTS

20 g (¾ oz) dried morels
100 g (4 oz) fresh wild mushrooms (chanterelles, girolles or whatever variety is available)
1×1.5 kg (3–3½ lb) free-range chicken
30 g (1¼ oz) unsalted butter
salt and freshly ground white pepper
300 ml (10 fl oz) dry sherry
300 ml (10 fl oz) double cream

METHOD

1 · Preparing the mushrooms

Wash the dried mushrooms very well in plenty of water, then cover with clean cold water and leave them to soak for about 3 hours. Drain well, but keep their soaking water.

Wash, dry and slice the fresh wild mushrooms (see p. 205).

2 · Preparing the chicken

Cut the chicken into 10 pieces: 2 legs, 2 thighs, 2 breasts (each cut in half) and 2 wings. Your butcher should do this for you. The meat should remain on the bone. (The carcase and the wings can be used in a chicken stock or soup, see p. 82).

3 · Cooking the fricassee

In a thick cast-iron saucepan large enough to hold all the chicken pieces in one layer, heat the butter on a medium heat until a rich golden colour and foamy. Add the chicken and cook for about 5 minutes to lightly brown. Season.

Add the rehydrated morels and sweat for 2–3 minutes, stirring from time to time. Spoon out the fat.

Add the dry sherry and bring to the boil. Reduce the heat and simmer until reduced by half. Add the water the morels soaked in, then the cream. Simmer for about 15 minutes until the sauce is thick and creamy. Check that the chicken is cooked.

4 · Serving

Add the fresh wild mushrooms to the casserole towards the end of cooking, and cook for 5 minutes. Serve to your guests.

VARIATIONS

A teaspoon of Marc de Bourgogne will give an extra layer of flavour if added to the sauce towards the end of cooking.

CHEF'S NOTES

If you cannot find wild mushrooms, use button mushrooms.

The reduction of the sherry is essential: bringing it to the boil will remove some of the alcohol and make it taste less sour.

Pan-fried Breast of Wild Pigeon with Stewed Red Cabbage and Blackcurrants

NUTRITIONIST'S NOTES

Chicken is high in protein and B vitamins and the meat is relatively low in fat. However, the overall fat content of this dish is increased due to the addition of the butter used to fry the chicken pieces and the cream in the sauce. Mushrooms are also low in fat and contain fibre and B vitamins, especially biotin. Since this dish contains very little carbohydrate, accompany it with potatoes or with a rice dish to balance out the high fat content.

Pan-fried Breast of Wild Pigeon with Stewed Red Cabbage and Blackcurrants

FOR 4 GUESTS

PREPARATION TIME: 20 minutes

MARINATING TIME: 12–24 hours

COOKING TIME: 2 hours for the cabbage; 5 minutes for the pigeon.

PLANNING AHEAD: The red cabbage can be made a day in advance; the pigeon needs to be marinated for a day, and the sauce can also be made a day ahead. Prepare the black currants at least 10 hours in advance.

INGREDIENTS
the breasts of 4 wild pigeons
1 tablespoon unsalted butter
salt and freshly ground
**   black pepper**

FOR THE MARINADE
400 ml (14 fl oz) red wine
100 ml (3½ fl oz) port
1 sprig of fresh thyme

½ bay leaf
½ garlic clove, peeled
2 juniper berries, crushed

FOR THE SAUCE
1 tablespoon butter
1 tablespoon groundnut oil
the chopped pigeon carcases
¼ onion, finely chopped
1 small carrot, finely
**   chopped**
1 tablespoon blackcurrant
**   jelly**
1 teaspoon cornflour or
**   arrowroot mixed with**
**   1 tablespoon water**

FOR THE GARNISHES
200 g (7 oz) Stewed Red
**   Cabbage (see p. 230)**
30 g (1¼ oz, or about 20)
**   blackcurrants, fresh or**
**   frozen**
2 tablespoons caster sugar

METHOD

1 · Marinating the pigeon breasts

Mix the marinade red wine and port together in a pan, and boil to reduce by half. Cool.

Place the wild pigeons in a container and mix in all the ingredients for the marinade, including the reduced wine and port, and cover with cling film. Refrigerate and marinate for between 12 and 24 hours.

Remove the pigeon breasts from the marinade, pat dry, and reserve. Reserve the wine and aromatics as well.

2 · Preparing the garnishes

Make in advance, or re-heat, the stewed red cabbage.

The blackcurrants must be steeped in the sugar for 10–12 hours. Cook them slowly on a gentle heat for 3–4 minutes. Taste, add a bit more sugar if necessary, then reserve.

3 · Preparing the sauce

In a roasting pan mix the butter and oil, and heat until rich golden in colour. Add the finely chopped carcasses, and sear and colour on a medium heat for 5 minutes. Add the chopped vegetables and cook for a further 5 minutes. Spoon out the fat.

Add the aromatics and the wine from the marinade, and barely cover the bones and vegetables with cold water. Transfer everything to a suitably sized pan, bring to the boil, skim and simmer for 20 minutes. Strain, pressing on the bones to extract as much juice as possible. Reduce the stock down on a brisk heat until there is 200 ml (7 fl oz) remaining. Add the black-currant jelly and bind the sauce with the diluted cornflour. Taste and correct seasoning. Reserve.

4 · Cooking the pigeon breasts

Pre-heat the oven to 180°C/350°F/Gas 4, or pre-heat the grill.

Heat the butter in a frying pan until it foams and reaches a rich golden colour, and sear the pigeon breasts for 1 minute on each side. Then, either place in the pre-heated oven or under the grill for 3 minutes. Season with salt and pepper.

5 · Serving

Re-heat the cabbage, the sauce and the blackcurrants.

Cut each breast lengthways. Place a mound of cabbage in the middle of each plate and arrange 4 half-breasts against it so that it looks like a pyramid. Pour the sauce over and around, and scatter with the blackcurrants.

VARIATIONS

The wild pigeon breasts can be replaced by grouse breasts.
The blackcurrants can be replaced by blueberries.

CHEF'S NOTES

Order the pigeons well in advance from your butcher as they
need to be hung for four to five days. Ask the butcher to remove
the skin and breast from the bone and to chop the bones and
legs finely (they will be needed for the sauce). The finer the
bones are chopped the quicker they will release their flavour,
shortening the cooking time and producing clearer flavours.

The pigeon breasts absorb wine whilst marinating. Pat them dry
so they do not stew in their own juices.

The carcases must be coloured well, but carefully, because the
degree of colour will determine how appetizing the sauce is.

Bringing the sauce to the boil will coagulate proteins which will
be carried to the surface. Simply spoon this out, then simmer.
If the sauce were allowed to boil, it would be cloudy and the
taste would also be affected – it would be coarser.

Breast of Chicken with Green Curry, Mango, Lime and Coconut

FOR 4 GUESTS

PREPARATION TIME: 5 minutes

COOKING TIME: 20 minutes

INGREDIENTS
**1 large teaspoon unsalted
  butter**
½ teaspoon curry powder
1 large pinch of turmeric
1 teaspoon honey
juice of 1 lime
**200 ml (7 fl oz) tinned
  coconut milk**
**100 ml (3½ fl oz) White
  Chicken Stock (see p. 54)
  or water**
1 lime leaf (optional)
2 sprigs of fresh thyme
salt and cayenne pepper
**4 chicken breasts, each cut
  into 5 pieces, wing bones
  removed**
50 ml (2 fl oz) double cream
**½ green mango, peeled and
  diced**

METHOD

1 · Preparing the cooking liquor

In a small casserole melt the butter, then add the curry powder and turmeric. Sweat for 1 minute. Add the honey and lime juice, and boil for a few seconds, then add the coconut milk, chicken stock or water, lime leaf (optional), thyme, salt and cayenne pepper. Simmer for 2 minutes so the flavours can infuse.

2 · Cooking and serving

Add the chicken pieces to the stock and cook at just under simmering point for 10 minutes. Check that the chicken is cooked.

At the last moment, mix in the cream and diced mango. Taste and correct seasoning, then serve to your guests.

VARIATIONS

Chopped cashew nuts could be added to the dish at the same time as the mango.

The chicken could be replaced by prawns or a firm fish such as monkfish.

CHEF'S NOTES

Lime leaves have such a magnificent and powerful scent, they are well worth looking for. You are likely to find them in an ethnic shop, fresh or dried. You can also dry them at home.

On no account must the curry powder be subjected to too strong a heat or it will burn, and the flavour of the dish ruined.

It is essential for the chicken to be cooked at just under simmering point, because the meat is off the bone and could easily dry out and shrivel. By applying a gentle heat the chicken will cook perfectly, remaining moist, and the flavours of all the ingredients mingle with each other.

Roast Breast of Mallard with Blackcurrant

NUTRITIONIST'S NOTES

Duck is a very fatty bird but, in fact, most of the fat is found just beneath the skin which means that the meat itself is not too high in fat. The duck pieces are fried in oil which will increase the fat content of the dish. However, the red wine and vegetables contain many useful nutrients with anti-oxidant properties. Overall, this dish is high in fat, protein, iron and B vitamins.

FOR 4 GUESTS

PREPARATION TIME: 20 minutes

COOKING TIME: 40 minutes

PLANNING AHEAD: The sauce can be prepared a day in advance.

INGREDIENTS
2 mallards
30 g (1¼ oz) unsalted butter
salt and freshly ground black pepper

FOR THE SAUCE
100 ml (3½ fl oz) ruby port
300 ml (10 fl oz) red wine
the chopped duck carcases and bones
4 tablespoons groundnut oil
1 small carrot, diced
¼ celery stick, diced
1 piece of orange peel
2 juniper berries
200 ml (7 fl oz) Brown Chicken Stock (see p. 54) or water
1 teaspoon blackcurrant jelly
1 teaspoon arrowroot or cornflour mixed with 1 tablespoon water

METHOD

1 · Preparing the mallards
Remove the breasts *on the bone* from the birds. Remove the wishbones. Chop the carcases, legs and thighs finely.

2 · Preparing the sauce
Mix the port and red wine together in a pan and boil to reduce by half. Cool.

Sear and colour the duck carcases and bones in the hot oil for about 5 minutes. Lower the heat to medium then add the carrot and celery and cook, stirring, for a further 5 minutes.

Add the orange peel, juniper berries, port and red wine reduction, brown chicken stock or water, and bring to the boil. Skim, then simmer for 20 minutes. Strain the juices, pressing on the bones to extract as much juice as possible.

Reduce to about 200 ml (7 fl oz). Add the blackcurrant jelly, taste and correct the seasoning. Bind the sauce with the diluted arrowroot or cornflour.

3 · Roasting the duck breasts
Pre-heat the oven to 190°C/375°F/Gas 5.

In a small roasting dish just large enough to hold the duck breasts, heat the butter until it foams and turns a rich golden colour. Sear the duck on the skin side for 5 minutes, then season with salt and pepper. Turn the breasts over and roast in the pre-heated oven for 5 minutes. Remove from the oven, spoon out the fat, and rest the meat, covered with foil, for 5 minutes.

4 · Serving
Carve the breasts, and season the cut sides with salt and pepper. Arrange on a warm serving dish and spoon the sauce over.

CHEF'S NOTES

Buy real wild duck, as the flavour will be much better.

The legs and thighs of wild duck are often very tough, so we use them in the sauce. Ask your butcher to cut the breasts off the bone and chop the carcases finely. This way they impart their flavour more quickly and so shorten the cooking time.

The duck cooking time is short to keep it between medium rare and medium. If overcooked, the duck will be dry and tough.

Sauté of Chicken with Ginger and Sesame Seeds

FOR 4 GUESTS

PREPARATION TIME: 20 minutes

MARINATING TIME: 12–24 hours

COOKING TIME: 20 minutes

PLANNING AHEAD: The dish can be prepared half a day in advance and re-heated.

INGREDIENTS
1×1.5 kg (3–3½ lb) free-range chicken, cut into 12 pieces
100 ml (3½ fl oz) sesame oil
4 tablespoons sesame seeds
1 handful of cashew nuts
1 head broccoli, cut into small florets
1 carrot, thinly sliced
1 leek, coarse outer leaves removed, halved lengthways, and cut into 1 cm (½ in) slices
12 asparagus spears (optional), trimmed and cut into 2.5 cm (1 in) pieces
4 tablespoons chopped fresh coriander

FOR THE MARINADE
30 g (1¼ oz) fresh ginger, peeled and finely sliced
2 garlic cloves, peeled and finely sliced
100 ml (3½ fl oz) rice wine or dry white wine
100 ml (3½ fl oz) soy sauce

METHOD

1 · Marinating the chicken

Boil the ginger in plenty of boiling water for 5 minutes. Drain well.

Mix all the marinade ingredients together in a suitable dish. Add the chicken pieces and marinate for 12–24 hours. Drain, reserving the marinade.

2 · Cooking and serving the chicken

Place the sesame oil in a large frying pan over a strong heat, add all the chicken pieces and pan-fry for 5–6 minutes, stirring all the time.

Add the sesame seeds, cashew nuts, all the vegetables and the ginger and garlic from the marinade. Cook for a further 2 minutes. Spoon out the fat, then mix in the marinade juices. Cover with a lid and cook for a further 8 minutes, stirring from time to time. Add the finely chopped coriander and serve to your guests.

VARIATIONS

This dish can be made with guinea fowl or with a firm fish such as fillets of sole or monkfish, or with shellfish such as scallops, lobster or prawns. The cooking time should be reduced to 5 minutes.

All sorts of herbs – such as lemon thyme, parsley or lemon grass – could be added to this dish.

CHEF'S NOTES

Your butcher should be willing to cut the chicken for you. Ask him to leave every piece on the bone.

No salt should be needed in this dish as the soy will hold enough. The ginger is blanched in order to remove some of its fire.

Meat

Navarin of Lamb
and Lambs' Tongues
(see p. 190)

Navarin of Lamb and Lambs' Tongues

—— ILLUSTRATED ON PAGE 188 ——

FOR 4 GUESTS

PREPARATION TIME: 20 minutes

COOKING TIME: 2 hours

PLANNING AHEAD: The navarin could be cooked in advance and then gently re-heated – at the same temperature for about 30 minutes.

INGREDIENTS

4 lambs' tongues in brine
1 large carrot, cut into 5 mm (¼ in) thick slices
12 shallots, peeled
8 garlic cloves, peeled
1 large leek, coarse outer leaves removed, cut in half lengthways and chopped into 2 cm (¾ in) pieces
2 medium turnips, peeled, each cut into 12 segments
8 black peppercorns
1 bouquet garni (1 sprig of fresh rosemary, 2 bay leaves, 2 sprigs of fresh thyme, tied together)
800 g (1¾ lb) new season neck of lamb
1 teaspoon salt

METHOD

1 · Preparing the tongues
Soak the tongues in cold running water for 30 minutes to remove excess salt in the brine. Drain and reserve.

2 · Cooking the navarin
Pre-heat the oven to 110°C/225°F/Gas ¼.

In a large casserole dish, place all the vegetables and aromatics, the tongues, then the neck of lamb. Barely cover with water – about 1 litre (1¾ pints) – and season with salt. Bring to the boil, skim, then cover with the lid. Cook at barely simmering point either on top of the stove on a very low heat, or in the pre-heated low oven for 3 hours.

Taste and correct seasoning. Remove the lambs' tongues and peel off the outer skin. Slice the tongues and replace in the broth.

3 · Serving
Heat through if necessary, then serve the dish to your guests directly from the casserole.

VARIATIONS
Shoulder of new season lamb could also be cooked in this way. New potatoes could be added to the dish after an hour, and

spring or summer vegetables such as spring greens, young peas or spinach could be cooked in the broth at the last moment.

CHEF'S NOTES

This dish is a perfect example of 'cooking by exchange': the flavours of the meat, the vegetables and the herbs will inter-react, creating wonderful tastes and flavours.

The stock must not boil as it will become very cloudy, the meat would shrink and become very tough, and the vegetables would disintegrate – this would make what is called a disaster!

Fillet of Beef with Basil and Deep-fried Capers

FOR 4 GUESTS

PREPARATION TIME: 15 minutes

COOKING TIME: 10 minutes

PLANNING AHEAD: Both the sauce and the Black Olive Purée can be prepared a day or two in advance. The capers can be deep-fried 2–3 hours in advance and kept on kitchen paper.

INGREDIENTS

4×150 g (5 oz) fillets matured beef (pure Aberdeen Angus if possible), or 4×175 g (6 oz) rump steaks
20 g (¾ oz) unsalted butter
salt and freshly ground black pepper

FOR THE BASIL SAUCE

40 g (1½ oz) Dijon mustard
100 ml (3½ fl oz) extra virgin olive oil
20 g (¾ oz) pickled capers, rinsed and patted dry
60 g (2¼ oz) fresh basil leaves with stalks, roughly chopped
2 garlic cloves, peeled and chopped

FOR THE GARNISHES

500 ml (17 fl oz) vegetable oil for deep-frying
32 pickled capers, rinsed and patted dry
25 g (1 oz) Black Olive Purée (see p. 61)

METHOD

1 · Preparing the basil sauce
This will make 200 ml (7 fl oz) of sauce. For this recipe you need only half of that, so keep the remainder in a small jar in the fridge. Added to pasta, it will be absolutely delicious.

Place the mustard in a small mixing bowl and slowly whisk

the olive oil in until well incorporated. Spoon the mixture into a liquidizer, add all the other ingredients and purée finely. Taste and season to taste with 2 pinches each of salt and pepper. Reserve in a small container.

2 · Preparing the garnishes
Heat the oil until it smokes lightly. Deep-fry the capers in a frying basket for 30 seconds, then drain well on kitchen paper.

Place the olive purée in a small casserole.

3 · Cooking the fillet steaks
Pre-heat the oven to 200°C/400°F/Gas 6.

Pan-fry the steaks in the foaming butter for 1 minute on each side until well coloured. Season with salt and pepper and roast in a single layer for a further 5 minutes (rare) or 8 minutes (medium rare) in the pre-heated oven. Correct the seasoning with salt and pepper, and leave to rest in a warm place for 2–3 minutes, loosely covered with foil.

4 · Serving
Place the basil sauce in a small casserole, and heat it up for a few minutes, stirring. Do the same with the olive purée (or heat both through in the oven for about 10 minutes).

Arrange the steaks on a flat serving dish and spoon the basil sauce over them, along with any escaped meat juices. Spoon a teaspoon of olive purée on top of each steak. Add one little turn of ground pepper, garnish with the capers and serve.

VARIATIONS
The beef can be replaced by fillet of lamb, lamb cutlets or chump of lamb. You can add vegetable garnishes such as Sautéed New Potatoes with Spring Onions (see p. 229) and Tomato Fondue (see p. 238).

C H E F ' S   N O T E S

The mustard in the basil sauce holds emulsifying agents which will facilitate the incorporation of the oil. The oil must be mixed very slowly to help the process. If the oil and mustard separate, take a little bit more mustard and start again with what you have done. The best instrument to do this with is a small whisk and not a spoon or fork.

When pan-frying the fillet steak the butter must reach a high temperature so the solid particles inside will start cooking and

Fillet of Beef with Basil
and Deep-fried Capers
(see p. 191)

browning. This process must not be carried beyond a rich gold colour, otherwise you will burn the butter (and your stomach!).

The fillet is pan-fried to achieve a good colour. The protein, albumen and sugars in contact with the hot fat will caramelize and produce a wondrous and tasty colour. Cook for no more than 1 minute, though, as the fat would overcook the outside.

You will notice that the steaks are seasoned twice, once after the pan-frying and again after being in the oven. This is because some of the first salt addition will not penetrate the beef and will run off the meat. The second seasoning is to adjust the balance.

A resting time after cooking is essential. During cooking the strong heat tenses all the fibres and muscles. Resting will allow those muscles to relax, making the meat very tender. It will also allow the residual heat within the meat to travel gently through the heart of the meat and partially cook it.

It is very difficult to determine a precise cooking time, as this will depend on the size of the steak and whether it is taken from the head or towards the tail.

Roast Chump of Lamb with Tomato Fondue

The success of this dish will depend very much on the quality of the lamb and on how long it has been hung. If hung properly, it will have both taste and tenderness.

FOR 4 GUESTS

PREPARATION TIME: 20 minutes

COOKING TIME: 30–35 minutes

INGREDIENTS
50 g (2 oz) unsalted butter
2×400–450 g (14–16 oz) chumps of lamb, well hung

salt and freshly ground black pepper
100 ml (3½ fl oz) water
6 large fresh basil leaves, finely chopped (and kept in a little water)
1 quantity Tomato Fondue (see p. 238)

1 quantity Tomato Fondue (see p. 238)

NUTRITIONIST'S
NOTES

Lamb is usually a fatty meat but if you use well-trimmed cuts, as in this recipe, the fat content is reduced substantially, from just over 20 to 10 per cent or less. The lamb is seared in butter but relatively little is absorbed due to the high temperature and excess fat is then removed. On the plus side, the dish is rich in protein, zinc, phosphorus and B vitamins. The Tomato Fondue contains vitamin C.

Meat requires resting after it has been roasted. During this time the heat on the outside of the meat – where the majority of the heat actually *met* the meat – will continue to be conducted through to the centre of the meat. This is why it is best only to cook in the oven to less than medium – the process of resting will 'cook' the meat to perfection, improving texture.

Meat which has not been rested will leak more precious juices when carved. During the resting period, the meat protein firms up a little, *retaining* the juices better. The juices which are left in the meat, mostly at the centre, can redistribute themselves throughout the whole joint, contributing to overall moisture and tenderness. (See also the Scientist's Note on p. 203.)

METHOD

1 · Preparing the lamb
Chumps of lamb are usually divided into chops, but they make a compact small roast. Get the butcher to trim them of all fat, and to bone them. They will need tying to keep a tidy shape.

2 · Searing and roasting the lamb
Pre-heat the oven to 180°C/350°F/Gas 4.

In a heavy cast-iron roasting pan, just large enough to hold the two pieces of lamb, melt the butter on a medium heat. When foaming and a blond colour, sear and colour the lamb in the pan. This will take about 6–8 minutes. Season with salt and freshly ground pepper.

Spoon out the butter, then place the pan in the pre-heated oven. Roast for 15–20 minutes.

Remove from the oven and place the lamb on a plate covered with aluminium foil. Leave to rest for 10 minutes.

3 · Preparing the sauce
Add the water to the roasting pan, and mix in with and scrape off the caramelized juices on the bottom. Bring to the boil, then strain the juice into a small casserole. Add the basil.

4 · Serving
Re-heat the tomato fondue, then spoon on to the middle of each plate.

On a board, cut the lamb into 1 cm ($^1/_2$ in) slices. Correct the seasoning, then divide and arrange the slices on top of the tomato. Add the juices that the lamb has released to the prepared lamb sauce. Pour over the lamb, and serve to your guests.

VARIATIONS
The tomato fondue could be replaced by an Onion and Garlic Purée (see p. 230).

CHEF'S NOTES

Chump of lamb deserves to be better known as a roasting joint as I find its flavour and texture very attractive. Usually, if not cut into chump chops, it is braised or stewed.

A lot of the juices will have slowly caramelized and formed a tasty deposit on the pan. By adding the water and scraping the bottom you will dilute this deposit and create the most delicious and simple juice.

Best End of Lamb with a Herb Crust

FOR 4 GUESTS

PREPARATION TIME: 15 minutes

COOKING TIME: About 1 hour

PLANNING AHEAD: The fennel purée and the herb-scented breadcrumbs can be made a day in advance. Ask your butcher to trim the lamb (French trim), and remove the chine bones and end of ribs. He should cut the fat off the upright rib bones, and chop the chine bones very finely.

INGREDIENTS
1 tablespoon olive oil
1 best end of lamb, about 8 ribs, perfectly trimmed
salt and freshly ground black pepper

2 tablespoons Dijon mustard
200 ml (7 fl oz) water

FOR THE BREADCRUMB COATING
100 g (4 oz) dried breadcrumbs, not too finely ground
1 tablespoon chopped fresh parsley
1 teaspoon dried thyme
½ teaspoon chopped fresh rosemary needles
2 tablespoons olive oil

FOR THE FENNEL PUREE
½ quantity Braised Fennel with Cardamom (see p. 234)
90 ml (3 fl oz) extra virgin olive oil

METHOD

1 · Preparing the breadcrumb coating
Mix all the dry ingredients together then add the olive oil. Mix until you have a sandy texture, and reserve on a small tray.

2 · Cooking the fennel purée
Cook the fennel as described on p. 234, then allow to cool. Purée in a liquidizer, adding the olive oil gradually. Taste and correct seasoning.

3 · Cooking the lamb
Pre-heat the oven to 230°C/450°F/Gas 8.

In a small roasting pan, heat the olive oil and sear and colour the lamb on all sides for about 5 minutes. Add and sear the small chopped chine bones at the same time. Season with salt and pepper.

Place the lamb on to the chine bones, so it does not touch the bottom of the pan, and roast in the pre-heated oven for about 10 minutes.

Remove the lamb from the oven, and spread mustard all over the meat part (not the bones). Press the meat into the breadcrumbs until it is completely coated. Roast for a further 12–15 minutes in the oven.

Remove the lamb from the oven, and reserve on a small plate for about 8–10 minutes, loosely covered with foil.

4 · Making the juice and serving

Remove most of the fat from the roasting pan, and add the water. Scrape off all the caramelized bits, stirring all the bones around, and simmer for 5 minutes until you obtain 100 ml ($3\frac{1}{2}$ fl oz) of juice. Strain and keep warm.

Gently re-heat the fennel purée.

You can either carve the lamb in front of your guests or do it in the privacy of your kitchen. Serve the purée and lamb juice separately.

VARIATIONS

You could also serve the lamb on a bed of simply cooked young vegetables as in the photograph on p. 196.

CHEF'S NOTES

The lamb should be hung for a minimum of 10 to 14 days otherwise it will have very little taste and it will be very tough.

The breadcrumbs should not be to finely ground; you want them to keep some texture.

The very finely chopped lamb bones are added to the roasting pan for two reasons:
a) They will prevent the lamb being in contact with the direct heat of the tray. This would dry out the lamb.
(b) The bones will caramelize during the roasting and will help provide a delicious juice when you add the water. (See also the Scientist's Notes about roasting on pp. 22 and 39.)

Personal Chef's Note
The French do not know how to cook lamb!

Braised Shin of Veal

FOR 4 GUESTS

PREPARATION TIME: 15 minutes

COOKING TIME: 3¼ hours

PLANNING AHEAD: Order the shin of veal well in advance, and ask your butcher to prepare it.

INGREDIENTS

1 shin of veal on the bone, prepared by your butcher
40 g (1½ oz) unsalted butter

100 ml (3½ fl oz) dry white wine
400 ml (14 fl oz) water
2 medium carrots, each cut into 4
1 large onion, peeled and cut into 8
2 medium parsnips, each cut into 4
2 medium leeks, trimmed
2 sprigs of fresh thyme
salt and freshly ground black pepper

METHOD

1 · Braising the veal

Pre-heat the oven to 140–150°C/275–300°F/Gas 1–2.

For the dish to be attractive, the knuckle must be sawn off the shin, and the flesh pushed along the bone.

In a large oval cast-iron dish, heat the butter until it foams and turns a rich gold. Sear and colour the shin of veal on medium heat until a rich brown, about 15 minutes. Pour off all the fat and deglaze with the white wine. Boil for 1 minute, then add half the water, all the vegetables, the thyme, salt and pepper. Cover with a lid and cook in the pre-heated oven for 3 hours. Add the remaining water half-way through the cooking time.

2 · Serving

Scatter the vegetables over a large hot serving dish. Place the shin of veal in the centre of the dish and serve the juice separately. The meat will come off the bone very easily.

VARIATIONS

Wild or button mushrooms could be added, as could green vegetables such as broccoli, green beans, spinach etc, but they need to be cooked separately and at the last moment.

CHEF'S NOTES

The searing and browning of the skin is a delicate operation. Too strong a heat and the butter will burn, dry the meat and discolour it, impairing its taste, so make sure the heat is medium so the butter remains at the 'hazelnut' stage (see p. 58).

Smoked Hock of Pork with Lentils

FOR 4 GUESTS

PREPARATION TIME: 10 minutes

COOKING TIME: $3^3/_4$ hours

PLANNING AHEAD: The dish can be made a day in advance and re-heated. It will re-heat very well. The hocks must be soaked for 24 hours, and the lentils for 2 hours.

INGREDIENTS

2×1 kg (2¼ lb) smoked hocks of pork
1 bouquet garni (1 sprig of fresh thyme, 1 bay leaf and 10 g/¼ oz parsley stalks, tied together)
1 onion, peeled and cut in half, each studded with 1 clove
2 large carrots, quartered, then each quarter cut in half
2 celery sticks, chopped into 2.5 cm (1 in) pieces
1 leek, cut into 2.5 cm (1 in) pieces
200 ml (7 fl oz) dry white wine
2 garlic cloves, peeled
½ teaspoon black peppercorns
salt
250 g (9 oz) Puy or green lentils

METHOD

1 · Soaking the hocks
Soak the hocks in cold water for 24 hours, changing the water frequently. Drain.

2 · Cooking the hocks
Pre-heat the oven to 110°C/225°F/Gas ¼.

Put the soaked hocks into a large round casserole dish. Cover with fresh cold water. You may need from 1 to 1.5 litres ($1^3/_4$–$2^1/_2$ pints), depending on the size of the casserole. Add the bouquet garni, the vegetables, wine, garlic, peppercorns and ½ teaspoon of salt. Bring to the boil, then transfer to the pre-heated oven and cook for 3 hours.

Remove the hocks from the stock, and reserve in a warm place.

3 · Cooking the lentils
Meanwhile, soak the lentils in cold water for 2 hours. Drain.

Strain the stock from the hocks and put it and the drained lentils into the rinsed-out casserole. Cover and put back in the oven for 40 minutes.

4 · Serving
Add the hocks to the lentils in the casserole and re-heat.

Smoked Hock of Pork
with Lentils

Arrange the lentils in a large serving dish and place the hocks on the top. Carve and serve to your guests.

VARIATIONS

This dish can be made with knuckle of veal or any cut of pork, smoked or unsmoked.

CHEF'S NOTES

The smoked hocks have been cured, and although they are soaked in water for some time, they will still release quite a lot of salt. Beware of adding too much salt – and do not add any more salt when cooking the lentils.

Lentils are traditionally soaked for up to 12 or even 24 hours. I find this process to be damaging both to taste and texture as the chlorinated water seeps into the lentils. The 2 hours' soaking is quite adequate. For soaking and cooking of pulses, see Scientist's Notes, p. 82.

It is essential that the oven is at the right, extremely low, temperature, as there must be no boiling whilst the hocks are cooking. This will avoid any shrinkage.

Roast Rib of Beef

FOR 4 GUESTS

PREPARATION TIME: 10 minutes

COOKING TIME: 2 hours

RESTING TIME: 20 minutes. The roast beef can actually be wrapped in aluminium foil and kept warm at 50°C (122°F) for up to 1½ hours. The longer the resting time the better the texture.

INGREDIENTS
100 g (4 oz) beef dripping
1×1.8 kg (4 lb) rib of mature beef (2 rib bones), well hung
500 g (18 oz) beef or veal trimmings
salt and freshly ground black pepper
2 garlic cloves, in their skins
300 ml (10 fl oz) water

METHOD

1 · Roasting the beef
Pre-heat the oven to 150°C/300°F/Gas 2.

When meat, red or white, starts to coagulate, it begins to look more opaque. It also exudes juices. This is the water content of the meat which is being forced and squeezed out by the coagulating proteins. If the meat were to be overcooked, it would lose too much of its natural juice content – thus the dryness of well-done meat. For perfect roast meat, there must be some juices left.

See also the Scientist's Note on p. 195 about resting meat.

Heat the beef dripping in a roasting tray and brown both the meat and the beef or veal trimmings for about 7–10 minutes.

Season the joint with salt and pepper. Arrange it on the trimmings so it is separated from the bottom heat. Add the garlic cloves to the pan. Roast in the pre-heated oven for 2 hours, basting from time to time.

2 · Resting the meat

Remove the joint from the oven, and remove from the tray. Season the meat with salt and pepper and wrap in aluminium foil. Rest for 20–30 minutes in a warm place, above the oven, for instance.

3 · Making the juice

Spoon most of the fat from the roasting tray. Add the water to the juices left in it. Bring to the boil and scrape and stir the caramelized juices stuck on the bottom of the pan to create a delicious juice.

Taste, correct seasoning, then strain and reserve.

4 · Serving

The meat can be carved in front of your guests or in the privacy of your kitchen. Serve to your guests.

VARIATIONS

You could serve a very delicious red wine sauce with the meat. Sweat 4 finely chopped shallots in butter for 2 minutes, add 500 ml (18 fl oz) red wine and reduce down to 200 ml (7 fl oz). Add this to the roasting pan instead of the water. Boil, then strain and whisk in 30 g (1¼ oz) unsalted butter. Season with salt and pepper.

CHEF'S NOTES

The success of this dish will be directly related to the quality of the meat and how long it has been hung (see Ingredients, p. 22). You have to trust your butcher for the quality. I believe that the best beef comes from a two-year-old animal. It will have had time to develop a marbling of fat within the meat, which will then translate into taste and good texture after cooking. Needless to say, a frozen Argentinian beef joint will be as different from a pure Aberdeen Angus joint as a burger is from a fillet steak. So ask for, and expect, quality.

I prefer to cook the joint on the bone as the meat keeps moister

and the bone adds extra flavour. Ask your butcher to prepare
and trim the ribs.

———————

Most cooks roast their beef joint at too high a temperature,
causing dryness, too much contraction of the tissue; too often
the meat is overcooked outside and undercooked inside.

———————

N U T R I T I O N I S T ' S
N O T E S

*Beef is very high in protein, B
vitamins, iron and zinc. It is
also high in fat but this can
be reduced, if you wish, by
trimming off any visible fat.
Beef dripping is extremely
high in saturated fat, so
reduce the amount you add if
you are concerned about your
fat intake. Most of the fat that
drains from the beef is
spooned out at the end of
cooking, which, again, helps
keep the fat content of the
finished dish down.*

It is impossible to define exactly how many minutes per pound
as it will depend on so many factors such as:

> thickness of the meat
> whether the animal was young or old
> how long it had been matured or hung
> quality of the meat
> whether your oven is ventilated or not.

So this recipe, as with so many, is only a guideline.

———————

The beef or veal trimmings will add more taste and help to
create a delicious juice. They will also isolate the joint from the
bottom heat of the roasting tray which would otherwise dry the
bottom of the meat.

———————

The basting will help the caramelization and the formation of
that delicious crust.

———————

Resting the meat is essential. When you take it out of the oven
it is medium rare. To reach medium, the residual heat within
the meat must travel slowly through the flesh to the centre,
cooking it to perfection. The fibres of the meat will relax as well,
giving tenderness.

———————

It is essential that the meat is completely sealed in aluminium
foil to prevent the heat from dissipating.

Pan-fried Lamb Sweetbreads with a Fricassee of Wild Mushrooms

FOR 4 GUESTS

PREPARATION TIME: 10 minutes

COOKING TIME: 20 minutes

INGREDIENTS

20 lamb sweetbreads (from the heart)
300 g (11 oz) wild mushrooms such as girolles (or button mushrooms)
3 tablespoons unsalted butter
salt and freshly ground white pepper

2 shallots, peeled and finely chopped

TO FINISH THE SAUCE
1 teaspoon lemon juice
50 ml (2 fl oz) water
1 tablespoon whipping cream
20 g (¾ oz) cold unsalted butter, diced
1 heaped tablespoon finely chopped fresh parsley
½ tablespoon finely snipped fresh chives

METHOD

1 · Preparing the sweetbreads

Soak the sweetbreads in cold water overnight, or thoroughly rinse under cold running water, to remove any traces of blood.

Blanch the sweetbreads in plenty of boiling water for 10 seconds. With a slotted spoon, remove and refresh in cold water. Drain, pat dry and, with a small knife, carefully peel off the membrane around each sweetbread. Reserve on a tea towel.

2 · Preparing the wild mushrooms

Scrape the cups and stalks of the wild mushrooms very gently with a small paring knife and cut off the base of the stalks. Wash them very briefly in plenty of water. Pat them dry, then quarter or halve according to size, and reserve.

3 · Cooking the sweetbreads

Over a medium heat, melt 2 tablespoons of the butter in a non-stick pan until it foams and becomes a rich gold. Add the sweetbreads and colour them for about 5 minutes on each side. Spoon out the fat, then season the sweetbreads with salt and white pepper. Keep warm, covered, and reserve.

4 · Cooking the wild mushrooms

Sweat the shallots in the remaining butter for 1 minute without colouring. Add the wild mushrooms, increase the heat, and cook for 2 minutes. Season with salt and white pepper.

5 · Finishing the sauce and serving

Add the lemon juice and water to the mushrooms, and bring to the boil. Add the cream, then whisk in the cold diced butter. Taste and correct the seasoning. Add the parsley and chives.

Serve five sweetbreads in the middle of each plate or dish, and spoon the wild mushrooms and the sauce around.

VARIATIONS

Other vegetables can be added to the wild mushrooms such as peas, French beans, button mushrooms, young spinach leaves, diced tomatoes etc. Other herbs can be added, such as basil, tarragon, chervil, etc.

C H E F ' S   N O T E S

For more information about sweetbreads, see p. 126.

Small insects and tiny worms often make their home in wild mushrooms, especially the larger ones, so check carefully and discard any that are heavily affected.

The mushrooms must be washed very fast otherwise the water would 'bloat' them and spoil both taste and texture.

Just 2 minutes will be enough to cook the wild mushrooms. If overcooked, they would shrivel and lose their beautiful texture.

The lemon juice has a dual role – to prevent oxidation and discolouring (see also p. 99) and to enhance the taste of both the sauce and the wild mushrooms.

Stuffed Cabbage

This dish belongs to the peasant cooking of my native Franche Comté. Despite its humble origins, though, it makes an elegant and wholesome winter or autumn dish.

NUTRITIONIST'S NOTES

Cabbage is brimming with many important vitamins, including vitamin C and beta-carotene, as well as other nutrients that have anti-oxidant properties. These help the body's defence system against free radicals, protecting against heart disease, certain cancers and the effects of ageing.

The filling of pork, butter and egg yolk is high in fat, protein and zinc. If you are concerned about fat, choose lean cuts of pork or trim off any excess. Eggs provide extra protein and vitamins.

FOR 4 GUESTS

PREPARATION TIME: 40 minutes

COOKING TIME: $1\frac{1}{2}$–2 hours

SPECIAL EQUIPMENT: A mincer; 6×40 cm (16 in) lengths of string.

PLANNING AHEAD: The chicken stock must be prepared in advance; the cabbage can be prepared and cooked in advance and re-heated gently.

INGREDIENTS
1 Savoy cabbage
salt and freshly ground black pepper
1 large onion, peeled and finely chopped
6 fresh sage leaves, finely chopped
30 g ($1\frac{1}{4}$ oz) unsalted butter
400 g (14 oz) belly pork, rinded, boned and cut into 2 cm ($\frac{3}{4}$ in) dice
400 g (14 oz) loin of pork, cut into 2 cm ($\frac{3}{4}$ in) dice
2 eggs

FOR THE POACHING LIQUOR
2.5 litres ($4\frac{1}{2}$ pints) White Chicken Stock (see p. 54)
2 sprigs of fresh thyme
2 bay leaves
2 garlic cloves, peeled

METHOD

1 · Blanching the cabbage
Discard the tough outside cabbage leaves. Trim the base of the root. With a small knife cut off each cabbage leaf at the base, taking care not to cut off the stem. Remove all the leaves until you reach the heart of the cabbage. Leave the heart as it is, still attached to the stem.

Bring 2 litres ($3\frac{1}{2}$ pints) of salted water to the boil. Boil the leaves for 30 seconds and the heart attached to its stem for 1 minute. Take them out and refresh in cold water.

Lie the leaves flat with the inside of the leaf facing upwards, and pat dry. Arrange the leaves, according to size, on a tray (i.e. small ones together, large ones together).

2 · Making the stuffing
In a cast-iron pan, sweat the chopped onion with the sage in the butter for 10–15 minutes until blond in colour. Cool.

Mix with the diced belly and loin, and then pass through the medium disc of a mincer. Mix in the eggs, then season.

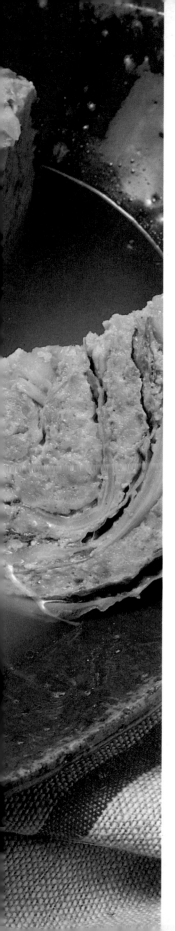

If you do not wish to taste the mince in its raw state, wrap a piece of cling film tightly round a teaspoon of the mince and poach for 5 minutes. Taste, then correct seasoning if necessary.

3 · *Assembling the stuffed cabbage*

This may sound difficult but it is quite easy and fun to do.

Spread the inside of each leaf with the mince. Wrap the first two smaller mince-lined leaves around the heart of the cabbage and continue to reconstruct the cabbage in this way, moving from the smaller to the larger leaves.

Now secure the cabbage with the string. Tie each piece of string around the cabbage so the 6 pieces form a star shape.

4 · *Poaching the stuffed cabbage*

Place the cabbage in a casserole, the base of the cabbage on the bottom, and cover with chicken stock. Add the thyme, bay leaves and garlic. Bring to the boil, skim, then cover with the lid. Cook at barely simmering point for about $1\frac{1}{2}$–2 hours, turning the cabbage over half-way through.

5 · *Serving*

Remove the cabbage from the stock. Place on a board and, with a sharp serrated knife, cut it into 4 or 6 portions. Discard the strings.

Pour the stock into large soup bowls and arrange the layered cabbage portions in the stock. Serve to your guests.

VARIATIONS

A garnish of root vegetables could be cooked in the stock (parsnips, swedes, carrots, etc.).

In my native Franche Comté, a glass of red wine is added to the stock towards the end, but this is an acquired taste.

About 2 tablespoons of chopped fresh chervil and a few fresh tarragon leaves could be added to the stock at the last moment.

C H E F ' S N O T E S

The cabbage leaves are boiled for a few seconds in the water in order to part-cook them. This removes the bitterness and also makes the leaves supple and easy to work with when re-assembling them.

It is essential that the stuffed cabbage is cooked for a long time so that there is an exchange of flavours between cabbage and stock. The stock remains clear as well, with the slow cooking.

Pan-fried Veal Steak with a Mustard and Herb Sauce

FOR 4 GUESTS

PREPARATION TIME: 20 minutes

COOKING TIME: 15 minutes

PLANNING AHEAD: The sauce can be completed up to the first stage a few hours in advance.

INGREDIENTS

1 tablespoon unsalted butter
4×200 g (7 oz) loin 'steaks' from milk-fed veal
salt and freshly ground white pepper

FOR THE SAUCE

2 shallots, peeled and finely chopped
20 g (¾ oz) unsalted butter

1 tablespoon white wine vinegar
100 ml (3½ fl oz) dry white wine
200 ml (7 fl oz) whipping cream
1 tablespoon Dijon mustard
½ tablespoon finely chopped fresh parsley
½ tablespoon finely snipped fresh chives
8 fresh tarragon leaves, finely chopped
4 tomatoes, skinned, seeded and diced
1 tablespoon small capers, rinsed in cold water

METHOD

1 · Preparing the sauce
Sweat the chopped shallot in the butter without colouring for a few minutes. Add the white wine vinegar and boil to reduce down almost completely. Add the white wine and boil to reduce by half. Add the cream, bring to the boil, then leave to cool. Reserve.

2 · Cooking the veal steaks
In a large non-stick pan, on medium heat, heat the butter until it foams and becomes a rich gold. Colour the veal steaks on both sides for about 5 minutes. Season with salt and freshly ground pepper. Remove the steaks to a small tray and keep warm.

3 · Finishing the sauce
Discard the butter from the veal cooking pan and add the sauce ingredients from stage 1. Bring to the boil, then whisk in the mustard. Add the herbs, the tomato dice, the capers and seasoning, then simmer for 1 minute.

4 · Serving

Arrange the veal steaks on a dish or plate. Pour the sauce over them, and serve to your guests.

VARIATIONS

The veal can be replaced by thin steaks of beef or pork.

CHEF'S NOTES

The sauce is completed in two stages which facilitates the serving of the dish.

The herbs must be added at the last moment so they do not lose their colour and taste.

Braised Venison with a Bitter Chocolate Sauce

FOR 4 GUESTS

PREPARATION TIME: 20 minutes

MARINATING TIME: 24 hours

COOKING TIME: $3\frac{1}{2}$ hours

PLANNING AHEAD: This dish actually gains from being cooked 24 hours in advance, then being re-heated at the same temperature for about 30 minutes.

INGREDIENTS
4 × 250 g (9 oz) pieces of venison shoulder
50 ml (2 fl oz) sunflower oil
salt and freshly ground black pepper

FOR THE MARINADE
1 bottle (750 ml/1¼ pints) red wine
8 juniper berries, crushed

12 black peppercorns, crushed
2 bay leaves
1 sprig of fresh thyme
1 strip of orange peel
1 medium carrot, diced
1 large onion, peeled and roughly chopped
4 garlic cloves, peeled
1 celery stick, chopped

FOR THE SAUCE
1 tablespoon tomato purée
350–400 ml (12–14 fl oz) water
1 tablespoon redcurrant jelly
30 g (1¼oz) bitter chocolate, grated

FOR THE GARNISH (optional)
24 chestnuts, prepared and cooked (see p. 235)

METHOD

1 · Marinating the venison

Put the red wine in a pan and boil to reduce by one-third. Allow to cool down to room temperature.

Place the venison in a large container and cover with the reduced wine and all the remaining marinade ingredients. Refrigerate and allow to marinate for 24 hours.

2 · Braising the venison

Pre-heat the oven to 110°C/225°F/Gas ¼.

Drain the venison and the vegetables and pat them dry. Reserve the wine.

In a non-stick pan, heat the sunflower oil until smoking and sear and colour both pieces of venison on all sides to a good deep brown. This operation will take about 10 minutes. Transfer the venison pieces to a cast-iron casserole.

In the oil remaining in the non-stick pan, colour the vegetables and seasonings lightly, about 5 minutes, then transfer them to the casserole with the venison. Add the tomato purée to the non-stick pan and cook for 1–2 minutes. Add the reserved red wine from the marinade, and bring to the boil. Pour over the venison, vegetables and seasonings in the casserole, and barely cover with the water. Season lightly with salt. Bring to the boil for 1 minute, skim, then cover with a tight lid. Braise in the pre-heated oven for 3½ hours.

3 · Finishing the sauce

Strain the juices into a large saucepan and reduce on full heat to about 300 ml (10 fl oz). Reduce the heat until the sauce barely simmers, then add the redcurrant jelly. Correct the seasoning and, finally, whisk in the grated chocolate.

4 · Serving

Mix the venison and vegetables back into the sauce, and re-heat gently. Add the chestnuts if using.

You may serve the venison from the casserole or transfer it to a nice serving dish. Serve to your guests.

VARIATIONS

The venison can be replaced by beef.

A parsnip purée could be served with this dish (see p. 224).

CHEF'S NOTES

The wine is reduced to remove most of its alcohol and to

Braised Venison with a
Bitter Chocolate Sauce
(see p. 211)

concentrate its colour and flavour. It will also be less aggressive and less tannic, giving a rounder flavour to the venison.

Only a little salt should be added before the meat is braised as the sauce will be reduced later on, when the seasoning can be corrected.

Use a bitter cooking chocolate and grate it before incorporating it into the sauce. It will impart a beautiful shine as well as a very special flavour.

Pigs' Kidneys with Mustard Sauce

FOR 4 GUESTS

PREPARATION TIME: 10 minutes

COOKING TIME: 15 minutes

PLANNING AHEAD: The sauce can be prepared a few hours in advance.

INGREDIENTS
4 pigs' kidneys, about 450 g (1 lb), trimmed
15 g (½ oz) unsalted butter

FOR THE SAUCE
6 shallots, peeled and thinly sliced
1 teaspoon unsalted butter
50 ml (2 fl oz) white wine vinegar
150 ml (5 fl oz) dry white wine
100 ml (3½ fl oz) whipping cream
1 tablespoon Dijon mustard
salt and freshly ground white pepper

METHOD

1 · Making the sauce
Sweat the shallots in the butter for about 8 minutes on a medium heat, without colouring.

Add the vinegar and boil to reduce to a syrup. Add the white wine, bring to the boil and boil to reduce by half. Add the whipping cream, and bring to the boil for 1 minute. Turn off the heat, whisk in the mustard, and season with salt and pepper.

Liquidize the sauce, then force through a fine strainer. Taste and correct seasoning. Reserve.

2 · Cooking and serving the kidneys
Slice the kidneys about 3 mm (⅛ in) thick.

In a large non-stick pan, heat the butter on a medium heat

until a blond colour. Turn the heat on to full, slide in all the kidney slices at once, stir and cook for about 3 minutes only.

Season with salt and pepper, and mix the kidneys with the sauce. Serve to your guests.

CHEF'S NOTES

Specify to your butcher that you want the kidneys to be pink or whiteish, with no traces of blood whatsoever. Never accept red kidneys.

The shallots are here to give taste and texture and to thicken the juices, so they need to be cooked thoroughly in order that they can be sieved easily.

The cooking of the kidneys must be very fast – 3 minutes will be ample to cook them to medium. (See the Scientist's Note below.)

SCIENTIST'S
NOTE

Some animal organs such as liver and kidney are not muscles, therefore they do not contain much connective tissue. Neither do they contain much fat. As a result, cooking must be brief and fairly gentle so that they do not dry out or toughen. Other organs, such as hearts, *are* actually muscles, and these would need long slow cooking to tenderize them. Heart muscle is actually the most active kind in most animals, and well-exercised muscle is always the toughest.

Pan-fried Lambs' Liver and Kidneys

There is a particular moment when lambs' livers and kidneys are a delicacy, as good as if not better than veal. It is obviously when the lamb is milk-fed, right at the beginning of the new season. Both liver and kidneys should be a creamy pink colour.

FOR 4 GUESTS

PREPARATION TIME: 10 minutes

COOKING TIME: 5 minutes

INGREDIENTS

4 new season, milk-fed lambs' kidneys, wrapped in their own fat

8 × 80 g (3¼ oz) slices of new-season, milk-fed lamb's liver

2 tablespoons unsalted butter

salt and freshly ground black pepper

FOR THE SAUCE

50 ml (2 fl oz) water or Brown Chicken Stock (see p. 54)

2 shallots, peeled and finely chopped

½ garlic clove, peeled and finely chopped

4 tablespoons finely chopped fresh parsley

Pan-fried Lamb's Liver
and Kidneys (see p. 215)

METHOD

1 · Preparing the kidneys

Trim off the excess fat around the kidneys, leaving a thin layer only, about 3 mm ($^1/_8$ in). Remove the cores. Slice each kidney 5 mm ($^1/_4$ in) thick. Reserve.

2 · Pan-frying the liver and kidneys

You need to pan-fry the liver and kidneys separately in two non-stick pans.

Divide the butter between the pans. Place on medium heat until the butter foams and reaches a rich golden colour. Add the liver slices to one pan and the kidneys to the other. Cook for 30 seconds, then turn both on to the other side and cook for a further 30 seconds. Take care that the butter does not burn.

Season with salt and pepper. Arrange the livers and kidneys on a warm serving dish and keep warm.

3 · Finishing and serving

Add the water or brown chicken stock to the pan in which the liver cooked, and immediately add the shallots, garlic and parsley. Cook for 10 seconds.

Either serve directly on individual plates, or place on a flat dish. Have the liver slices overlapping each other and the kidney slices scattered around. Pour the sauce over.

VARIATIONS

Some new-season lamb's sweetbreads could be added to this dish. They need to be blanched before being pan-fried (see p. 205).

Peas with Lettuce and Bacon (see p. 242) would be a delightful accompaniment to this dish.

CHEF'S NOTES

The cooking time is very short as the liver and kidney slices are cut thinly – this will be cooked to medium rare. For medium to medium well done, cook for another 30 seconds.

Add the parsley, shallot and garlic mixture at the very last moment, so that it does not lose colour or taste.

Roasted Pork Fillet with Onion and Garlic Purée

FOR 4 GUESTS

PREPARATION TIME: 20 minutes

COOKING TIME: 15 minutes

RESTING TIME: 20 minutes

PLANNING AHEAD: The purée can be prepared a day in advance. The fillets and the juice can be prepared 30 minutes in advance, kept warm covered with aluminium foil.

INGREDIENTS
50 g (2 oz) unsalted butter

2×400 g (14 oz) pork fillets, trimmed of all sinews
300 g (11 oz) pork spare ribs, finely chopped
1 garlic clove, peeled and chopped
1 sprig of fresh thyme
salt and freshly ground black pepper
200 ml (7 fl oz) water

TO SERVE
1 quantity Onion and Garlic Purée (see p. 230)

METHOD

1 · Cooking the pork fillets
Pre-heat the oven to 180°C/350°F/Gas 4.

On a medium heat, in a small roasting tray, heat the butter until it foams. Sear and colour the fillets and the spare ribs on all sides for approximately 10 minutes until both fillets and bones are beautifully caramelized to a golden brown.

Add the garlic and thyme, season with salt and pepper, and roast in the pre-heated oven for 5–7 minutes.

Spoon out the fat. Remove the fillets, season them again, and keep warm covered with aluminium foil.

2 · Making the sauce
Place the roasting tray on a medium heat, add the water and bring to the boil. Scrape the bottom of the pan to dilute all the caramelized juices. Simmer for 5 minutes before straining into a casserole. On full heat reduce the liquid for 5 minutes, until you have about 150 ml (5 fl oz). Taste and correct seasoning.

3 · Serving
Re-heat the Onion and Garlic Purée.

Pour the liquid which the fillets will have released into the sauce. Heat through.

Re-heat the fillets in the oven for 2 minutes if necessary.

Carve into thin slices and arrange in a warm serving dish. Pour the sauce over and serve to your guests with the onion and garlic purée offered separately. Or you could spread the onion and garlic purée on the middle of each plate, and fan the fillet slices over. Serve the sauce separately.

VARIATIONS
This dish can be prepared with veal fillets.

CHEF'S NOTES

The spare ribs must be cut into tiny pieces so they lend their flavour more readily, and the simmering time will be shortened.

The short cooking means that the seasoning will not have time to permeate the meat, so you need to re-season.

Vegetables

Braised Fennel with
Cardamom (see p. 234)

Cabbage with Smoked Bacon and Caraway Seeds

FOR 4 GUESTS

PREPARATION TIME: 10 minutes

COOKING TIME: 15 minutes

INGREDIENTS
1 Savoy cabbage

**salt and freshly ground
white pepper**
**150 g (5 oz) smoked streaky
bacon, cut into fine strips**
1 tablespoon unsalted butter
**2 teaspoons caraway seeds,
crushed**

NUTRITIONIST'S NOTES

Cabbage is an excellent source of beta-carotene, vitamin C and other anti-oxidant nutrients. On its own it can be rather dull but, combined with other flavoursome ingredients, it becomes much more interesting and palatable. This dish is also high in fibre and moderate in fat due to the addition of the bacon and butter.

METHOD

1 · Preparing and blanching the cabbage

Cut the stem off the cabbage, and remove the coarse outer leaves. Halve the cabbage, cut out the cores and chop each half finely into 3 mm ($^1/_8$ in) thick slices. Wash in plenty of water, drain well and reserve.

Bring 2 litres ($3^1/_2$ pints) of water to a full boil with 30 g ($1^1/_4$ oz) of salt, and boil the shredded cabbage for 5 minutes. Refresh in cold water, drain and reserve.

2 · Finishing and serving the cabbage

In a large cast-iron pan, sweat the bacon in the butter for 2 minutes. Add the cabbage and crushed caraway seeds, and stir together. Cover and cook for a further 5 minutes. Taste and correct the seasoning, then serve to your guests.

CHEF'S NOTES

Personally, I prefer to blanch the cabbage to remove some of its very powerful taste.

It is always better to buy bacon which is in the piece rather than the already pre-cut slices; or get your butcher to slice bacon in front of you. Newly sliced bacon will have a much better taste and texture.

Spinach and Watercress Purée

FOR 4 GUESTS

PREPARATION TIME: 15 minutes

COOKING TIME: 4 minutes

PLANNING AHEAD: The purée can be made about an hour or so in advance.

INGREDIENTS
20 g (¾ oz) unsalted butter

300 g (11 oz) spinach, washed, drained and tough stalks removed
200 g (7 oz) watercress, washed, drained and leaves picked from the stalks
salt and freshly ground black pepper
100 ml (3½ fl oz) whipping cream (optional)

NUTRITIONIST'S NOTES

Both spinach and watercress are super sources of anti-oxidants and anti-cancer nutrients, containing large quantities of beta-carotene. They also contain valuable amounts of the minerals iron and calcium, as well as fibre. In this recipe they are cooked only very briefly which means most of the vitamins will be retained.

METHOD

1 · Cooking the spinach and watercress
In a large pan heat the butter until it starts to foam. Add the spinach and watercress, ½ teaspoon of salt and a pinch of pepper, and cook for 3 minutes, covered.

2 · Finishing and serving the purée
Pour the mixture into the liquidizer, add the cream, if using, and mix for about 10 seconds until a rough texture is achieved. Place in a warm serving dish and serve to your guests.

VARIATIONS
A little grated nutmeg could be added.
    About 50 g (2 oz) of flat parsley leaves, blanched for 3 minutes in boiling water, could also be added, as could puréed garlic, of course.

CHEF'S NOTES

The texture of the spinach is important as we do not want it to revert to baby food consistency.

If you do not serve the purée straight away, cool it down on ice so that it retains both colour and flavour. Re-heat at a later stage.

SCIENTIST'S NOTES

Refreshing a green vegetable in cold water stops the cooking immediately. Immersion in water is not practical for a purée, so cooling down rapidly with the ice serves much the same purpose.

Celeriac Purée

This purée goes particularly well with game and roast meats.

NUTRITIONIST'S NOTES

Celeriac has a mild diuretic effect and contains several anti-cancer compounds. It is very low in calories, although in this recipe it is puréed with cream and butter which increase the fat and calorie content of the dish. Milk is an excellent source of calcium.

FOR 4 GUESTS

PREPARATION TIME: 15 minutes

COOKING TIME: 30 minutes

INGREDIENTS
500 g (18 oz) celeriac, peeled

500 ml (17 fl oz) milk
50 ml (2 fl oz) double cream
30 g (1¼ oz) unsalted butter
**salt and freshly ground
  white pepper**
lemon juice

METHOD

1 · Preparing and cooking the celeriac
Chop the celeriac roughly into 1 cm (½ in) cubes. Simmer these cubes in the milk for 15–20 minutes until tender. Strain and purée in a food processor.

2 · Finishing the purée
Add the cream and butter to the purée, then taste, and season with salt and pepper. Add a dash of lemon juice and serve.

VARIATIONS
Parsnips can be puréed in the same way but replace the milk with water.

French Beans in Butter

This very simple dish can turn into the most nightmarish, tired-looking and tasteless dish unless you follow and understand the method and a few very simple principles which are explained in the Notes.

FOR 4 GUESTS

PREPARATION TIME: 5 minutes

COOKING TIME: 5–6 minutes

PLANNING AHEAD: The beans can be blanched and refreshed a few hours in advance.

INGREDIENTS
25 g (1 oz) salt
**400 g (14 oz) French beans,
  topped and tailed**
40 g (1½ oz) butter
2 tablespoons water
freshly ground black pepper

French Beans in Butter

METHOD
Bring 1.5 litres (2½ pints) of water to the boil with the salt. Cook

the beans for 3–3½ minutes, according to size. Taste, and if ready, drain and plunge them into cold water for 5 minutes, to arrest the cooking process, then drain again. Reserve.

To finish the dish, heat the butter and water together to emulsify. Add the French beans, toss, then taste, season with salt and pepper, and cook for 1 minute. Serve to your guests.

VARIATIONS

Swiss chard leaves can be cooked in this way as well. Cook broccoli florets for 6–8 minutes, according to size; similarly with asparagus stalks.

CHEF'S NOTES

In the past vegetables were totally overcooked, now the trend is to undercook them, which is equally wrong. The cooking time is proportional to the size of the beans and the texture should be firm, but not crunchy.

During cooking do not place a lid on a pan of green vegetables. There are certain acids contained in vegetables which are released; when the lid is on, these acids in the water will attack the colour of the vegetables which will be lost.

Refreshing beans and other green vegetables in cold water arrests the cooking and preserves taste, colour and texture. This can be done in advance and it also saves time and effort when serving your complete dish. Just re-heat them as above and serve.

The emulsion of butter and water is important, since water creates steam which heats the vegetables quickly and thoroughly. The water must not evaporate totally or the vegetables will be too greasy; they should simply be coated with a fine film of the butter and water emulsion. The final seasoning should be light to allow the taste of the vegetables to come through.

Purée of Potatoes

The potato is often branded 'the poor man's food', and dismissed as stodge. In fact, however simple their preparation, potatoes often provide the most delicious accompaniment for any meat.

FOR 4 GUESTS

PREPARATION AND COOKING TIME:
About 20 minutes

INGREDIENTS
800 g (1¾ lb) potatoes (choose Estima, King Edward, Maris Piper, Désirée or Bintje)
salt and freshly ground white pepper
100 ml (3½ fl oz) milk
50 g (2 oz) unsalted butter

METHOD

1 · Preparing the potatoes
Pre-heat the oven to 180°C/350°F/Gas 4.

Peel the potatoes and cut them into 2.5 cm (1 in) cubes. Bring 1 litre (1¾ pints) water to the boil with 15 g (½ oz) salt, and add the potatoes. Cook them at simmering point for about 9–10 minutes. Drain them in a colander then place in the pre-heated oven for 2 minutes to remove surplus moisture. Purée them in a vegetable mill.

2 · Finishing the purée
In a pan on a low heat or in a bowl over a pan of hot water or in a bain-marie, add the milk then the butter to the purée. Taste and correct seasoning with about ½ teaspoon salt and a pinch of white pepper. Serve to your guests.

VARIATIONS
The butter can be replaced by olive oil.

The purée can be given more volume by adding some cream. It can also be made more austere by not adding the butter. To enrich the purée you can also add a free-range egg yolk.

CHEF'S NOTES

Some potatoes are starchy and some are very close textured. Try to find varieties which are ideal for this dish: Estima, King Edwards, Maris Piper, Désirée or Bintje.

Cooking at simmering point avoids damaging the potato.

When re-heating the purée do not bring it to the boil or the starch in the potatoes will create a very elastic texture.

***

The old-fashioned mouli-légumes, or vegetable mill, is perfect for this purée. Do not use a food processor as it would make the purée very elastic and unpalatable.

***

Do not use an aluminium casserole or the potatoes will turn grey. Always use a stainless-steel pan for potatoes.

Sautéed Potatoes

FOR 4 GUESTS

PREPARATION AND COOKING TIME:
20 minutes

INGREDIENTS
600 g (1¼ lb) potatoes (Desirée, King Edward, Cara or Maris Piper)
2 tablespoons corn or sunflower oil

2 tablespoons unsalted butter
½ teaspoon salt
2 large pinches of black pepper
1 shallot, peeled and finely chopped (optional)
20 g (¾ oz) chopped fresh parsley mixed with ½ garlic clove, peeled and puréed (optional)

METHOD

1 · Preparing the potatoes
Wash and peel the potatoes, and dice into 1 cm (½ in) cubes. Wash again in plenty of cold water. Drain well and pat dry in a cloth.

2 · Cooking the potatoes
Pan-fry the potatoes in the hot oil on a medium to high heat, turning them from time to time. This will take about 8 minutes.

Spoon the oil out, add the butter, and cook on for a further 2 minutes. Season with the salt and pepper.

About 2 minutes before the end of cooking, if you like, you can add the finely chopped shallot and, at the very last moment, the parsley and garlic. Serve to your guests.

VARIATIONS
The possible additions are endless – bacon, ham, tomatoes, eggs, cheese, etc.

Try to use a non-stick pan as some potato starch will seep out; the non-stick coating will prevent any sticking because of this.

It may seem odd to wash the potato *before* peeling, but all too often I have seen young commis chefs (apprentices) peeling potatoes covered with earth; once peeled the potato still looked as if it had just come from the ground.

You must also wash and dry potatoes once they are diced. The washing removes excess starch which gathers where the potato has been cut. If this were left, the diced potato would stick together. The patting dry is simply to remove any moisture; this prevents the oil spitting. (See also the Scientist's Note on pp. 232.)

SCIENTIST'S NOTES

Although new potatoes are waxy and therefore brown too quickly when fried, here the slices are very thin so they will cook and brown at the same time.

NUTRITIONIST'S NOTES

New potatoes are rich in vitamin C, and also good sources of thiamin and fibre. Sautéing them in oil helps seal in the vitamins and pre-vents them leaching out into any cooking liquor. Most of the vitamin content is under-neath the skin so, again, this is not destroyed because the skins are left on.

New potatoes and freshly bought contain more vitamin C than old potatoes which have been stored for a long time. Use potatoes fairly soon after purchase since the vitamin C content reduces faster if kept in a warm kitchen. Frying in hot oil helps preserve the vitamins and minimize the amount of oil that can be absorbed.

Sautéed New Potatoes with Spring Onions

FOR 4 GUESTS

PREPARATION TIME: 10 minutes

COOKING TIME: 20 minutes

INGREDIENTS
500 g (18 oz) new potatoes, washed not peeled

50 ml (2 fl oz) sunflower oil
2 tablespoons unsalted butter
8 spring onions, very finely chopped
salt and freshly ground black pepper

METHOD
Slice the potatoes into 5 mm (¼ in) rounds.

Heat the oil in a large non-stick pan and sauté the potatoes for about 5 minutes.

Spoon out the oil and add the butter. Cook for a further 10 minutes until the potatoes have reached a golden brown colour, stirring continuously.

Add the finely chopped spring onions in the last 5 minutes. Season with salt and pepper, and serve to your guests.

Onion and Garlic Purée

This purée goes particularly well with lamb or any Provençale dish.

NUTRITIONIST'S NOTES

Both onion and garlic are exceptionally strong anti-oxidants. They are full of numerous anti-cancer agents, and onions have been specifically linked to the inhibition of stomach cancer. Both help to 'thin' the blood, lower total cholesterol, raise the good HDL cholesterol, ward off colds and help fight infections. Both are also anti-inflammatory and antibiotic, and help boost the immune system.

FOR 4 GUESTS

PREPARATION TIME: 5 minutes

COOKING TIME: 30 minutes

PLANNING AHEAD: The purée can be made a day in advance.

INGREDIENTS
12 large garlic cloves, peeled
700 g (1 lb 6 oz) onions, or 2 large onions, peeled and chopped

50 ml (2 fl oz) olive oil
4 sprigs of fresh thyme
100 ml (3½ fl oz) double cream
50 ml (2 fl oz) extra virgin olive oil
salt and freshly ground white pepper

METHOD
Cut the garlic in half lengthways, and remove and discard the central green germ, which is bitter. Simmer the garlic in 1 litre (1¾ pints) of water for 12–15 minutes. Drain well and reserve.

In a covered cast-iron pan, over a gentle heat, sweat the onion in the olive oil for about 15–20 minutes. Do not colour. Stir from time to time. Add the garlic, thyme and cream, and cook for a further 10 minutes.

Cool, remove the thyme, then liquidize to a purée. Enrich with the extra virgin olive oil, then taste and season.

Stewed Red Cabbage

FOR 4 GUESTS

PREPARATION TIME: 10 minutes

COOKING TIME: 2½ hours

PLANNING AHEAD: The cabbage can be cooked a day in advance and gently re-heated.

INGREDIENTS
500 g (18 oz) red cabbage

60 g (2¼ oz) unsalted butter
100 ml (3½ fl oz) red wine
200 ml (7 fl oz) ruby port
salt and freshly ground black pepper
2 tablespoons blackcurrant jelly
caster sugar (optional)

NUTRITIONIST'S
NOTES

*Red cabbage is a prime source
of various anti-oxidants, including sulphur-containing
compounds that have an anti-
cancer activity. It also provides fibre, potassium and
surprisingly high quantities of
vitamin C. Cooking in red wine
enhances the anti-oxidant
content even further, as this is
also recommended by scientists as a good way of com-
bating heart disease and
cancer.*

NUTRITIONIST'S
NOTES

*Carrots are a very rich source
of beta-carotene which is a
powerful anti-oxidant. Beta-
carotene can also be con-
verted into vitamin A in the
body. A small amount of
butter is used to fry and sweat
the carrots and this helps to
bring out the flavour. You can
use a little less if you wish to
reduce your fat intake.*

METHOD

1 · Preparing the cabbage

Cut the cabbage in half and remove the central cores. Remove any torn or bruised outside leaves if necessary. Chop each half finely into 3 mm ($\frac{1}{8}$ in) thick slices.

2 · Cooking and serving the cabbage

In a cast-iron saucepan, sweat the shredded cabbage in the butter for about 10 minutes, stirring from time to time. Add the red wine, and simmer to reduce by half. Add the ruby port, salt, pepper and blackcurrant jelly. Cover with a lid and cook on a very slow heat for a further 2 hours.

Taste and correct seasoning, adding a little bit of sugar if necessary. Serve to your guests.

Baton Carrots

FOR 4 GUESTS

PREPARATION AND COOKING TIME:
About 20 minutes

INGREDIENTS
30 g (1$\frac{1}{4}$ oz) unsalted butter
**400 g (14 oz) carrots, peeled
and cut into batons
3 cm × 5 mm (1$\frac{1}{4}$ × $\frac{1}{4}$ in)**
200 ml (7 fl oz) water

$\frac{1}{2}$ teaspoon salt
**a pinch of freshly ground
black pepper**
1 teaspoon caster sugar
**1 sprig of fresh tarragon,
blanched and finely
chopped**
**1 tablespoon very finely
chopped fresh parsley**

METHOD

Melt the butter in a pan and sweat the carrots for 1 minute. Then add the water, salt, pepper and sugar. Cover the pan and cook for about 15 minutes on a very gentle simmer.

Add the tarragon and parsley at the last minute. The carrots should be beautifully glazed.

CHEF'S NOTES

Too often carrots are cooked in plenty of boiling water and thereby lose texture and flavour. The small amount of water used here will reduce whilst cooking to create a very tasty and shiny glaze around the vegetables.

Pancake Potatoes

FOR 4 GUESTS

PREPARATION TIME: 10 minutes

COOKING TIME: 40 minutes

INGREDIENTS
500 g (18 oz) potatoes, peeled and quartered (use Désirée, King Edward, Cara or Maris Piper)

salt and freshly ground white pepper
4 eggs, lightly beaten
50 g (2 oz) plain flour, sifted
100 ml (3½ fl oz) milk
100 ml (3½ fl oz) double cream
freshly grated nutmeg
50 g (2 oz) unsalted butter

METHOD

1 · Preparing the potatoes

Cover the potatoes with salted water and bring to the boil. Simmer for 20 minutes. Drain well, then pass the potatoes through a vegetable mill into a casserole dish, and cool slightly.

Add the whole eggs, stirring all the time, then the flour, milk and cream. Season with salt, pepper and grated nutmeg.

2 · Cooking the potatoes

Melt the butter in a large non-stick pan on a medium heat until it becomes rich gold in colour and foamy. Using a dessertspoon, gently spoon five or six little potato mixture pancakes into the pan; these will shape themselves. Cook for 1 minute on each side, turning them with a palette knife. Drain and serve to your guests.

VARIATIONS

Very finely chopped ham, pan-fried smoked bacon strips or chives would be pleasant additions.

CHEF'S NOTES

According to the starch content of the potato you may need to add a little bit more milk.

The texture of the mixture should be quite loose. Do a little test: pan-fry a tiny piece, and if this is too thick, add a little more milk.

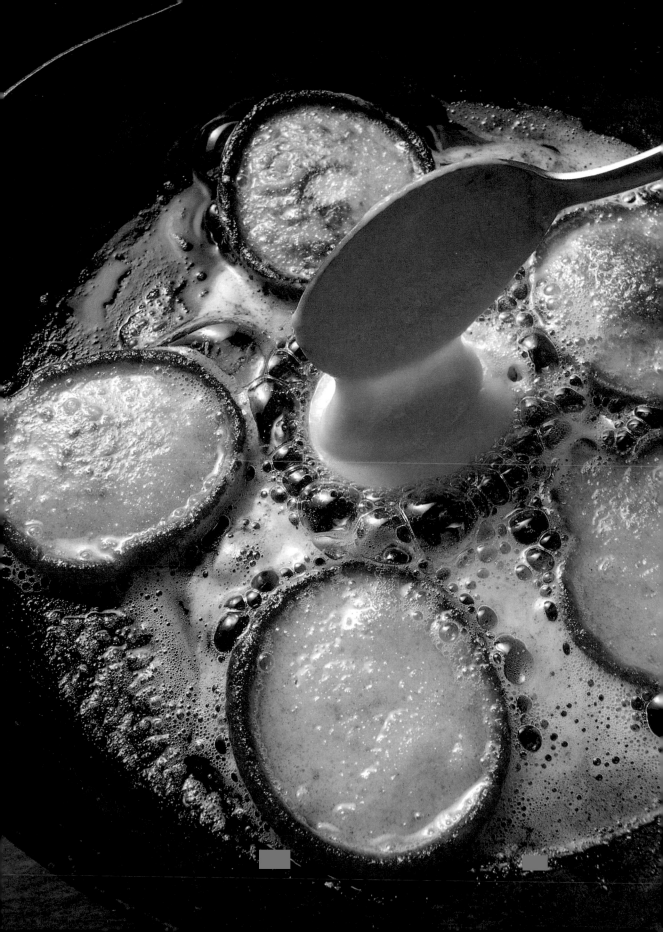

Braised Fennel with Cardamom

—— ILLUSTRATED ON PAGE 220 ——

FOR 4 GUESTS

PREPARATION TIME: 10 minutes

COOKING TIME: 2 hours

PLANNING AHEAD: This can be made one to two days in advance and kept in the fridge.

INGREDIENTS

500 g (18 oz) baby fennel bulbs, or large bulbs cut into 4 or 6, according to size

50 ml (2 fl oz) extra virgin olive oil
2 garlic cloves, peeled and sliced
2 sprigs of fresh thyme
4 black olives, stoned
3 cardamom pods, lightly crushed
500 ml (17 fl oz) water or White Chicken Stock (see p. 54)
salt and freshly ground white pepper

METHOD

Pre-heat the oven to 180°C/350°F/Gas 4.

Sweat the fennel for about 10 minutes in the olive oil in a flameproof casserole. Add the garlic, thyme, black olives, cardamom and water or stock. Season with salt and pepper. Bring to the boil, cover with a lid then cook in the pre-heated oven for 1½–2 hours. Serve to your guests.

VARIATIONS

The fennel can be served whole, as a vegetable, but it can also be puréed, to serve as a vegetable purée (good with lamb) or as a sauce (good with red mullet).

CHEF'S NOTES

The best olives are the ones in olive oil with Provençal herbs. The ones kept in brine are not so tasty.

The sweating of the fennel will remove its coarse taste and extract the sugar. Do not colour.

The cooking time for the fennel may seem very long, but it is essential to cook it thoroughly so a proper exchange of flavours can take place.

Braised Chestnuts

FOR 4 GUESTS

PREPARATION TIME: 30 minutes

COOKING TIME: 20 minutes

INGREDIENTS
500 g (18 oz) fresh chestnuts
¼ onion, peeled and chopped
1 celery stick, chopped
20 g (¾ oz) unsalted butter

water or White Chicken Stock (see p. 54) to cover, about 300 ml (10 fl oz)
juice of ¼ lemon
1 heaped teaspoon caster sugar
1 teaspoon salt
freshly ground white pepper

METHOD

1 · Preparing the chestnuts
With a small knife make an incision through the skin around the chestnuts. Bring to the boil 2 litres (3½ pints) of water, add the chestnuts and cook for 30 seconds. Drain in a colander and remove both the hard outer shell and the thin inner skin.

2 · Cooking the chestnuts
Sweat the onion and celery in the butter in a medium-sized pan for a few minutes. Add the shelled chestnuts and cover with the water or chicken stock. Add the lemon juice, sugar, salt and pepper, cover with a lid, and cook at just under simmering point for 20 minutes.

3 · Serving
Drain off and discard the liquid, and serve the chestnuts in a warmed serving bowl.

C H E F ' S   N O T E S

It is important to score all the way around the chestnuts. This allows the boiling water to react and soften both skins, so they can be easily removed.

I have tried many ways of making the task of shelling chestnuts easy – roasting, deep-frying, microwaving – but found that blanching is the best and by far the easiest method.

The chestnuts must be cooked at just under simmering point. If the heat is too strong it will overcook and break up the chestnuts.

SCIENTIST'S NOTE

Chestnuts have a very high carbohydrate content. If you gather them yourself, fresh from the tree, allow them to mature at room temperature for a couple of days before using. This allows some of the starch to be converted into sugar, and will improve the flavour.

NUTRITIONIST'S NOTES

Fresh chestnuts, unlike other nuts, are low in fat and calories, less than 3 per cent fat by weight and around 170 calories per 100 g (4 oz). They are high in potassium, with reasonable amounts of B vitamins, zinc, protein and vitamin E. The total fat content of the dish is low but the salt content is fairly high. Adjust this to suit your palate if you have high blood pressure.

Potato Soufflées

This recipe makes from 28 to 38 potato soufflées, according to the size of potato used.

FOR 4 GUESTS

PREPARATION TIME: 10 minutes

COOKING TIME: About 18 minutes

SPECIAL EQUIPMENT: A mandoline; 2 deep-frying pans with baskets (16–18 cm/6½–7¼ in in diameter); 1 oil thermometer.

PLANNING AHEAD: The potatoes can be 'blanched' in advance, kept in a tea towel, and chilled. The second deep-frying must be done at the last moment.

INGREDIENTS

4 medium potatoes (Maris Piper, Desirée or Cara), peeled, washed and patted dry
3 litres (5¼ pints) vegetable oil for deep-frying
salt and freshly ground white pepper

METHOD

1 · Preparing the potatoes
Shape the potatoes into cylinders 6 cm (2½ in) in diameter, and slice them with a mandoline to 3–5 mm (⅛–¼ in) thickness. Wash them briefly to remove excess starch, then pat dry. Reserve in a damp tea towel.

2 · Cooking the potato slices
Divide the oil between the two pans. If fully cooking the potatoes at this stage, heat both pans, one to 160°C (290°F), and the other to 190°C (374°F). Otherwise heat the lower temperature pan only.

'Blanch' – deep-fry – eight slices of potato at a time in the oil at the lower temperature, and cook for 4 minutes, stirring them lightly. Remove with a slotted spoon and allow to cool down on absorbent paper for 1 minute.

Slide the cooled blanched slices into the second, hotter pan of oil. They will puff out, or soufflé, to a crispy golden brown. Remove from the fat with a slotted spoon and place on absorbent paper. Season with salt and pepper and serve to your guests.

Tomato Fondue

These tomatoes are 'stewed' to an intense red paste.

FOR 4 GUESTS

PREPARATION TIME: 20 minutes

COOKING TIME: 30 minutes

PLANNING AHEAD: This garnish dish can be made a day in advance.

INGREDIENTS
½ **medium onion, peeled and finely chopped**
50 ml (2 fl oz) olive oil
1 tablespoon tomato purée

500 g (18 oz) Roma tomatoes, seeded and finely chopped
2 sprigs of fresh thyme
1 bay leaf
2 garlic cloves, peeled and crushed
1 teaspoon caster sugar
salt and freshly ground black pepper
100 ml (3½ fl oz) extra virgin olive oil

METHOD

Pre-heat the oven to 200°C/400°F/Gas 6.

In a roasting tray on top of the stove, sweat the onion in the olive oil for 8–10 minutes. Do not colour. Add the tomato purée and cook for a further 5 minutes. Add the chopped tomatoes, thyme, bay leaf, garlic, sugar, salt and pepper. Bring to the boil and cook uncovered in the pre-heated oven for 20 minutes, stirring from time to time.

Place the tomato fondue in a casserole and trickle and whisk in the extra virgin oil to enrich it. Make sure it is smooth and amalgamated. Serve or chill.

CHEF'S NOTES

Obviously for this dish you need beautifully ripe tomatoes. If you want a more refined stew, first blanch the tomatoes in boiling water for 10 seconds and peel off the skin before seeding and chopping.

The tomatoes must be cooked in a large roasting tray, so as much water as possible can evaporate. This concentrates the taste of the tomato. The addition of extra virgin olive oil at the end will enrich the taste of the tomato which, during its long cooking, has turned from acid to sweet.

Spinach in Butter

So often spinach is cooked in plenty of boiling water, refreshed then wrung out in a cloth, then cooked again. This is definitely one of the sacrileges of cooking.

NUTRITIONIST'S
NOTES

Spinach is possibly one of the most nutrient-packed vege-tables you can eat. It is burst-ing with beta-carotene, iron and potassium and gives a pretty hefty dose of calcium, vitamin C and vitamin E too. So it's a great vegetable to include in your diet as much as possible.

No water is added to the spinach in this recipe which will help minimize vitamin losses. Quick cooking over a high heat keeps more of the nutrients in.

FOR 4 GUESTS

PREPARATION TIME: 10 minutes

COOKING TIME: 3 minutes

INGREDIENTS
400 g (14 oz) spinach leaves
25 g (1 oz) unsalted butter
salt and freshly ground
**   black pepper**

METHOD

Remove the tough stalks from the centre of the leaves. Wash the leaves in plenty of cold water, twice if necessary, and drain.

In a large pan, melt the butter and add the spinach leaves. Season with salt and pepper. Cover and cook at a full boil for 2–3 minutes. Remove the lid, stir and cook for a further 1 minute. Taste, correct the seasoning and serve to your guests.

CHEF'S NOTES

If you are having a dinner party, prepare the spinach ready in a casserole dish with butter and cook at the last moment.

Baby Onions

NUTRITIONIST'S
NOTES

Baby onions, like ordinary onions, have many health-giving properties, mainly attributable to their anti-oxidant nutrients. They can help fight colds and infec-tions. In this recipe they are cooked in a caramelized but-tery sauce which raises the fat content just a little but adds a wonderful flavour.

FOR 4 GUESTS

PREPARATION AND COOKING TIME:
20 minutes

PLANNING AHEAD: The onions can be cooked a day in advance and re-heated.

INGREDIENTS
20 g (³/₄ oz) unsalted butter
20 silverskin onions, peeled
4 large pinches of caster
**   sugar**
1 sprig of fresh thyme
salt and freshly ground
**   black pepper**
50 ml (2 fl oz) sherry vinegar

METHOD

Melt the butter in a pan and lightly cook until rich golden brown and foamy. Add the onions, sugar, thyme, salt and pepper and slowly caramelize for 15 minutes, shaking the pan occasionally. Finally deglaze with the sherry vinegar. Serve.

Grilled Summer Vegetables

NUTRITIONIST'S NOTES

Summer vegetables are brimming with vitamin C, folate and beta-carotene. Grilling is one of the healthiest ways of cooking vegetables as it preserves the valuable vitamins and, along with the olive oil, imparts a wonderful flavour. The olive oil is rich in monounsaturated fatty acids.

FOR 4 GUESTS

PREPARATION TIME: 20 minutes

MARINATING TIME: 6–12 hours

COOKING TIME: 10 minutes plus

SPECIAL EQUIPMENT: A ridged cast-iron grill pan

PLANNING AHEAD: The vegetables can be grilled a few hours before the meal and re-heated.

INGREDIENTS

2 courgettes, cut lengthways into 3 mm (⅛ in) slices
1 aubergine, cut widthways into 5 mm (¼ in) slices

1 red pepper, skinned, halved, seeded, each half cut in two
2 tomatoes, skinned, halved and seeded
salt and freshly ground black pepper
2 tablespoons balsamic vinegar

FOR THE MARINADE
100 ml (3½ fl oz) extra virgin olive oil
2 garlic cloves, peeled and sliced
4 sprigs of fresh thyme or a large pinch of dried thyme
6 fresh basil leaves

METHOD

1 · Marinating the vegetables
Mix all the prepared vegetables with the ingredients of the marinade. Stir so they are coated with the olive oil. Cover with cling film and marinate at room temperature for 6–12 hours.

2 · Grilling the vegetables
Brush the pan with the marinade, place on medium heat and grill:
      courgettes and tomatoes, 2 minutes on each side;
      aubergines and peppers, 4 minutes on each side.

3 · To finish
Taste and season with salt and pepper. Place on to a serving dish and sprinkle with the balsamic vinegar. Serve to your guests.

VARIATIONS
Other vegetables such as lettuce, chicory and fennel grill very well but need to be blanched first for 30–60 seconds.

CHEF'S NOTES

See Cooking Techniques, Marinating, p. 42.

The short cooking time helps to keep the vegetables firm.

Grilled Summer
Vegetables

Carrots with Parsley

FOR 4 GUESTS

PREPARATION TIME: 10 minutes

COOKING TIME: 20 minutes

INGREDIENTS

1½ tablespoons unsalted butter

2 shallots, peeled and finely chopped

4 large carrots, sliced about 3 mm (⅛ in) thick

½ garlic clove, peeled and crushed

100 ml (3½ fl oz) water

salt and freshly ground white pepper

2 tablespoons finely chopped fresh parsley

100 ml (3½ fl oz) whipping cream (optional)

NUTRITIONIST'S NOTES

Carrots are packed with beta-carotene and in this recipe are served with parsley, also an excellent source of anti-oxidants. Eating parsley after garlic helps to neutralize your breath! The cream is optional, so you can control your fat intake.

METHOD

Melt the butter in a pan and sweat the shallot in this for 2–3 minutes. Add the carrots and stir so they are all coated in the butter. Add the garlic and water, cover with a lid and cook for 15–20 minutes over a gentle heat. Season with salt and pepper.

Add the chopped parsley and the cream, if using, and cook for a further 3 minutes. Serve to your guests.

CHEF'S NOTE

Too often recipes stipulate that the parsley should be chopped then wrung out in a cloth. I find this method uninspired as it removes most of the taste and the lovely texture. Wash and dry the parsley first, *then* chop.

Peas with Lettuce and Bacon

FOR 4 GUESTS

PREPARATION AND COOKING TIME: 20 minutes

INGREDIENTS

1 English lettuce

100 ml (3½ fl oz) water

30 g (1¼ oz) unsalted butter

salt and freshly ground black pepper

1 teaspoon caster sugar

400 g (14 oz) very young podded peas

2 tablespoons very finely chopped smoked streaky bacon

NUTRITIONIST'S NOTES

Peas contain good amounts of protein, fibre, beta-carotene and vitamin C. The soluble type of fibre in peas can help to reduce high blood cholesterol levels and also control blood sugar levels. The younger the peas, the higher the vitamin C content.

SCIENTIST'S
NOTES

The quality of peas depends on how long they have been away from the parent plant. The cells in vegetables carry on working after they are removed from the source of food and water, and this changes the internal composition of the vegetable. Peas can become drier and starchier, losing up to 40 per cent of their sugar, in less than half a day of being picked. Like corn on the cob, peas really should be picked and popped into the pot straight away.

Peas which are to be frozen are blanched within a few hours of picking. This stops the internal enzyme activity and keeps the peas sweet.

NUTRITIONIST'S NOTES

Parsley is very rich in iron, folate and beta-carotene. In large quantities, it can have a natural diuretic effect, helping prevent or alleviate excessive water retention. Deep-frying parsley obviously adds fat and calories, but it is the healthy polyunsaturated type of fat. Corn oil is also high in vitamin E.

METHOD

1 · Preparing the lettuce

Discard the outer leaves of the lettuce, cut off the root, free the leaves and wash them in plenty of water. Drain and reserve.

2 · Cooking the dish

In a pan, mix together the water, butter, a pinch each of salt and pepper and the sugar. Add the lettuce leaves, cover and cook for 30 seconds.

Add the peas and bacon, cover and cook for 2 more minutes. Taste and correct seasoning. Serve to your guests.

CHEF'S NOTES

In this recipe, very young peas are used which need hardly any cooking. However, if you use more mature peas, increase the cooking time accordingly. (If using frozen peas, obviously follow packet instructions.)

Deep-fried Parsley

FOR 4 GUESTS

PREPARATION AND COOKING TIME:
About 5 minutes

INGREDIENTS
8 sprigs of fresh parsley
500 ml (17 fl oz) corn oil

METHOD

Pick the parsley into smaller sprigs. Wash thoroughly in cold water, then dry even more thoroughly.

Heat the oil to 160°C (325°F). Deep-fry the parsley for 30 seconds only, then drain well on kitchen paper.

VARIATIONS

Other green herbs, such as basil and sage, can be deep-fried as well.

CHEF'S NOTES

Parsley contains very large amounts of vitamin C. This vitamin, or ascorbic acid, is water-soluble, and is easily lost when cooked in water. Deep-frying parsley, therefore, actually preserves more of the herb's vitamin content than stirring it, chopped, into a hot braise or sauce.

Desserts

Medley of Summer Fruits
in Raspberry and Strawberry Sauce
(see p. 280)

Vanilla Crème Brûlée

The traditional recipe, made with double cream, is rich and delicious, but punishment soon follows. This recipe tastes as good but is much lighter. Although we use milk, the richness in texture and colour is achieved by binding the milk with egg yolks, to give a wonderful result ... and no guilt either!

FOR 4 GUESTS

PREPARATION TIME: 15 minutes

COOKING TIME: 30 minutes

SPECIAL EQUIPMENT: 4 ramekins 10 cm (4 in) in diameter, or 2 white china egg dishes (Apilco size 2).

PLANNING AHEAD: This dish can be prepared 3 or 4 hours in advance.

INGREDIENTS
1 vanilla pod
300 ml (10 fl oz) milk
4 free-range egg yolks
40 g (1½ oz) caster sugar
40 g (1½ oz) demerara sugar

NUTRITIONIST'S NOTES

Replacing the double cream in the traditional recipe with milk dramatically reduces the fat content. What's more, it improves the nutrition score a good deal too. Milk is one of the best sources of bone-strengthening calcium. The amount used in this dish will supply around one-half of an adult's daily needs for calcium. Milk also gives you protein, B vitamins and other minerals.

Egg yolks contain some fat but they are also rich in many vitamins and minerals, especially B vitamins and vitamins A and D.

METHOD

1 · Preparing the cream
With a small sharp knife, split the vanilla pod lengthways. With the back of the blade, scrape off all the seeds which are inside the pod. Chop the pod finely. Bring the milk to the boil in a pan with the vanilla seeds and chopped pod. Cook for a further 5 minutes at a gentle simmer. Turn off the heat and reserve.

In a mixing bowl, whisk the egg yolks and caster sugar together until a pale straw colour. Pour the hot milk on to the egg yolk mixture. Mix well, then strain the milk and egg yolk mixture through a fine sieve into a clean pan, pressing on the vanilla pods and seeds to extract as much flavour as possible. Spoon off any foam from the surface. Reserve.

2 · Cooking the cream
Pre-heat the oven to 140°C/275°F/Gas 1.

Pour equal quantities of the mixture into each of the four ramekins or egg dishes. Line a deep roasting tray or dish just large enough to hold the ramekins, with kitchen paper. Place the filled ramekins into this, on top of the paper. Add enough boiling water to the tray or dish to reach three-quarters of the height of the ramekins. Place the tray into the pre-heated oven and cook for about 30 minutes until the mixture has just set.

When the mixture has set, remove each ramekin from the water and allow to cool down at room temperature. When cold, chill for at least 1 hour.

3 · Caramelizing the cream

Pre-heat the grill.

Sprinkle the demerara sugar over the top of each cream, and caramelize under the pre-heated hot grill for 2–3 minutes according to its strength. Leave to cool and set.

4 · Serving

Place the ramekins on serving plates, and serve to your guests.

VARIATIONS

You can achieve different flavours by adding grated lemon rind, lemon or orange juice, or any liqueur to the cream.

CHEF'S NOTES

Demerara sugar is untreated cane sugar. It holds certain impurities, and its melting point is lower than caster sugar, so it will caramelize more easily.

———

Boiling the milk kills all bacteria and germs. Simmering gently for 5 minutes releases the essential oils contained within the vanilla seeds and pod.

———

Placing kitchen paper under the ramekins whilst cooking will serve as a form of insulation against the strong heat from the oven and prevent it from overcooking them.

———

The water must be boiling when poured into the bain-marie or water-bath tray. It is important that the water level reaches three-quarters up the height of the ramekins. Too often mistakes occur when the dry heat of the oven overcooks the cream, losing that magic melting texture.

———

You need to pre-heat the grill so the heat is very strong and will caramelize the sugar very quickly. If the heat is not strong enough, it will heat the cream up and overcook it. The idea is to create a delightful layer of crisp caramel on top.

Blackcurrant Mousse

FOR 6 GUESTS

PREPARATION TIME: About 1 hour

COOKING TIME: About 15 minutes

RESTING TIME: At least 4 hours

SPECIAL EQUIPMENT: A cake ring 16 cm (6¼ in) in diameter and 4 cm (1½ in) high; a cake board of the same diameter; a piping bag and a large plain nozzle, 8 mm (¾ in) in diameter; a baking tray 30×40 cm (12×16 in); a sugar thermometer; greaseproof paper.

PLANNING AHEAD: This dessert can be made the day before and kept in the fridge covered with cling film to prevent any alteration of flavour.

INGREDIENTS

FOR THE SPONGE
2 eggs, separated
40 g (1½ oz) caster sugar
40 g (1½ oz) plain flour
40 g (1½ oz) icing sugar, sifted

FOR THE BLACKCURRANT PUREE
1 kg (2¼ lb) whole blackcurrants

FOR THE SYRUP
30 g (1¼ oz) caster sugar
2 tablespoons water

50 g (2 oz) blackcurrant purée or Crème de Cassis liqueur (see step 5)

FOR THE BLACKCURRANT MOUSSE
2 gelatine leaves, soaked in cold water to soften, or ¼ teaspoon powdered gelatine
150 g (5 oz) blackcurrant purée
40 g (1½ oz) caster sugar
50 ml (2 fl oz) whipping cream

FOR THE ITALIAN MERINGUE
60 g (2¼ oz) caster sugar
2 tablespoons water
1 egg white
50 g (2 oz) blackcurrant purée

FOR THE GLAZE
50 g (2 oz) blackcurrant purée
20 g (¾ oz) caster sugar
½ gelatine leaf, soaked in cold water to soften

FOR THE BLACKCURRANT COULIS
AND GARNISH
350 g (12 oz) blackcurrant purée
50 g (2 oz) caster sugar
100 g (4 oz) whole fresh blackcurrants

METHOD

1 · Preparing the sponge mixture (see also Sponge-making, p. 47)
On a medium speed, beat the egg whites to form soft peaks. Gradually add the caster sugar and continue to beat until firm peaks are achieved.

At a lower speed, add the egg yolks, and carry on beating

until well mixed in. With a spatula, fold the flour in gently until well incorporated. Do not try to achieve a perfect mix.

2 · Piping the sponge

Place ¹/₂ teaspoon of the sponge mixture on to each corner of the baking sheet and place a sheet of greaseproof paper securely on the top. This holds the paper in place whilst baking.

Place the sponge mixture into the piping bag and pipe sponge fingers on to the paper 10 cm (4 in) in length. These should be touching each other and will form a strip 25 cm (10 in) wide. With the remaining sponge, pipe one disc of sponge 14 cm (5¹/₂ in) in diameter beside the sponge fingers. These measurements are important, as the sponge strips and disc will be used to fill the cake ring exactly.

3 · Baking the sponge

Pre-heat the oven to 180°C/350°F/Gas 4.

Dust the strips of sponge with icing sugar then leave for 30 minutes. Dust them again with icing sugar and then bake in the pre-heated oven for about 8–10 minutes. Cooking times can vary according to the type of oven used; but you want a light blond colour and a spongy texture.

When cooked, remove the sponge from the oven and then from the baking tray on to a wire rack to cool. Reserve at room temperature.

4 · Making the blackcurrant purée

Bring about 3 litres (5¹/₄ pints) of water to the boil and blanch the blackcurrants in this for about 20 seconds. Drain well, then liquidize and rub through a fine sieve, extracting as much purée as you can. You should have about 650 g (a scant 1¹/₂ lb) purée: 50 g (2 oz) for the syrup, 150 g (5 oz) for the mousse, 50 g (2 oz) for the meringue, 50 g (2 oz) for the glaze, and 350 g (12 oz) for the coulis. Reserve.

5 · Making the syrup

In a small pan, bring the caster sugar and water to the boil. Add the measured amount of blackcurrant purée, and reserve. If you use the Cassis instead of the purée, use it as it is, do not add water or sugar.

6 · Preparing the sponge base

Place the cake ring on the cake board.

Pull the greaseproof paper carefully from the sponge strips and disc. Trim both ends of the strips slightly with a serrated

NUTRITIONIST'S NOTES

Blackcurrants, the main ingredient in this recipe, are a superb source of vitamin C – far richer than oranges on a weight-for-weight basis. However, some of the vitamin content is lost during cooking so ensure that you blanch them for the briefest time only. Overall, this recipe is low in fat as it contains only a small amount of cream. It is high in sugar but this is needed to counteract the acidity and tartness of the blackcurrants.

knife, and slice lengthways into two halves. Place both halves of the sponge strips around the inside of the cake ring, top crust facing outwards and the wavy edges at the top. Soak with some of the blackcurrant syrup or Crème de Cassis liqueur.

Place the sponge disc carefully into the sponge-sided ring. Using a pastry brush, soak the sponge disc with the remaining blackcurrant syrup (or Crème de Cassis) Reserve.

7 · *Starting the blackcurrant mousse*

If using the gelatine powder, dilute with a little hot water.

Bring the mousse blackcurrant purée, plus the caster sugar, up to 40°C (104°F). Add the softened gelatine leaves or powder and stir in. Reserve.

8 · *Making the Italian meringue*

Bring the caster sugar and water to the boil and cook up to 120°C (248°F).

On a high speed, whisk the egg white to soft peaks then pour the cooked sugar syrup on to the egg white, between the beaters and edge of bowl. Carry on beating on a medium speed until the mixture is cold.

When cool, still beating, add the meringue blackcurrant purée and carry on beating for 1 minute. Beat for a further 2 minutes to increase the volume of the egg white mixture even more.

9 · *Finishing the mousse*

Whip the cream to a soft peak, and fold in the gelatine and blackcurrant mixture, and then the Italian meringue. Pour all this into the sponge-lined ring, and smooth the top with a small palette knife. Reserve in the fridge for at least 4 hours.

10 · *Glazing the cake*

In a stainless-steel pan, bring the glaze blackcurrant purée and caster sugar to 40°C (104°F), and add the softened gelatine. Leave to cool until at room temperature.

Remove the cake from the fridge and pour the glaze on to it. Swirl the cake round until the glaze covers the whole top. Replace the cake in the fridge to allow the glaze to set.

11 · *Making the blackcurrant coulis and garnish*

Mix the coulis blackcurrant purée and the caster sugar together, and reserve in the fridge.

For the garnish, place 1 tablespoon of the blackcurrant coulis in a small container. Add the fresh blackcurrants and toss gently so the blackcurrants are well coated.

Remove the glazed cake from the fridge and scatter the coated fruit over the top.

12 · *Serving*

Heat the blade of a knife and cut the cake into six equal portions. Place each portion on a plate and pour the blackcurrant coulis around. Serve to your guests.

VARIATIONS

You could serve this dessert with Vanilla Ice-cream (see p. 279).

If you want to simplify the dish, omit the sponge completely, and serve the blackcurrant mousse by itself in glass bowls.

C H E F ' S   N O T E S

The first coating of icing sugar on the sponge will melt a little bit (as the first snow would). The second will not, and it will create a nice shiny and crunchy crust which will also give some strength to the sponge strips.

Placing the blackcurrants into boiling water for 20 seconds and then draining them straight away will only partly cook the fruit, thus retaining some of its freshness.

Black Cherry Tart

Black Cherry Tart

FOR 4 GUESTS

PREPARATION TIME: 45 minutes

COOKING TIME: 40 minutes

SPECIAL EQUIPMENT: A tart tin with removable base, 18 cm (7½ in) in diameter, 2.5 cm (1 in) in height.

PLANNING AHEAD: The sweet pastry must be made at least 2 hours in advance, but can also be prepared the day before. This type of pastry is suitable for freezing.

INGREDIENTS
20 g (¾ oz) unsalted butter, softened
2 tablespoons caster sugar
1 tablespoon plain flour
350 g (12 oz) black cherries, pitted

FOR THE SWEET PASTRY
60 g (2¼ oz) unsalted butter
30 g (1¼ oz) icing sugar
2 egg yolks
120 g (4½ oz) plain flour

METHOD

1 · *Making the sweet pastry*

In a bowl, beat the butter until a white 'cream' has formed.

Beat in the icing sugar and egg yolks. Sift in the plain flour and, with your fingertips, rub in until you obtain a sandy texture. Press together. Place on your work surface and with the palm of your hand knead the dough until smooth. Wrap the dough in cling film and allow to rest in the fridge for at least 2 hours.

2 · Lining the tart tin

With a pastry brush grease the inside of the tart tin with the softened unsalted butter. Reserve.

On a lightly floured surface, roll the sweet pastry out into a 25 cm (10 in) circle. Place the circle on to the tart tin and press it down into the tin using your thumb. Use the blade of a knife to trim any excess at the top on the rim.

3 · Cooking the tart

Pre-heat the oven to 180°C/350°F/Gas 4.

Mix together the sugar and the plain flour and sprinkle the mixture over the bottom of the pastry-lined tin. Place the pitted cherries on the base of the tart tin, and bake in the pre-heated oven for about 30–40 minutes. Remove from the oven and allow to cool on a wire rack.

4 · Serving

Remove the sides of the tin, and place the tart on a serving dish. Present to your guests, then cut into wedges.

VARIATIONS

Black cherries can be replaced by Morello cherries, plums or apricots. You might have to alter the amount of sugar sprinkled on the base of the tart, according to the sweetness of the fruit used.

CHEF'S NOTES

The cherries will release some of their juices whilst cooking. The flour will absorb this moisture and thicken to produce a cream, thus preventing the pastry from becoming soggy. The sugar will act as a sweetening agent in this cream.

NUTRITIONIST'S
NOTES

Black cherries are naturally high in fruit sugars so need relatively little extra sugar to bring out their flavour. They provide modest amounts of fibre to this dish as well as vitamin C, potassium and beta-carotene. The extra egg yolks in the sweet pastry add some useful vitamins, but they also bump up the overall fat content of the pastry.

Apple Mousse with Apple and Vanilla Sauce

NUTRITIONIST'S NOTES

Much of the sweetness of this recipe comes from the natural sugars in the apples. Very little extra sugar needs to be added to the apple mousse since the apples and the cider or juice provide plenty of flavour and sweetness. Apples also provide fibre and potassium and small amounts of vitamin C. The mousse is fairly high in saturated fat due to the whipping cream.

FOR 8 GUESTS

PREPARATION AND COOKING TIME: 1 hour

SPECIAL EQUIPMENT: A cake tin, 20 cm (8 in) in diameter and 4.5 cm ($1^{3}/_{4}$ in) high.

PLANNING AHEAD: The dessert can be made the day before and kept in the fridge, covered with cling film.

INGREDIENTS

FOR THE APPLE MOUSSE
400 ml (14 fl oz) dry farm cider or good-quality apple juice
4 small Granny Smith apples
175 ml (6 fl oz) water

20 g ($^{3}/_{4}$ oz) caster sugar
a dash of lemon juice
4 gelatine leaves, soaked in cold water to soften
300 ml (10 fl oz) whipping cream
50 ml (2 fl oz) calvados

FOR THE CARAMELIZED APPLE
4 Granny Smith apples
80 g ($3^{1}/_{4}$ oz) caster sugar
4 teaspoons calvados

FOR THE APPLE AND VANILLA SAUCE
4 Granny Smith apples
100 ml ($3^{1}/_{2}$ fl oz) water
50 g (2 oz) caster sugar
juice of $^{1}/_{4}$ lemon
$^{1}/_{2}$ vanilla pod, halved

METHOD

1 · Preparing the caramelized apple
Peel, quarter and core the apples. Cut each quarter into three wedges.

Place a non-stick frying pan over a strong heat. Add the caster sugar and cook to a blond caramel. Place in the apple segments and sauté, turning them from time to time to allow even caramelization and cooking.

Lower the heat and carry on cooking until the apple pieces are *al dente*.

Remove from the heat and pour in the calvados. Remove the caramelized pieces of apple to a plate, allow to cool, then reserve.

2 · Lining the cake tin
Place the caramelized apple segments in the tin, flat edges down, covering the base and the sides of the cake tin. The caramel on the apple pieces should make them stick to the tin.

3 · Preparing the mousse
Boil to reduce the cider or apple juice until 6 tablespoons are left. Reserve.

Apple Mousse (see p. 255)

Peel, core and cut the apples into pieces, and place them in a pan. Add the water, sugar and lemon juice and bring to the boil. Simmer for about 10 minutes or until the apples have softened.

Liquidize in a blender, then rub through a sieve. Add the softened gelatine and reduced cider, stir and allow to cool down at room temperature.

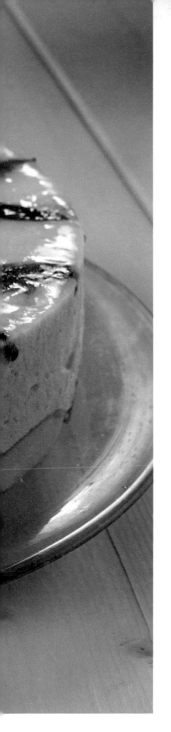

Whip the cream to soft peaks, and fold into the apple compote mixture along with the calvados.

Pour the mixture carefully into the tin lined with the caramelized apple. Smooth the top and allow to set in the fridge for a minimum of 2 hours.

4 · Making the sauce

Peel, core and chop the apples into 1 cm (½ in) cubes. Place the cubes in a saucepan with the water, sugar, lemon juice and vanilla pod and seeds, and simmer for 10 minutes. Liquidize and push the sauce through a fine sieve. Cool, then reserve.

5 · Serving

Place some hot water in a large bowl. Dip the cake tin carefully in this up to the rim, then turn the tin upside down on to a serving plate. Lift the cake tin up and away from the mousse.

Pour the apple sauce into a sauceboat.

Present and serve a wedge of mousse to your guests, with a side accompaniment of apple and vanilla sauce.

VARIATIONS

Apple Sorbet with Dried Apple Slices (p. 272) could also be served as an accompaniment for this dessert.

Apple jelly or apricot jam can be slightly heated and brushed all over the apple mousse.

CHEF'S NOTES

Strong heat is necessary to ensure that the caramelization of the sugar, then of the apple, takes place. Lowering the heat will allow the cooking process to continue without burning the apples. Cooking the apples until *al dente* only, brings some texture to the whole dish.

Adding calvados at the end of the caramelization of the apple segments will dissolve the caramel stuck in the pan and nicely coat each piece of apple.

Reducing the cider concentrates the apple flavour.

Dipping the cake tin into hot water right up to the rim, slightly melts the inside coating and makes the removal of the mousse very much easier.

Bitter Chocolate Charlotte

FOR 6 GUESTS

PREPARATION TIME: About 30 minutes

COOKING TIME: 8–10 minutes

CHILLING TIME: 1 hour

SPECIAL EQUIPMENT: A cake ring 16 cm (6$\frac{1}{4}$ in) in diameter; a cake board the same size; a piping bag and a large plain nozzle, 8 mm ($\frac{3}{4}$ in) in diameter; a sheet of greaseproof paper; a baking tray 30×40 cm (12×16 in); a sugar thermometer.

PLANNING AHEAD: This dessert can be made the day before and kept in the fridge covered with cling film to prevent any alteration of flavour.

INGREDIENTS

FOR THE SPONGE
2 eggs, separated
40 g (1$\frac{1}{2}$ oz) caster sugar
40 g (1$\frac{1}{2}$ oz) plain flour
40 g (1$\frac{1}{2}$ oz) icing sugar, sifted
1 quantity Stock Syrup (see p. 66)

FOR THE CHOCOLATE MOUSSE
120 g (4$\frac{1}{2}$ oz) very best extra bitter chocolate
175 ml (6 fl oz) whipping cream

FOR THE GLAZE
35 ml (1$\frac{1}{4}$ fl oz) whipping cream
25 g (1 oz) very best extra bitter chocolate

METHOD

1 · Preparing the sponge mixture (see also Sponge-making, p. 47)
On a medium speed, beat the egg whites to form soft peaks. Gradually add the caster sugar and continue to beat until firm peaks are achieved.

At a lower speed, add the egg yolks, and carry on beating until well mixed in. With a spatula fold in the flour gently until well incorporated. Do not try to achieve a perfect mix.

2 · Piping the sponge
Pre-heat the oven to 180°C/350°F/Gas 4.

Place $\frac{1}{2}$ teaspoon of the sponge mixture on to each corner of the baking tray, and place the sheet of greaseproof paper securely on the top. This holds the sheet of paper in place, whilst baking. If you like, mark the shapes of sponge required (see below) in pencil on the paper.

Place the sponge mixture into the piping bag and pipe sponge fingers on to the paper, 10 cm (4 in) in length. These should be touching each other and will form a strip 25 cm (10 in) wide.

NUTRITIONIST'S
NOTES

Keep this dessert for special occasions as it's rather high in fat and sugar! The chocolate and cream bump up the calorie and fat content, but it's more important to enjoy the taste than worry about the nutritional value here!

With the remaining sponge, pipe one disc of sponge 14 cm (5½ in) in diameter beside the sponge fingers. These measurements are important, as the sponge strips and disc will be used to fill the cake ring exactly.

3 · Baking the sponge

Lightly dust the strips of sponge with icing sugar then leave for 30 minutes. Dust them again with icing sugar and then bake in the pre-heated oven for about 8–10 minutes until light blond in colour. The icing sugar will give a nice shiny crunchy crust, and also gives the sponge some strength.

When cooked, remove the sponge from the oven, and then from the baking tray on to a wire rack to cool. Reserve at room temperature.

4 · Preparing the sponge base

Pull the greaseproof paper carefully from the sponge strips and disc. Trim both ends of the strips slightly with a serrated knife, and slice in half lengthways.

Place the cake ring on the cake board. Place both halves of the sponge strips around the inside of the cake ring, top crust facing outwards and the wavy edges at the top. Using a pastry brush, soak the sponge with the syrup. Place the sponge disc into the ring, and soak it with syrup as well.

5 · Making the chocolate mousse

On a low heat melt the chocolate in a bowl over a pan of simmering water, or in a bain-marie, up to 45°C (84°F), then remove from the heat and cool a little.

While the chocolate is melting, whip the cream up to soft peaks. Add one-third of the whipped cream to the melted chocolate and mix in very well. Add the remaining cream and fold in with a spatula until well incorporated but not overmixed. Pour the chocolate mousse into the sponge-lined ring and smooth the top with a palette knife. Place in the fridge for about an hour.

6 · Glazing the charlotte

In a pan, bring the cream to the boil. Flake the chocolate, then pour the boiling cream on top of it. Leave the chocolate mixture to one side for 2 minutes and then stir until smooth.

Remove the cake from the fridge and pour the glaze on to it. Swirl the cake round until the glaze covers the whole top. Replace the cake in the fridge until the glaze has set.

7 · Serving

Remove the cake ring carefully, and present and serve to your guests.

C H E F ' S   N O T E S

The sponge cooking time can vary depending on the make and type of oven used. However, the light blond colour you can see of the sponge, through the greaseproof paper, and its spongy texture, are foolproof methods of checking that the sponge is correctly cooked.

Placing the sponge on a wire rack will prevent it from drying out on the heat of the hot baking tray. It will also cool down much more quickly.

If the chocolate were subjected to a strong heat, it would become grainy. The occasional stirring will help to distribute the heat evenly.

Adding a third of the whipped cream to the melted chocolate and mixing it very well, ensures the future smoothness of the mousse: it dilutes the chocolate, which will then not set so easily.

Whipped cream is a delicate and unstable foam. If overmixed, the chocolate mousse will split, you will lose at least one-third in volume, and the texture will be heavy and grainy.

Only 2 minutes are necessary for the heat of the cream to go through the chocolate pieces and ensure the smoothness of the glaze.

Millefeuilles of Shortbread and Raspberries

SCIENTIST'S NOTES

The purple and red colours of fruits and vegetables are caused by a group of compounds called anthocyanins. These compounds are not stable as they depend on how acid or alkaline the mixture is. Increasing acidity, say, by adding lemon juice, will normally make the colour more red-purple, and reducing the acidity (making it more alkaline) will move the colour towards green-yellow. (Litmus paper works just like this.) A simple experiment with some fresh red fruit juice or red cabbage water, vinegar and sodium bicarbonate, will show spectacular results.

NUTRITIONIST'S NOTES

Shortbread is traditionally high in fat with the proportion of butter to flour almost equal. In this recipe, the fresh raspberries not only add vibrant colour but they provide a real nutritional boost: lots of vitamin C and extra fibre. There is roughly the same amount of vitamin C in an average 100 g (4 oz) serving of raspberries as in the average orange.

FOR 4 GUESTS

PREPARATION TIME: 30 minutes

COOKING TIME: 10–15 minutes

RESTING TIME: 2 hours

SPECIAL EQUIPMENT: A fluted pastry cutter, 9 cm (3½ in) in diameter.

PLANNING AHEAD: The shortbread pastry must be made at least 2 hours in advance, but can also be prepared the day before. This type of pastry is suitable for freezing.

INGREDIENTS
300 g (11 oz) fresh raspberries
20 g (¾ oz) icing sugar

FOR THE SHORTBREAD PASTRY
50 g (2 oz) icing sugar, sifted
1 egg yolk
100 g (4 oz) unsalted butter, creamed
a pinch of salt
135 g (4¾ oz) plain flour, sifted

FOR THE RASPBERRY SAUCE
250 g (9 oz) fresh raspberries
40 g (1½ oz) caster sugar
juice of ¼ lemon

METHOD

1 · Making the shortbread pastry
In a bowl, mix together the icing sugar, egg yolk, creamed butter and salt. Add the flour and rub together using your fingertips until sandy in texture. Press together to a fairly soft dough.

Lightly flour your work surface and place the dough on it. Knead with the palm of your hand until it is well blended. Wrap in cling film and chill for at least 2 hours to allow it to firm up.

2 · Making the raspberry sauce
Place the raspberries, sugar and lemon juice in a bowl and slightly mash them with a fork. Marinate for about an hour.

When marinated, liquidize in a blender and then rub through a sieve into a bowl, pressing out as much purée as possible with a ladle. Reserve in the refrigerator.

3 · Preparing the shortbread pastry discs
Pre-heat the oven to 160°C/325°F/Gas 3.

On a lightly floured surface, roll the shortbread pastry out into a rectangle 37 × 28 cm (14¾ × 11¼ in). With a fluted pastry cutter, cut out 12 discs. Using a palette knife, carefully slide the discs on to a baking tray, slightly apart to allow for spread. Bake in the pre-heated oven for 10–15 minutes or until a light blond colour. Remove from the oven and allow to cool on a wire rack.

4 · Preparing the raspberries

Pour 2 tablespoons of the raspberry sauce into a very large bowl, then add the fresh raspberries. Shake to coat the raspberries. Reserve.

5 · Serving

Divide the marinated raspberries into two portions. Take four of the pastry discs and place in the centre of four plates. Divide one-half of the raspberries evenly among the four discs. Place another pastry disc on top of the layer of raspberries. Divide the remaining raspberries evenly among the discs.

Slightly dust the four remaining shortbread discs with icing sugar and place them on the top of the last layer of raspberries. Pour the remaining raspberry sauce around the dessert and serve to your guests.

VARIATIONS

Raspberries can be replaced by an equal quantity of any red fruit, maybe a medley of them, or poached pear or peach, using one half poached fruit per layer.

CHEF'S NOTES

Ripeness of the fruit is important otherwise the dish will be flavourless and even unexciting.

Coating the grains of flour with fat keeps the pastry very short, and prevents the gluten developing and linking together. This stops the pastry from becoming tough.

Refrigerating will allow the butter to firm up, which will make the pastry rollable.

Marinating the raspberries with the lemon juice and sugar allows the flavour to increase and also gives to the coulis a deeper red colour.

Using a large bowl will prevent too much mashing of the raspberries.

Sticky Rice with Coconut Milk and Mango

This dish, which is from Thailand, is suitable for a vegan diet. The caramel cages can be rather difficult, which is why they are optional, but they make the dessert look spectacular.

NUTRITIONIST'S NOTES

High in carbohydrate and low in fat, this dish also provides a good balance of vitamins and minerals. The basis of the recipe is rice, a terrific source of complex carbohydrates. Unlike the actual nut, coconut milk is very low in calories and almost fat-free. The pineapple and mangoes contain vitamin C and beta-carotene.

FOR 4 GUESTS

PREPARATION TIME: 1¼ hours

SOAKING TIME: A minimum of 6 hours

STEAMING TIME: 10–15 minutes

COOKING TIME: 20 minutes

SPECIAL EQUIPMENT: The optional items of equipment are for the caramel cages: a rice steamer; a 10 cm (4 in) ladle (optional); a sugar thermometer (optional); and a copper saucepan, 12 cm (4¾ in) in diameter (optional).

PLANNING AHEAD: The rice can be soaked and steamed the day before and re-heated before serving. The pineapple sauce can be made the day before and re-heated before serving.

The caramel cages (if used) can also be prepared the day before, but they must be kept in an airtight container with silica gel crystals (these help absorb moisture, thus avoiding ruining the wonderful work you have done).

The mangoes can be prepared before your guests arrive, and kept chilled until you are ready to serve.

INGREDIENTS

FOR THE RICE
80 g (3¾ oz) glutinous rice
500 ml (17 fl oz) cold water
120 ml (4 fl oz) tinned coconut milk
25 g (1 oz) caster sugar

FOR THE PINEAPPLE SAUCE
1 baby pineapple, approx. 350–400 g (12–14 oz) in weight
50 ml (2 fl oz) tinned coconut milk
1 tablespoon Malibu (coconut liqueur)
1 small pinch of finely ground black pepper
1 level teaspoon cornflour

FOR THE MANGO GARNISH
2 ripe mangoes
juice of ¼ lime

FOR THE CARAMEL CAGES (optional)
6 tablespoons water
250 g (9 oz) caster sugar
50 ml (2 fl oz) liquid glucose syrup
a little vegetable oil

METHOD

1 · Soaking the rice
Place the rice and cold water in a bowl and allow to soak for at least 6 hours.

2 · *Steaming the rice*

Drain the rice from its soaking water and rinse it under cold running water. Place in the steamer over boiling water. Steam for about 10–15 minutes until tender.

Place the rice in another pan with the coconut milk and sugar. Stir in and reserve.

3 · *Making the pineapple sauce*

Peel the baby pineapple, chop it into small pieces and liquidize to a pulp in a food processor. Place the pulp in a pan and add the coconut milk, Malibu, black pepper and cornflour. Bring to the boil, stir well, then sieve into a bowl. Reserve.

4 · *Preparing the mangoes*

Peel the mangoes and cut them into halves on either side of the stone. Place the half mango (flat side down) on a chopping board and chop into 5 mm (¼ in) slices, lengthways *or* widthways. Squeeze a few drops of lime juice on to each sliced half, and reserve.

5 · *Preparing the caramel cages (optional)*

Place 2 litres (3½ pints) of cold water in a bowl. This will be used to cool down the outside of the sugar pan.

Bring the measured water and the sugar to the boil together, then add the glucose syrup and carry on cooking until a light blond caramel colour is reached. Check, using the sugar thermometer, that it is 165°C (330°F).

Place the caramel pan into the bowl of cold water up to the sugar content level for about 30 seconds. Ensure that no cold water goes into the cooked sugar in the pan. The sugar must be hot and runny enough to make the caramel cages.

6 · *Making the caramel cages (optional)*

With your hand, spread a thin film of oil over the back of the ladle (or a large spoon). Have a fork or a spoon ready.

Dip your fork or spoon into the caramel and trickle the thread from it into a thin trellis over the back of the ladle, covering this evenly. The distance between ladle and the fork or spoon must be about 20 cm (8 in). If too far away, the sugar will have time to harden. If too near, the sugar will be too runny and you will not be able to control the flow of the caramel.

Very carefully twist the cage free from the ladle – this can be quite tricky – and place it into the airtight box with the silica gel crystals (not necessary if you serve immediately). By now the

Sticky Rice with
Coconut Milk and Mango
(see p. 263)

caramel left in the pan will have hardened so return it to the heat until softened and repeat the process until you have made four cages.

7 · *Serving*

Re-heat both rice and sauce in two different pans. Divide the rice evenly between warmed plates, making a little dome in the centre. Top with a half of sliced mango. Pour the sauce around the rice. Finally place the caramel cages over the dome of rice and mango, and serve to your guests.

CHEF'S NOTES

Soaking the rice first allows it to be moist and to be cooked by steaming; during the soaking it will absorb some water.

Rinsing the rice after soaking will remove the starch covering the grains of rice after draining.

Adding coconut milk prevents the drying of the steamed rice, but mostly it gives a fine flavour and a creamy texture.

Boiling the sugar and water together before adding the glucose syrup allows the sugar crystals to melt into a syrup. If the glucose syrup were added before, it would coat the sugar crystals and thus stop them melting. You would end up with a grainy caramel.

Below 165°C (330°F) the sugar syrup will still have a high water level, when it will be sticky and will not hold the shape of the cage for very long. If the sugar is boiled past 170°C (338°F), the caramel will lose its strength and then become runny. A caramel which is overcooked will also have a very bitter flavour.

To make the caramel cages with a spoon or fork is not easy, I know, so I have devised a piece of a equipment which makes it child's play – no skill is necessary. A wire coat hanger from the dry cleaners can become very useful. Cut the straight wires (base) into 8 × 25 cm (10 in) length pieces. Bind 8 wires together tightly with either wire or string at the top. Open up the 'teeth' of the wires in a circular shape, then the whole process becomes very easy. Dip into the caramel and with short wrist movements thread the caramel on to the ladle.

Poached Pears with Cassis Coulis

FOR 4 GUESTS

PREPARATION TIME: 30 minutes

COOKING TIME: 15 minutes

COOLING TIME: 2 hours

SPECIAL EQUIPMENT: A potato peeler; a Parisian scoop; an 18 cm (7 in) stainless steel saucepan; an 18 cm (7 in) disc of greaseproof paper.

PLANNING AHEAD: The pears have to be poached at least 2 hours in advance to allow them to cool down in their juices; they can be poached the day before and kept in the fridge until served. The blackcurrant coulis can be prepared up to a day in advance and kept in the fridge until served.

INGREDIENTS

4 ripe pears, about 175 g (6 oz) each (Guyot or Williams)
1 litre (1¾ pints) water
200 g (7 oz) caster sugar
½ vanilla pod
juice of ½ lemon

FOR THE BLACKCURRANT COULIS

1 litre (1¾ pints) water
250 g (9 oz) fresh blackcurrants (weighed after picking from stalks)
50 g (2 oz) caster sugar

NUTRITIONIST'S
NOTES

Both pears and blackcurrants contain vitamins, minerals and fibre. Blackcurrants are one of the best sources of vitamin C which helps keep our gums and blood vessels healthy, boosts the immune system and helps make healthy red blood cells. In fact, just 25 g (1 oz) will give you all you need for one day.

This recipe is very low in fat which would make it a good choice for ending a rich meal. The sugar content is fairly high, but this helps balance out the acidity of the black-currants.

METHOD

1 · Preparing and cooking the pears

With a potato peeler, peel the pears very carefully, leaving the stalk on and not marking the fruit too deeply. Reserve.

In the stainless steel pan, bring the water, caster sugar and vanilla pod to the boil. Place the peeled pears and lemon juice into the pan and cover with the greaseproof paper disc. Bring back to the boil and simmer for 4–6 minutes.

Remove the pan from the heat and leave the pears to cool for about 2 hours in the cooking juices or until they are at room temperature. Reserve in the fridge if you are not serving the pears immediately.

2 · Preparing the blackcurrant coulis

Bring the water to the boil in a large pan. Put 200 g (7 oz) of the blackcurrants into the boiling water for about 20 seconds, then drain through a sieve. Place the partly cooked blackcurrants into a liquidizer or food processor and liquidize. Pass through a sieve into a bowl, pressing as much as you can out of the purée. Stir in the sugar and if the purée is too thick, loosen with a little water.

3 · Serving

Drain the pears from their cooking juices. If you like, using a Parisian scoop, you can very carefully remove the core from each pear. Trim the wide bottom of each pear slightly to allow them to stand up. Place each one in the centre of a plate.

In a small container, place 2 tablespoons of the blackcurrant coulis and the remaining fresh blackcurrants. Mix gently to coat the blackcurrants. Pour the remaining blackcurrant coulis equally around each pear, then sprinkle around the coated fresh black-currants. Serve to your guests.

VARIATIONS
A Chantilly cream – sweetened cream flavoured with something like vanilla or Champagne – or fresh cream can be served with the pears.

C H E F ' S   N O T E S

The lemon juice will stop the pear turning a rusty colour, and will bring up the pear flavour. (See also the Scientist's Note on p. 99.)

The disc of greaseproof paper on the top of the pears keeps them in the liquid, allows them to cook evenly and, particularly important, prevents brown rings on the pears due to them floating whilst cooking.

Leaving the pears to cool in their own juices is part of the cooking process: this allows the heat to filter through to the core of the pear.

You might need to add more sugar or water to the blackcurrant coulis depending on the sugar or pectin level. If it tastes too acidic, add sugar; if it is too thick (due to a high pectin level), add 1 tablespoon of water.

Cooking the pears *with* the cores allows the pears to keep their shape. The cores are also easier to remove when cooked, because they are slightly softened.

Apple Fritters with Vanilla and Cinnamon Sauce

FOR 4 GUESTS

PREPARATION TIME: 30 minutes, plus
1 hour proving.

COOKING TIME: 30 minutes

SPECIAL EQUIPMENT: An apple corer;
an oil thermometer.

PLANNING AHEAD: This dessert can
be prepared a few hours in advance,
but the *beignets* must be cooked at
the last minute.

INGREDIENTS

90 ml (3 fl oz) beer
1 egg yolk
a pinch of ground cinnamon
1 teaspoon dried yeast
100 g (4 oz) plain flour
2 teaspoons caster sugar
3 egg whites
a few drops of lemon juice
2 teaspoons caster sugar
 mixed with ¼ teaspoon
 salt

FOR THE APPLES
5 Granny Smith apples,
 about 675 g (1½ lb)
50 g (2 oz) unsalted butter
50 g (2 oz) caster sugar
1 tablespoon calvados
 (optional)
1 litre (1¾ pints) vegetable
 oil for deep-frying
200 g (7 oz) plain flour

FOR THE VANILLA AND
CINNAMON SAUCE
1 vanilla pod
250 ml (8 fl oz) milk
¼ cinnamon stick
3 egg yolks
40 g (1½ oz) caster sugar

TO FINISH
100 g (4 oz) icing sugar,
 sifted

METHOD

1 · Preparing the batter base

In a bowl, mix together the beer, egg yolk, cinnamon and yeast. Add the flour and caster sugar and mix well again. It will be fairly thick.

Place a piece of cling film on top of the mixture and allow it to prove for 1 hour at room temperature (at about 22–24°C/71–75°F).

2 · Preparing the apples

Peel and core the apples. Slice the apples across into 5 mm (¼ in) rings. Reserve.

On a medium heat, in a non-stick frying pan, cook the butter and sugar together until you have a blond caramel. Pan-fry each apple ring in this on both sides for 1 minute. Add the calvados,

SCIENTIST'S
NOTES

Apples, like other fruits, consist mainly of water and of carbohydrates, the latter amounting to just under 10 per cent of the total. Firmness and its retention in cooking depends on the relative proportions of the three types of carbohydrates: starch, sugar and cellulose (fibre). During ripening these proportions change; in particular, starch is converted into sugar.

.

Yeasts are organisms whose cells contain a variety of enzymes which trigger off the chemical reaction known as fermentation. In alcoholic fermentation, sugar or starch is converted into alcohol, while 'baker's yeast' transforms starch into sugar, generating carbon dioxide gas which forms the bubbles in the dough: hence its being termed a 'raising agent'. Enzyme activity is sensitive to temperature. If this is too high (say above 50°C/122°F), the enzyme may be destroyed; if it is too low, the activity becomes sluggish. Yeast only acts in a liquid medium (water, milk) and for maximum efficiency it must be well dispersed. Yeast must not be confused with baking powder, another raising agent consisting of two or three simple chemical compounds which when dissolved and heated also generate carbon dioxide.

if using, turn off the heat and rest the apples for a couple of minutes in their own cooking juices. Reserve on a plate.

3 · Making the vanilla and cinnamon sauce

Cut the vanilla pod in half lengthways and scrape out all the seeds. Chop the pod finely. Combine the milk, cinnamon stick, vanilla seeds and chopped pod in a heavy-based pan. Bring to the boil and simmer for about 5 minutes. Remove from the heat.

In a large mixing bowl, whisk together the egg yolks and sugar until a pale straw colour. Pour the hot milk on to the egg and sugar mixture, whisking continuously, then return the mixture to the pan on a medium heat; stir for a few minutes until it thickens and coats the back of a wooden spoon. Strain immediately into a bowl through a fine sieve. Stir for a few minutes, then place the bowl into a bowl of ice to cool it down quickly. When cold, keep in the fridge.

4 · Finishing the batter

In an electric mixer, whisk the egg whites with a few drops of lemon juice to soft peaks. Add the caster sugar and salt, and carry on whisking until the whites form to firm peaks.

Using a spatula, briskly fold half of the whipped egg white into the proved batter base. Then delicately fold in the other half of the egg white.

5 · Deep-frying the apple rings

Pre-heat the oil to 160°C (325°F).

Roll each of the apple rings in the plain flour, and shake off any excess. Dip as many rings as will fit into your deep-fryer at one time into the batter mixture, completely covering them, and deep-fry in batches for about 4 minutes, turning them over twice whilst cooking.

Remove from the oil, and lift the apple fritters on to kitchen paper. Transfer to a serving plate and dust with icing sugar. Deep-fry the remaining apple slices in the same way.

6 · Serving

Present the fritters on a dish lined with a napkin and serve the vanilla and cinnamon sauce separately.

VARIATIONS

The apple can be replaced by pears, apricots, peaches, figs etc., or pineapple rings poached in lemon syrup.

N U T R I T I O N I S T ' S
N O T E S

The total amount of fat in this recipe is high, coming from the oil in which the apples are fried, the caramel and also the sauce. The apples themselves contain useful amounts of fibre and small amounts of vit-amins. The recipe also in-cludes nutritious ingredients like eggs and milk, so it has a reasonable content of cal-cium and protein.

In this recipe I use Granny Smith apples as I find that they hold their shape very well whilst cooking and develop a delicious taste.

_____

The quantity of yeast must be carefully measured: too little, and it would not lighten the dough; too much, and the dough would be very bitter and unworkable.

_____

The apple rings need to be pre-cooked as the deep-frying time will be too short to thoroughly cook them. They can be cut 3 mm ($\frac{1}{8}$ in) thick, in which case they will not need to be pan-fried.

_____

It is important to pan-fry the slices of apple very quickly when caramelizing, otherwise they will already be cooked and too soft to be dipped into the batter.

_____

Although this recipe is very simple, there are still a few difficulties. If the egg yolks are subjected to too strong a heat, the sauce will curdle. The partial cooking of the yolk binds and thickens the sauce. Stir constantly to distribute the heat and watch carefully – there is a precise moment when the sauce will be ready. Even when strained, the sauce can still curdle, so continue stirring for 1–2 minutes until tepid.

_____

The yeast releases gas within the batter, and creates an extremely light mixture with thousands of air bubbles. The further incor-poration of the egg white lightens it still further. This emulsion is not stable, but, once in contact with the hot oil, the protein in the batter will coagulate and solidify around the air bubbles, creating a very light coating for the apple.

Apple Sorbet with Dried Apple Slices

FOR 4 GUESTS

PREPARATION TIME: 40 minutes

DRYING TIME: 3 hours

FREEZING TIME: 20 minutes, but this depends on the power of your machine.

SPECIAL EQUIPMENT: A machine with an attachment that will slice 2 mm (scant $^{1}/_{8}$ in) thick (a Robot-Coupe for instance), or a very sharp knife; an ice-cream machine; 2 non-stick baking trays, 30 × 40 cm (12 × 16 in).

PLANNING AHEAD: The dried apples can be prepared the day before and kept in an airtight container. The sorbet can also be prepared the day before.

INGREDIENTS

4 Granny Smith apples, about 600 g (1¼ lb) in weight
juice of 1 lemon
50 g (2 oz) apple jelly (or crab-apple jelly or apricot jam)
50 g (2 oz) caster sugar
20 ml (¾ fl oz) calvados

FOR THE DRIED APPLE SLICES

1 Granny Smith apple, about 150 g (5 oz) in weight
juice of ¼ lemon
100 ml (3½ fl oz) water
1 tablespoon caster sugar

METHOD

1 · Preparing the apple slices

Do not peel or core the apples. Chop the tops of the apples off and then slice them into the thinnest possible slices, no thicker than 2 mm (a scant $^{1}/_{8}$ in). Ideally, you should have about 30 slices from the apple. Place these slices into a bowl, squeeze the lemon juice over them and reserve.

In a pan, bring the water and sugar to the boil and pour this boiling syrup over the apple slices. Stir to allow the syrup to penetrate into the slices, cover with cling film and allow to marinate until the mixture has cooled.

2 · Making the apple sorbet

Do not peel or core the apples. Chop the apples into 1 cm ($^{1}/_{2}$ in) cubes and place them in a food processor with the lemon juice, apple jelly, sugar and calvados. Liquidize until completely puréed. Pass through a fine sieve then churn in the ice-cream machine. Reserve in the freezer until ready to serve.

3 · *Drying the apple slices*

Pre-heat the oven to its lowest setting, about 80°C (176°F).

Drain the syrup from the apple slices and place them next to one another on the non-stick trays. Place both trays in the pre-heated oven and cook slowly for 2–3 hours until the apples have

SCIENTIST'S
NOTES

Apples are a rich source of pectin. Pectus will only form a jelly in the presence of both acid and sugar. Lemon juice provides the acid.

.

Silica gel is an amorphous silica, the most abundant of all minerals (one type of which is the semi-precious opal!) Like a white sand, it attracts and converts moisture, and therefore is used as a drying and dehumidifying agent, and as an anti-caking agent in cosmetics.

dried. Check occasionally to make sure they do not darken.

Remove the trays from the oven and whilst still hot, use a palette knife to slide the apple slices off the trays. Place in an airtight container, cool, then cover and reserve.

4 · Serving

With two small oval spoons, scoop out and shape 20 small ovals of sorbet. Place on a tray and put them back in the freezer.

Use six slices of dried apple and five sorbet balls per guest: you are trying to create an upright fan shape, standing vertically from the plate.

Put the first slice of dried apple in the centre of the plate. Place one sorbet ball in the centre of this apple slice. Arrange a second slice of dried apple to one side of the base of the first dried apple slice – they should touch – and covering the sorbet at an angle. Place a ball of apple sorbet at the centre of this second apple slice. Repeat this process for the remaining apple slices and sorbet balls. You will end with the sixth dried apple slice, standing almost at right angles to the horizontal plate. Serve quickly to your guests.

VARIATIONS

With this dessert, you could serve the Apple and Vanilla Sauce on p. 255.

The dried apple slices can be replaced by pineapple slices (prepare in exactly the same way, and see p. 275).

You could make the assembly easier by simply layering sorbet between slices of dried apple as in the photograph.

CHEF'S NOTES

The apple jelly is used in this recipe to add some pectin to the sorbet; this will prevent it crystallizing into flakes of ice and a runny syrup. Crab apple jelly or apricot jam would also be suitable.

Pouring the boiling syrup on to the sliced apples partly cooks them. It also allows the apple slices to keep their original colour.

The dried apples must be kept in an airtight container to stop them softening due to humidity in the air. It would be advisable to place some silica gel crystals (which you can buy at the chemist) inside the container to ensure the lowest humidity level possible in it.

Iced Pineapple Parfait and Kirsch Biscuit with Pineapple Sunflowers

FOR 5 GUESTS

PREPARATION TIME: 40 minutes

DRYING TIME: 3 hours

FREEZING TIME: 3 hours

SPECIAL EQUIPMENT: A machine with an attachment that will slice 1–2 mm thick (a Robot-Coupe, for instance), or a very sharp knife; 2 non-stick baking trays 30 × 40 cm (12 × 16 in); 1 tray 30 × 20 cm (12 × 8 in), and a piece of grease-proof paper the same size; 1 pastry cutter, 6 cm (2½ in) in diameter; 1 sugar thermometer.

PLANNING AHEAD: The dried pineapple can be prepared the day before and kept in an airtight container. The parfait and the sauce can also be prepared the day before.

INGREDIENTS

FOR THE DRIED PINEAPPLE SLICES
1 small pineapple, about 350–400 g (12–14 oz)
juice of ¼ lemon
100 ml (3½ fl oz) water
15 g (½ oz) caster sugar

FOR THE CANDIED PINEAPPLE
½ baby pineapple, about 175–200 g (6–7 oz), diced

50 ml (2 fl oz) water
50 g (2 oz) caster sugar

FOR THE PARFAIT
75 g (3 oz) candied pineapple (see above)
100 g (4 oz) caster sugar
40 ml (1½ fl oz) water
2 egg whites
juice of 1 lemon
100 ml (3½ fl oz) whipping cream
4 teaspoons kirsch

FOR THE PINEAPPLE SAUCE
1 baby pineapple, about 350–400 g (12–14 oz)
50 ml (2 fl oz) tinned coconut milk
1 tablespoon Malibu (coconut liqueur)
a small pinch of freshly ground black pepper

FOR THE CHERRY GARNISH
25 black cherries, pitted
4 teaspoons kirsch
30 g (1¼ oz) caster sugar
a dash of lemon juice
a small pinch each of freshly ground black pepper, ground cloves and ground cinnamon

METHOD

1 · Preparing the pineapple slices
Peel the pineapple. You should have peeled fruit of about 7.5 cm (3 in) in length and 6.5 cm (2¾ in) width. Slice it into the thinnest possible slices, no thicker than 2 mm (a scant ⅛ in). Place these slices into a bowl, and sprinkle with the lemon juice.

Bring the water and sugar to the boil together in a small pan, then pour this boiling syrup over the slices. Stir to allow the syrup to coat all the slices, then cover with cling film and allow to marinate until the mixture has cooled.

2 · *Drying the pineapple slices*

Pre-heat the oven to the very lowest it will go, about 80°C (176°F), and proceed as outlined in the recipe on p. 273, stage 3.

3 · *Making the candied pineapple*

Peel the baby pineapple, and cut out and discard the hard central core. Chop the remaining flesh into 5 mm (¼ in) cubes.

Bring the water and sugar to the boil together in a suitable pan, and when the sugar has dissolved, pour it over the pineapple cubes. Allow to marinate for a few hours.

4 · *Making the parfait*

Drain the candied pineapple cubes, and discard the syrup.

Place the parfait sugar and water in a pan, heat to dissolve the sugar, and cook the syrup to 120°C (248°F). Check using the sugar thermometer.

Whilst the sugar syrup is cooking, whisk the egg whites to soft peaks. Reduce the speed of the machine and pour the cooked sugar syrup in between the side of the bowl and the whisk (this will prevent spitting). Whisk until incorporated, then allow to cool, still whisking. Gradually, and still whisking, add the lemon juice to the egg white mixture.

Separately, whisk the cream to soft peaks. Fold in the kirsch and the drained candied pineapple cubes. Reserve.

Add one-third of the egg white mixture to the whipped cream, and mix in. Return the mixture to the remaining two-thirds of egg white and carefully fold together.

Line the 30 × 20 cm (12 × 8 in) tray with the sheet of grease-proof paper. Spread the parfait mixture evenly over this. Place in the freezer for about 3 hours, or until it has hardened.

5 · *Preparing the pineapple sauce*

Peel and chop the pineapple, then purée. Place in a small pan and add the remaining ingredients. Bring to the boil, then pass through a fine sieve. Reserve.

Iced Pineapple Parfait and
Kirsch Biscuit with
Pineapple Sunflowers
(see p. 275)

Pineapple is good for aiding digestion as it contains an enzyme called bromelain. It contains vitamin C, manganese and potassium, and is said to have antibacterial properties. The total sugar content of this dish is quite high, coming from both the natural sugars in the fruit as well as sugars added for the candied pineapple and the sauce. The black cherries also provide vitamin C and potassium.

6 · Cooking the cherry garnish

Place all the ingredients for the cherry garnish in a saucepan, cover with a lid, and place on a medium heat for about 3 minutes. Remove the lid and carry on cooking for a further 5 minutes. Remove from the heat and leave to cool in a bowl.

7 · Serving

We want to create a flower pot with sunflowers made out of pineapple, drawing the stalk and the pot with cherry juice. (See also the photograph on p. 276.)

Cover the bottom of five plates with pineapple sauce. Each plate should be 18 cm (7¼ in) in diameter without the rim.

Pour about 1 teaspoon of cherry juice on the base of the plate and, dipping the tip of the spoon into the cherry juice, draw a flowerpot shape by running the cherry sauce into the pineapple sauce. Also, still dipping the tip of the spoon into the cherry juice, draw three stalks.

Place three dried pineapple slices per plate at the top end of each stalk. Cut out 15 discs of pineapple parfait with the pastry cutter. Place one disc on the top of each dried pineapple slice. Top each disc of parfait with another slice of dried pineapple.

Place three cherries on to the base of each flowerpot and one cherry or two in between each flower. Serve to your guests.

VARIATIONS

The cherry stalks in the photograph are not made with cherry juice but with pulled sugar. Pulled sugar is an extremely skilled technique and requires handling hot caramel; it is also time-consuming. Cherry juice has therefore been used in this recipe.

CHEF'S NOTES

Marinating the candied pineapple cubes for the parfait allows the hot sugar syrup to penetrate into the pineapple flesh. The sugar will stop the pineapple cubes freezing hard in the frozen parfait.

Cooking the cherries with the lid on prevents caramelization, allows steam to develop and the cherries to release their own juices in which they will cook. Later, removing the lid allows the cherry juice to reduce and to concentrate the flavour.

Vanilla Ice-cream

For this recipe you will need an ice-cream machine. It will be a very good investment as you will be able to prepare so many easy ice-creams, sorbets or desserts in very little time. These are very much better than many bought versions, most of which are full of emulsifiers, additives, colourings, flavourings and far too much sugar. One of the best machines is a Magimix Gelato Machine.

SCIENTIST'S NOTES

The principle involved in making ice cream is to produce the smallest possible ice crystals and to wrap each one individually in fat.

Ice-cream making is a three-stage process: making the mixture, or custard, freezing and hardening. Freezing is the trickiest part to do at home, but the ingredients in this recipe help the process. You have to make sure plenty of air is mixed in during the freezing because ice cream is frozen foam. The more protein the mix contains, the better it will foam. The protein comes from the egg yolks and the milk, but adding some dried milk will also increase the protein without making the mixture runny. Sugar in the mixture lowers its freezing point and increases the separation of the tiny ice crystals. The fat also helps to keep the ice crystals separate and give the ice cream a smooth, rich, mouth-feel.

FOR 6–8 GUESTS

PREPARATION AND COOKING TIME: 15 minutes

COOLING TIME: 10 minutes

FREEZING TIME: 15 minutes, but this depends on the power of your machine.

SPECIAL EQUIPMENT: An ice-cream machine.

PLANNING AHEAD: The ice cream can be made in advance.

INGREDIENTS
8 egg yolks
120 g (4½ oz) caster sugar
4 teaspoons dried milk
500 ml (17 fl oz) milk
1 vanilla pod

METHOD

In a large mixing bowl, cream together the egg yolks, sugar and dried milk until a pale straw colour.

Place the milk in a heavy-based pan. Halve the vanilla pod and scrape the seeds out into the milk. Chop the pod very finely, and add to the milk as well. Bring to the boil, and simmer for about 5 minutes.

Bring the milk back to the boil and pour it on to the egg, sugar and dried milk mixture, whisking continuously. Return the mixture to the pan on medium heat. Stir the custard until it thickens and coats the back of your spoon. Strain immediately into a bowl through a sieve, pressing down on the vanilla to get as much flavour as possible, then stir for a few minutes. Place the bowl into another bowl filled with ice, and cool, before churning in the ice-cream machine.

VARIATIONS

Instead of the vanilla, you could add a variety of other flavours. The choices are virtually endless.

Cinnamon Ice-cream Add 1 cinnamon stick to the milk during simmering.

Chocolate Ice-cream Add 50 g (2 oz) good-quality chocolate, broken into small pieces, to the milk during simmering.

Coffee Ice-cream Add 20 g (³/₄ oz) instant coffee to the milk during simmering.

Pistachio Ice-cream Add 50 g (2 oz) pistachio nut purée to the milk during simmering.

Orange or Lemon Ice-cream Add the finely grated zests of 2 oranges or lemons to the milk during simmering.

CHEF'S NOTES

Cooling the cream down on ice will bring the temperature of the mixture down below 4°C (39°F) very quickly and thus prevent the formation of any harmful bacteria. You could also cool the mixture in the ice-cream machine itself but, depending on the power of the machine, it will then take some time to freeze.

———

Maturing the cream in the fridge for 24 hours will improve both its taste and texture.

———

The dried milk enriches the texture of the ice-cream.

———

Never re-freeze ice-cream (or indeed any other frozen product) after it has been defrosted.

Medley of Summer Fruits in Raspberry and Strawberry Sauce

—— ILLUSTRATED ON PAGE 244 ——

FOR 4 GUESTS

PREPARATION TIME: 20 minutes

PLANNING AHEAD: This dessert should be prepared a maximum of 5 hours in advance of your meal.

INGREDIENTS
2 ripe peaches
1 small melon (Charentais)
8 fresh mint leaves

100 g (4 oz) each of raspberries, strawberries, blackcurrants and blackberries

FOR THE RED FRUIT SAUCE
200 g (7 oz) raspberries
200 g (7 oz) strawberries
100 g (4 oz) caster sugar
juice of ¹/₂ lemon
100 ml (3¹/₂ fl oz) Champagne (optional)

METHOD

1 · Preparing the sauce

Trim, wash and drain the fruit, then place in the blender. Add most of the sugar and lemon juice and purée, then force the pulp through a fine sieve into a large mixing bowl. Taste, add more sugar and juice if necessary, then reserve.

2 · Preparing the fruit

Wash and drain the fruit and mint leaves. Remove the stems from the latter.

Cut each peach into 8 segments and reserve. Halve the melon, remove the seeds and divide each half into 6. Remove the peel, and cut each piece into 2 (36 pieces in all) lengthways. Cut large strawberries in halves and quarters, leaving smaller ones whole.

Mix all the fruit together and place in the sauce.

Chop the mint leaves very finely and mix with the fruit. Cover with cling film and chill for at least 1 hour.

3 · Serving

Place the fruit and sauce into a glass bowl and serve, while very cold, to your guests.

VARIATIONS

Various fruits can be added or substituted – wild strawberries, grapes, mango, pears, etc.

You can add a festive note by pouring a little Champagne on to each fruit medley in front of your guests. This will produce a beautiful foam and add to the freshness of the dish.

C H E F ' S   N O T E S

The fruit must be of the very best quality, and very ripe. If the blackberries are too acidic, sprinkle them with 20 g (³/₄ oz) caster sugar and marinate for 2–3 hours.

———————

After chilling, taste the fruit mixture and add a little sugar if necessary.

———————

Prepare the dessert at least an hour in advance, but not more than 5 hours or the fruit will go soft.

Chocolate Fondant

The fragrant bitter-sweet taste of this dessert will delight you.

FOR 6 GUESTS

PREPARATION TIME: 45 minutes

RESTING TIME: At least 1 hour

COOKING TIME: 35–45 minutes

SPECIAL EQUIPMENT: This dessert can be made in two ways: using ring moulds or by piping the fondant onto the chocolate biscuits. The only difference is that the presentation will be better with the ring moulds. The equipment needed varies according to which method of presentation you choose so be sure to get the appropriate equipment.

With ring moulds: 6 stainless-steel ring moulds 6–7 cm (2¼–2¾ in) in diameter and 4 cm (1½ in) high; pastry cutter (unfluted) of the same diameter as the rings; baking tray, 30 × 40 cm (12 × 16 in); grease-proof paper.

Without ring moulds: pastry cutter 7–8 cm (3–3¼ in) in diameter; 1 baking tray, 30 × 40 cm (12 × 16 cm); greaseproof paper; piping bag and plain nozzle, 1 cm (½ in) in diameter.

PLANNING AHEAD: This dessert can be made a few days in advance as it is kept frozen and only baked at the last minute to be served hot.

INGREDIENTS
160 g (5½ oz) very best bitter chocolate
75 g (3 oz) unsalted butter, diced
1 teaspoon instant coffee powder or granules
1 tablespoon cocoa
50 ml (2 fl oz) boiling water
3 eggs, separated
30 g (1¼ oz) caster sugar

FOR THE MOULDS (optional)
20 g (¾ oz) unsalted butter
30 g (1¼ oz) extra bitter chocolate, finely grated
1 tablespoon cocoa

TO SERVE
200 ml (7 fl oz) whipping cream
50 g (2 oz) blanched pistachios, chopped

METHOD

1 · Preparing the base for the mousse and biscuits
On a low heat, melt the chocolate in a bowl over a pan of simmering water or in a bain-marie with the diced unsalted butter. Stir from time to time. Cool slightly.

Mix the coffee powder or granules with the cocoa and dilute with the boiling water. Cool, then add the egg yolks, and stir until you have a perfect mix. Reserve.

On a medium speed, beat the egg whites to form soft peaks, then gradually add the sugar. Continue to beat at a fast speed until firm peaks are achieved.

N U T R I T I O N I S T ' S
N O T E S

Chocolate, butter, eggs and cream are delicious ingredients but combined together make a dessert which is rather high in fat. There are a few good points nutritionally, though: dark bitter chocolate provides you with several valuable minerals such as iron and magnesium, and it is lower in sugar than ordinary chocolate. Egg yolks are a very good source of most vitamins, especially A, D and the B group, and a number of minerals including iron and zinc. Even cream has a fair amount of vitamin A in it.

Whisk the egg yolk, coffee and cocoa mixture into the melted chocolate butter. Fold the egg whites into the chocolate mixture. Do not try to achieve a perfect mix. Chill for at least 1 hour or up to 3 hours maximum.

2 · Spreading and baking the chocolate biscuit
Pre-heat the oven to 160°C/325°F/Gas 3.

Place a ½ teaspoon of the chocolate mixture into each corner of the baking tray and place the sheet of greaseproof paper securely on top. This holds the paper on to the tray, especially useful if you have a fan-assisted oven!

Take about a quarter to one-third of the chocolate mousse mixture and spread it on the paper, to about 14 × 21 cm (5½ × 8½ in) in area, and about 5 mm (¼ in) thick. Return the rest of the mixture to the fridge. Cook the mixture in the pre-heated oven for 15 minutes or, if you want a very dry biscuit, for 20 minutes. Remove from the oven, place on a cooling rack and allow to cool. Peel off the paper carefully.

3 · Preparing the moulds (optional)
Place the moulds in the fridge or freezer. When cold, spread the insides generously with the butter. Keep at room temperature for at least 10 minutes, then cover the insides with the grated chocolate and cocoa.

4 · Assembling the dessert
With a cutter, very carefully cut out six rounds of the chocolate biscuit: if using the rings, cut the biscuit to the same diameter as the rings, if not cut to 7–8 cm (3–3¼ in) in diameter, and delicately detach them with a palette knife. The biscuit is very fragile, so proceed with great care.

If you are not using the rings, fill the piping bag with the chilled chocolate mixture. Place the chocolate biscuit rounds on a tray. Pipe the chocolate mousse mixture on to each biscuit, starting from the middle and moving in a circular motion up to 1 cm (½ in) from the edge of the biscuit and 2 cm (¾ in) high. Freeze the layered desserts on the tray for at least 1 hour, until firm.

If using the rings, place them on the tray, place a round of biscuit in the bottom of each and spoon in the chocolate mixture two-thirds up the height of the ring. Freeze as above.

5 · To finish and serve
Pre-heat the oven to 180°C/350°F/Gas 4.

Lightly whip the cream and chill.

Remove the chocolate desserts from the freezer and cook in the pre-heated oven for about 15 minutes; for 20 minutes if you are using the rings.

Divide the whipped cream between six dessert plates and sprinkle with the chopped pistachios. Remove the desserts from the oven (and the rings, if used). Arrange on the cream. Serve.

VARIATIONS

You can create a delicious chocolate mousse by stopping at the end of stage 1 and using 5 egg whites instead of 3. (See Dark Chocolate Mousse with Orange, p. 290.)

C H E F ' S   N O T E S

If chocolate is subjected to a strong heat, it will become granular. An occasional stir will help to mix both butter and chocolate, and equally distribute the heat.

It is essential to mix the chocolate and instant coffee with hot water so that the mixture dissolves.

You must use a large spatula in order to gently mix the chocolate butter mixture and egg whites. If you mix it too fast you may deflate the volume by up to one-third. The whipped egg whites are made of millions of air bubbles which will burst if handled too roughly. You do not want a perfect mix for the same reason.

The refrigeration of this chocolate mousse will give a firmer texture and make it easier to handle later. Beyond 3 hours the texture will be too firm as the butter fats will go solid.

If the biscuit mixture is applied too thinly to the paper on the tray, it will be impossible to lift because it will be too fragile. If too thick it will simply be unpleasant.

Freezing the moulds instant sets the thick layer of butter. This eases the removal of the mould at the later stage. The mould is then brought back to room temperature as it would be impossible to fix the chocolate and cocoa on butter that was too cold.

The freezing of the mousse is essential as it will solidify it resulting in a crusty outside and a melting inside.

Chocolate Fondant
(see p. 282)

Blood Orange Gratin

Blood oranges are at their best in January and February, but the gratin *can* be made with 'ordinary' oranges.

FOR 4 GUESTS

PREPARATION TIME: 45 minutes

COOKING TIME: 5 minutes

SPECIAL EQUIPMENT: 4 egg dishes, 15 cm (6 in) in diameter, or 4 oven-proof plates, 20 cm (8 in) in diameter; a sugar thermometer.

PLANNING AHEAD: The sabayon, blood orange segments and orange zests can be made in advance and kept separately in the fridge until ready to serve.

INGREDIENTS
8 blood oranges

50 g (2 oz) caster sugar (optional)
icing sugar to dust

FOR THE CANDIED ORANGE ZEST (optional)
100 ml (3½ fl oz) water
50 g (2 oz) caster sugar

FOR THE SABAYON
2 egg yolks
50 g (2 oz) caster sugar
250 ml (8 fl oz) water
300 ml (10 fl oz) whipping cream
2 tablespoons Grand Marnier

METHOD

1 · Preparing the candied orange zest (optional)
With a potato peeler, remove the peel thinly from two of the blood oranges. With a chopping knife, cut the peel into fine julienne sticks.

In a pan, place 1 litre (1¾ pints) of cold water and the orange peel julienne. Bring to the boil, skim and cook for about 6–8 minutes, then strain and refresh under cold running water. Drain and reserve.

In a small pan, bring the measured water and sugar to the boil together. When the sugar has melted, add the drained orange julienne and simmer gently for about 8–10 minutes. Remove from the heat and allow the julienne to cool in the cooking syrup. Reserve.

2 · Segmenting the oranges
With a very sharp knife, carefully peel the blood oranges, not leaving any white pith on them. Remove any pith from the already peeled oranges. With a small sharp knife remove the segments. Hold one orange in your hand over a bowl. Cut down on either side of each piece of membrane separating the

segments, and release the denuded segments. Do this to all the oranges and put the segments in the bowl. Squeeze in the juice from the 'skeletons'. Taste the oranges. If they are too acid, sprinkle with a little caster sugar.

3 · Making the sweet sabayon

Place the egg yolks into the bowl of an electric mixer and whisk on a medium speed until a pale straw colour.

Meanwhile, place the caster sugar and water in a small pan and bring to the boil. Using a sugar thermometer, cook the syrup to 120°C (248°F).

Lower the whisking speed slightly, and carefully pour the cooked syrup on to the yolks, in between the beaters and the side of the bowl. Whisk until the mixture is cold.

Whip the cream to form soft peaks and fold it delicately with a spatula into the egg yolk and syrup mixture, along with the Grand Marnier. Reserve in the fridge, covered with cling film.

4 · Finishing the dish

Pre-heat the grill.

Separately drain into two different colanders the orange zest julienne and the orange segments. Leave for about 15 minutes. Keep the blood orange juice.

Arrange the blood orange segments attractively on the egg dishes. Place tablespoons of flavoured sabayon on to the orange segments, and dust with icing sugar.

At the very last minute, place the dishes under the red-hot grill, at a distance of about 8 cm (3¼ in) from the heat, and glaze for about 1 minute or until a light blond colour. Divide the drained zest julienne equally among the tops of the gratins. Serve to your guests.

VARIATIONS

The Blood Orange Gratin can be served with Hot Orange Buns (see p. 308). The buns can be ready in their moulds to be cooked, and then cooked while you are eating the main course. If possible, I prefer to do this just before glazing the gratin.

This gratin can also be made with strawberries, raspberries, peaches, cooked apricots, pears, etc.

Orange segments, whether blood or ordinary oranges, can also be replaced by Granny Smith apple segments, pan-fried with butter, sugar and calvados. The quantity required for this alternative will be 600 g (1 lb 5 oz) segments, 40 g (1½ oz)

unsalted butter, 50 g (2 oz) caster sugar and 1 tablespoon calvados. Use calvados instead of Grand Marnier in the sabayon as well. Replace the orange and lemon zest in the bun mixture with vanilla seeds scraped from a vanilla pod. Follow the method as above.

CHEF'S NOTES

Boiling the julienne of orange zest will slightly cook it, but also remove the powerful taste, leaving you with a very delicate flavour. Refreshing under running cold water will stop the cooking instantly, and rinse the julienne.

Simmering the orange julienne for 10 minutes is necessary to both cook and candy the zest. Simmering as opposed to boiling prevents the evaporation of the water in the sugar syrup and stops it caramelizing.

Cooking the sugar to 120°C (248°F) ensures that the egg yolks are cooked properly, and that the texture of the sabayon is correct. If the sugar syrup has not been cooked enough, and is not hot enough, the egg yolks will not thicken as they should, and the sabayon will be runny. If the sugar syrup is *overcooked*, the volume of the sabayon will be lessened, and the texture will be very heavy.

Using a sugar thermometer will help you obtain the correct temperature, but you can also dip a teaspoon into the cooking sugar syrup and then drop some of it into cold water. The syrup will solidify on contact with the cold water and show you the concentration of sugar in the syrup. You are looking for a 'soft ball'. If too soft, carry on cooking and repeat the process. If too hard, add a drop of water to the syrup until the right texture is obtained.

There is an emulsifier, called lecithin, in the egg yolk. The volume of egg yolk will develop due to air incorporated by the whisking. The hot syrup poured in will partly cook the egg yolk and make the sabayon stable. The operation must be done with

Blood Orange Gratin
(see p. 286)

great care; if the syrup trickles against the side of the bowl it will solidify; if poured over the beaters the syrup could 'spit' and burn you. In both instances, the balance of the recipe would be incorrectly altered.

———

Fat is notorious for absorbing other flavours, and as cream is one of the main ingredients of the sabayon, then covering it with cling film will stop it absorbing any foreign flavour present in your fridge – melon, cheese, fish, etc.

———

Blood orange juice can be served in a fresh fruit juice cocktail as an aperitif or as drink with a dessert if poured into small chilled glasses.

———

Glazing the gratin under the grill has to be done at the very last moment. The grill has to be pre-heated so that it can instantly caramelize the top without *cooking* the sabayon, but also allow the fruit to warm up a little.

Dark Chocolate Mousse
with Orange

———

FOR 6 GUESTS

PREPARATION TIME: 10–15 minutes

SETTING TIME: At least 2 hours

SPECIAL EQUIPMENT: A large serving bowl or 6 individual mousse dishes or ramekins.

PLANNING AHEAD: This dessert must be prepared a few hours in advance to allow it to set in the fridge.

INGREDIENTS
200 g (7 oz) best extra bitter chocolate
8 egg whites
75 g (3 oz) caster sugar
3 egg yolks
1 teaspoon finely grated orange zest (optional)
¼ teaspoon finely grated lemon zest (optional)
40 ml (1½ fl oz) Cointreau (optional)

METHOD
Break the chocolate into pieces and, on a low heat, melt in a bowl over a pan of simmering water or in a *bain-marie* at 40°C (104°F). Cool slightly.

Beat the egg whites until they form soft peaks. Add the sugar gradually, and continue whisking until firm peaks are formed.

Stir the egg yolks, citrus fruit zests and Cointreau, if using, into the melted chocolate. Briskly whisk one-third of the whipped egg white into the chocolate mixture, then fold the remainder in very gently. Pour the chocolate mousse into a large serving bowl or into individual dishes. Place in the fridge and allow to set for at least 2 hours.

A very nice garnish can be served along with the chocolate mousse: madeleines or Hot Orange Buns (see p. 308).

CHEF'S NOTES

The 5 egg yolks left over can be used in other recipes such as Vanilla Cream (see p. 64).

If the chocolate is subjected to strong heat, it will become granular. An occasional stirring will help to distribute the heat evenly. Adding ingredients other than those high in fat content in small quantities (i.e. water, alcohol, etc.), makes the chocolate solidify after 1 or 2 minutes and unable to be worked again.

Orange and lemon zests have to be very finely grated to spread the flavour evenly through the mousse. Over-large pieces of raw citrus fruit are not pleasant to eat.

When adding the yolks and Cointreau to the chocolate, you must have the egg whites already whipped. When adding the third of the whipped egg white to the chocolate and yolk mixture, you must work very briskly, as the water contained in the egg white would otherwise 'seize' the chocolate and solidify it. This process also eases the further incorporation of the remaining egg white.

Boiling the grated orange zest will slightly cook it but also remove the powerful taste and leave you with a very delicate flavour. Refreshing under running cold water will stop the cooking instantly, and rinse the grated zest. Simmering the grated orange zest for 10 minutes will both cook and candy the zest. Simmering as opposed to boiling prevents the evaporation of the water in the sugar syrup and stops it caramelizing.

Apple Charlotte

FOR 8 GUESTS

PREPARATION TIME: 45 minutes

COOKING TIME: 50–60 minutes

RESTING TIME: About 1 hour

SPECIAL EQUIPMENT: An earthenware dish or charlotte mould, 18 cm (7¼ in) in diameter, 8 cm (3¼ in) high.

INGREDIENTS
1 kg (2¼ lb) Granny Smith apples (about 10)
40 g (1½ oz) unsalted butter, clarified

60 g (2¼ oz) caster sugar
40 ml (1½ fl oz) calvados (optional)
a pinch of ground cinnamon (optional)

FOR THE CHARLOTTE MOULD
about 15 cm (6 in) of a large unsliced white loaf
30 g (1¼ oz) unsalted butter, softened
30–40 g (1¼–1½ oz) caster sugar
100 g (4 oz) unsalted butter, clarified

METHOD

1 · Preparing the bread
You want a thin lining of bread for the entire mould. The following is how we did it, in some considerable detail, but you may find a more straightforward way!

With a sharp serrated knife, slice 16 very thin slices from the piece of bread. Trim the crust from each slice to leave a 9 cm (3½ in) square.

Cut each of four slices into four triangles. You will obtain 16 triangles.

Cut each of seven slices into halves. You will obtain 14 fingers, 9 × 4.5 cm (3½ × 1¾ in).

Reserve the two remaining slices whole, to be used later in the centre of the apple charlotte.

2 · Preparing the apples
Peel the apples, cut them into quarters and remove the core. Cut each quarter into halves again. You will obtain eight segments from each apple. Reserve.

3 · Caramelizing the apples
Please note that this is done in two batches because of the large number of apple segments which need to be caramelized. The ingredients are therefore halved.

Place half of the clarified butter in a large non-stick frying pan over a strong heat, and add half the sugar. Throw in half the segmented apple, and pan-fry and sauté, stirring and shaking the pan, until the sugar has caramelized and the apples are coated.

Deglaze with half the calvados, if using, then add a tiny pinch of cinnamon, if using. Take care not to overcook the apple segments, but keep them slightly crisp. Remove from the pan on to a plate.

Clean the frying pan and repeat with the remaining apple segments and ingredients.

4 · Preparing and lining the charlotte dish
Using a pastry brush, grease the charlotte dish with the softened butter and sprinkle over the caster sugar. When distributed over all of the dish, shake off the excess sugar.

Brush eight of the bread triangles with some of the clarified butter and place them, slightly overlapping, on the base of the dish (the triangles must meet at the centre point).

Brush all the bread fingers with clarified butter, then arrange, like soldiers and slightly overlapping, around the edge of the dish. Reserve.

5 · Filling the dish
Place one-third of the caramelized apple segments into the bread-lined mould. Top with one of the reserved whole bread slices. Add a second third of caramelized apple and top with the second reserved whole bread slice. Top with the remaining caramelized apple.

Brush the eight remaining bread triangles with the remaining clarified butter and place them on the top of the charlotte, slightly overlapping (the triangles must meet at the centre point).

6 · Cooking the charlotte
Pre-heat the oven to 180°C/350°F/Gas 4.

Cover the charlotte tightly with a buttered piece of foil and bake in the pre-heated oven for 50–60 minutes or until the apples are tender. (Check by slipping a thin-bladed knife right into the heart of the charlotte.) Remove from the oven and allow to rest for a minimum of an hour, or until tepid.

Remove the piece of foil, place a plate on top of the apple charlotte and turn upside down. The charlotte should release from its mould. Serve to your guests.

VARIATIONS
A nice accompaniment could be Vanilla Cream (p. 64), Vanilla

Ice-cream (p. 279), or simply a large spoon of clotted Cornish cream or best Jersey double cream.

C H E F ' S   N O T E S

The best apples to use for this recipe are Granny Smiths, Juno Gold, Bramleys or Golden Delicious.

A strong heat will allow the sugar to caramelize and fry the apple, not turn it into a compote.

The caramel coating the apple will give an additional flavour to the dessert.

Deglazing with calvados adds an extra flavour to the dish, but will also dissolve the cooking juices stuck in the pan. Those cooking juices will glaze and flavour the apple segments.

Keeping the apples slightly crisp is important, as this will ensure a pleasant texture in the finished dish. Those segmented apples will be subjected to another hour in the oven.

The clarified butter allows the bread to toast whilst cooking; it sticks the triangles and fingers together and gives the dish a nice buttery taste!

The bread slices will absorb the moisture coming out of the apple whilst cooking which then allows the charlotte to hold its shape when removed from its mould.

Foil will retain the flavoured steam escaping from the apple charlotte whilst cooking. The steam will also make the bread and apples stick together.

Apple charlotte needs to rest and cool down before being turned out, otherwise it might not hold its shape.

Poached White Peaches with Orange Sabayon and Wild Strawberries

FOR 4 GUESTS

PREPARATION TIME: 45 minutes

COOKING TIME: 15–20 minutes

COOLING TIME: 2 hours

SPECIAL EQUIPMENT: 4 large Burgundy glasses or 4 glass serving bowls; an electric mixer; a disc of greaseproof paper to fit the diameter of your stainless steel saucepan.

PLANNING AHEAD: The peaches can be poached the day before, and the sabayon can be made a few hours in advance.

INGREDIENTS

FOR THE PEACHES
1 × 750 ml (1¼ pints) bottle dry white wine
120 g (4½ oz) caster sugar
½ vanilla pod
4 orange slices, 5 mm (¼ in) thick, skin included
4 lemon slices, 5 mm (¼ in) thick, skin included
4 ripe peaches, about 150 g (5 oz) each

FOR THE SABAYON
300 ml (10 fl oz) peach cooking juices
2 egg yolks
50 ml (2 fl oz) whipping cream
1 tablespoon Grand Marnier

FOR THE WILD STRAWBERRIES
80 g (3¼ oz) wild strawberries (or strawberries)
1 teaspoon caster sugar
a dash of lemon juice

METHOD

1 · Poaching the peaches

In a stainless-steel saucepan, bring the wine, sugar, vanilla pod, orange and lemon slices to the boil. When boiling, add the peaches, cover with the greaseproof paper disc, and bring back to the boil. Simmer for 4–5 minutes.

Remove from the heat and leave the peaches to cool in their cooking juices until at room temperature. Carefully place in a suitable container and reserve in the fridge until required.

2 · Preparing the sabayon

In a medium saucepan, bring to the boil the measured peach cooking juices, then lower the heat. Allow the juice to reduce gently to 100 ml (3½ fl oz).

While the juice is reducing, place the egg yolks into an electric mixer bowl, ready to be beaten. You can also whip the cream up to soft peaks in a separate bowl, and reserve in the fridge.

When the juice has reduced to the correct volume, switch the electric mixer on to its highest speed and carefully pour the boiling juice on to the egg yolks in between the side of the bowl and the beaters. Beat until completely cold.

Remove the cream from the fridge, and fold it delicately into the yolk and syrup mixture along with the Grand Marnier. Cover with cling film and reserve in the fridge.

3 · Marinating the strawberries

Place the wild strawberries, sugar and lemon juice in a bowl and shake the bowl gently to coat the fruit completely. Allow them to marinate for up to 1 hour.

4 · Serving

Drain the peaches from their remaining juices and skin them. Quarter each peach and very carefully remove each quarter from the stone. Arrange four quarters in each glass, and spoon equal quantities of the sabayon on top. Sprinkle over the marinated wild strawberries, then serve to your guests.

VARIATIONS

You could serve the peaches as 'forbidden fruit', trapped within the confines of a caramel cage (see pp. 264–65).

CHEF'S NOTES

Pouring the syrup in between the side of the bowl and the beater will prevent the syrup spitting all over the side of the bowl. This would considerably change the balance of the recipe. It will also prevent painful burns if the mixture spits on you!

Marinating the wild strawberries with the lemon juice will increase the flavour. The sugar in the marinade will also coat the fruit and make it very shiny. Do not marinate the fruits for more than an hour, though, or they will 'cook' to a mush.

Poached White Peaches with
Orange Sabayon and Wild
Strawberries (see p. 295)

Strawberry Sorbet

SCIENTIST'S NOTES

Many soft fruits such as strawberries are best eaten raw and do not freeze well. Strictly speaking, the fact is that they do not defrost well. As they freeze, the tiny ice crystals in the fruit start to expand and pierce the cell walls so that when they defrost you end up with an unsatisfactory mush. (Raspberries freeze better because they are formed of many individual little seed pods which are not so affected by ice crystals.)

A sorbet, such as this, is a good way of preserving the lovely flavour of fresh strawberries.

NUTRITIONIST'S NOTES

This simple recipe is an excellent source of vitamin C. Strawberries contain far more vitamin C than citrus fruit weight for weight, so take advantage of the fresh variety when they are in season. You will also get a good amount of potassium.

FOR 3–4 GUESTS

PREPARATION TIME: 10 minutes, plus 30 minutes' marinating time.

FREEZING TIME: 10–15 minutes, but this depends on the power of your machine.

SPECIAL EQUIPMENT: An ice-cream machine.

PLANNING AHEAD: The sorbet can be prepared well in advance.

INGREDIENTS
450 g (1 lb) ripe strawberries
80 g (3¼ oz) caster sugar
a dash of lemon juice

METHOD

Wash the fruit briefly under cold running water while the stems are still in place. Drain and dry on kitchen paper. Pull or cut off the stems, then slice the fruit. Place in a bowl and sprinkle with caster sugar and lemon juice. Mix and leave to marinate for 30 minutes at room temperature.

Liquidize the strawberry mixture and pass it through a fine stainless-steel sieve. Place in the ice-cream machine and churn until frozen. Reserve in the freezer until ready to serve.

CHEF'S NOTES

The fruit must be perfectly ripe, otherwise the sorbet will be tasteless and colourless.

When slicing some varieties of strawberries you may discover a hole in the centre. It is for this reason that you do not remove the stem before washing the fruit; otherwise more water might enter the strawberry.

Marinating the fruit with sugar and lemon juice will enhance its flavour and the colour.

Straining the purée may not be necessary for home use: I like to do it because the end result is smoother and finer.

Stuffed Poached Figs
with Port Ice-cream

SCIENTIST'S NOTES

Many of the foods we cook are acidic, especially fruit. Even weak acids will attack ordinary metals if they are left in contact for long periods. Stainless steel is a very unusual material in that it resists corrosion. It's made largely of iron, which rusts easily, but the addition of substantial amounts of chromium makes it stainless and resistant to many acids.

Plain iron pots are thought to be a useful source of iron in the diet.

FOR 6 GUESTS

PREPARATION TIME: 1 hour

COOKING TIME: 40 minutes

MARINATING TIME: 24 hours

FREEZING TIME: 10–15 minutes, but this depends on the power of your machine.

SPECIAL EQUIPMENT: An ice-cream machine; a stainless steel pan, 28–30 cm (11$\frac{1}{4}$–12 in) in diameter, plus a circle of greaseproof paper the same diameter.

PLANNING AHEAD: The figs must be marinated for 24 hours in advance.

INGREDIENTS
500 ml (17 fl oz) dark cooking port
500 ml (17 fl oz) Sauternes or other sweet white wine
50 g (2 oz) whole blackcurrants, crushed
24 figs (purple are the best)

FOR THE PORT ICE CREAM
4 egg yolks
50 g (2 oz) caster sugar
50 ml (2 fl oz) double cream
2 teaspoons dried milk
250 ml (8 fl oz) milk
250 ml (8 fl oz) fig purée (see below)

METHOD

1 · Poaching and marinating the figs

Bring the port, Sauternes and blackcurrants to the boil in the stainless steel saucepan. Add the figs, top them with the circle of greaseproof paper, and bring back to the boil. Simmer for 2–5 minutes, then allow to cool to room temperature. Allow to marinate for 24 hours.

2 · Preparing the figs

Drain the figs from their marinating juices. Trim off the stalks and, placing the figs sideways on your work surface, chop off the top third of each, creating a little hat. Do this to 18 figs only. Reserve the remaining six figs for the fig purée.

Placing the hats sideways, and using the flat part of the blade of a knife, push out the fig flesh, keeping the outside skin intact. This is a delicate process. Reserve the trimmings, flesh and seeds.

Place the bases, still holding their flesh, and the 'empty' hats on a small tray, and keep in the fridge until required.

3 · Preparing the port and fig purée

Sieve the cooking juices into a container, pressing on the

blackcurrants with a ladle to obtain as much juice as possible (you should have approximately 1 litre/1¾ pints of juice).

Place the cooking juices, the fig trimmings and the six remaining figs into a pan, bring to the boil and reduce down slowly to 500 ml (17 fl oz). Liquidize then reserve.

4 · Preparing the port ice-cream

Follow the Vanilla Ice-cream recipe on p. 279, adding the hot *unflavoured* milk to the egg yolk mixture.

When the sauce has cooled, whisk in 250 ml (8 fl oz) of the port and fig purée. Churn in the ice-cream machine for about 10–15 minutes. Reserve in the freezer.

5 · 'Stuffing' the figs and serving

Divide the remaining fig purée between six serving plates. Using a teaspoon, cover each fig base with port ice-cream. Top each fig with a hat, allowing the ice-cream to be seen, and arrange three of these per prepared plate. Serve to your guests.

C H E F ' S   N O T E S

For why the figs are covered while poaching with a disc of greaseproof paper, see the Chef's Note on p. 268.

Marinating the figs for 24 hours allows them to be flavoured by the port, Sauternes and blackcurrant.

Reducing slowly allows a concentration of flavour while avoiding the risk of caramelization: this would completely destroy the deep flavours of the cooking juice.

Stuffed Poached Figs
with Port Ice-Cream
(see p. 299)

Banana Soufflé

FOR 4 GUESTS

PREPARATION TIME: 30 minutes

COOKING TIME: 8–10 minutes

SPECIAL EQUIPMENT: 4 ramekins, 9 cm (3½ in) in diameter, 4.5 cm (1¾ in) deep.

SPECIAL NOTE: This dish is suitable for those on a gluten-free diet or for diabetics if sugar is used neither to coat the inside of the mould, nor in the banana soufflé mix. The butter can be replaced by unsalted margarine.

INGREDIENTS

275 g (10 oz) very ripe banana flesh (about 3 bananas)
juice of ½ lemon
4 egg whites
30 g (1¼ oz) caster sugar

FOR THE RAMEKINS
30 g (1¼ oz) unsalted butter or margarine, softened
20 g (¾ oz) caster sugar

NUTRITIONIST'S NOTES

This low-fat dessert is a dieter's dream although, of course, it can be enjoyed by anyone less concerned about their fat intake! Bananas are not fattening – they contain carbohydrate (not fat) – and have good levels of potassium and many vitamins. Ripe bananas are sweeter because more of their starch has been converted into sugar, but their calorie content is exactly the same as unripe bananas.

The egg whites increase the protein value of the dish, making it a good balance of nutrients.

METHOD

Pre-heat the oven to 170°C/325–350°F/Gas 3–4.

1 · Preparing the ramekins

With a pastry brush, butter the inside of each ramekin, then sprinkle in the caster sugar, if using. Swirl the sugar around until each ramekin is coated. Reserve.

2 · Making the soufflé mixture

Chop the bananas, then liquidize them with half the lemon juice until you obtain a very fine purée. Reserve.

Place the egg whites and a few drops of the remaining lemon juice into an electric mixer and whisk the whites to soft peaks. Gradually add the caster sugar (if using) and the remaining lemon juice and whisk until firmer peaks are reached.

Whisk one-quarter of the whipped egg whites into the banana mixture, then fold in the remainder carefully until well incorporated.

Fill the lined soufflé dishes with the soufflé mixture and smooth over the top with a palette knife. Run your thumb around the edge of the soufflé to push the mixture away from the sides.

3 · Cooking the soufflés

Place the soufflés on a baking tray and into the pre-heated oven for 8–10 minutes. Serve immediately to your guests.

For further advice on soufflé-making see Cooking Techniques, p. 45.

———

For the soufflé to be successful and for the banana flavour to come through, the fruit must be perfect. If they are over-ripe, the soufflé will not be appealing, as the flesh will be too dark.

———

Lemon juice prevents oxidation and discoloration of the banana; it also enhances its taste. (See also the Scientist's Note on p. 99.)

Apricot Clafoutis

FOR 8 GUESTS

PREPARATION TIME: 30 minutes

COOKING TIME: 30 minutes

SPECIAL EQUIPMENT: An ovenproof dish, 28 cm (11¼ in) in diameter, 5 cm (2 in) high; and a non-stick frying pan with a lid, 30 cm (12 in) in diameter.

PLANNING AHEAD: This dish must be prepared an hour in advance and served tepid.

INGREDIENTS
20 g (¾ oz) **unsalted butter, softened**
30 g (1¼ oz) **plain flour**

500 g (18 oz) **fresh apricots, ripe but still firm (or tinned apricots, see Variations)**
50 g (2 oz) **caster sugar**
50 ml (2 fl oz) **water**
juice of ¼ lemon
icing sugar to dust

FOR THE BATTER
100 ml (3½ fl oz) **milk**
½ **vanilla pod**
150 ml (5 fl oz) **whipping cream**
60 ml (2¼ fl oz) **Amaretto liqueur**
4 **eggs**
120 g (4½ oz) **caster sugar**
a pinch of salt
25 g (1 oz) **plain flour**

METHOD

1 · Preparing the dish
With a pastry brush, spread the softened butter all over the inside of the ovenproof dish, and sprinkle this with flour. Shake off the excess flour, and reserve the dish.

2 · Preparing the fresh fruit
With a knife, split the apricots into halves. Stone and reserve.

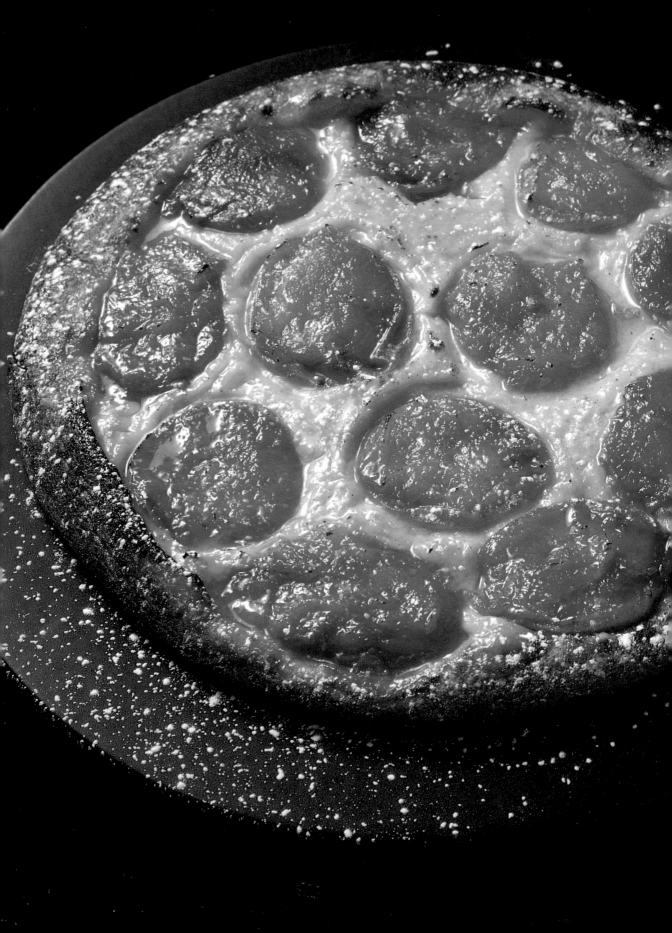

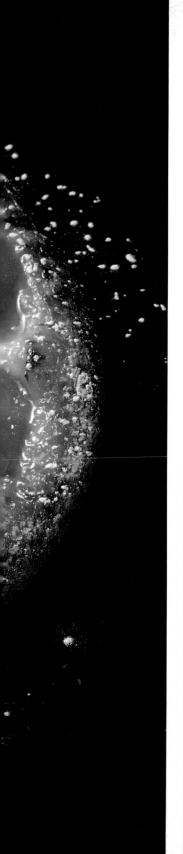

Place the frying pan over a medium heat with the sugar, water and lemon juice. Add the apricot halves, stone side down. Cover with the lid and cook gently for about 3 minutes. Turn the apricot halves over and repeat the cooking process for a further 3 minutes. Remove from the heat and allow to cool in the covered frying pan.

3 · Preparing the batter

Bring the milk and vanilla pod to the boil in a pan. Remove from the heat and allow to cool and infuse for 5 minutes.

Add the cream and Amaretto to the milk, and strain into a suitable container. Reserve.

Whisk the eggs, sugar and salt until the mixture triples in volume. Fold in the flour, and then the milk mixture.

4 · Cooking the clafoutis

Pre-heat the oven to 180°C/350°F/Gas 4.

Arrange the apricot halves in the bottom of the buttered and floured dish, and pour over the batter. Place in the pre-heated oven and bake for 30–35 minutes, until just set. Remove from the oven, allow to cool until slightly warm, then dust sparingly with icing sugar. Serve to your guests.

VARIATIONS

If fresh apricots are not available you can use 25–30 apricot halves tinned in a light syrup. In this case you do not need to use the sugar, water and lemon juice.

Other types of fruits such as pineapple, plums, cherries, apples, etc. can be used. Obviously the Amaretto should be replaced by an alternative liqueur appropriate to the fruit used.

CHEF'S NOTES

Ripe apricots are important for flavour and for the quality of the dish. If the apricots are over-ripe they will not keep their shape when cooking.

Cooking the apricots gently over a medium heat will prevent the sugar from caramelizing. You need to concentrate the delicate apricot flavour, not change it to one of caramelized fruit.

Cooling the apricots with the lid on is part of the cooking process. The steam and heat will finish poaching the apricots.

Creole Pancakes

This pancake recipe is suitable for any type of pancake. Multiply the recipe by two or three, using any type of filling you fancy, and have a pancake party! The pancakes can be cooked a couple of hours before being served.

FOR 4 GUESTS

PREPARATION TIME: About 10 minutes, plus 30 minutes' resting

COOKING TIME: About 25 minutes

SPECIAL EQUIPMENT: 1 pancake frying pan; a non-stick frying pan, 20–25 cm (8–10 in) in diameter.

PLANNING AHEAD: The pancake batter can be made half a day in advance.

INGREDIENTS
55 g (2¼ oz) unsalted butter

**1 egg
1 tablespoon caster sugar
a small pinch of salt
50 g (2 oz) plain flour, sifted
175 ml (6 fl oz) milk
finely grated zest of ¼ lemon**

FOR THE GARNISH AND SAUCE
**500 g (18 oz) ripe peeled
 bananas (about 4–6)
75 g (3 oz) unsalted butter
60 g (2¼ oz) demerara sugar
20 ml (¾ fl oz) dark rum
juice of ½ lemon
150 ml (5 fl oz) water**

METHOD

1 · Making the pancake batter
Heat 25 g (1 oz) of the butter in a small pan until it foams, and has a delicate nutty colour and smell. Pour into a mixing bowl and leave to cool.

Add the egg, sugar, salt, and sifted flour to the butter. Mix thoroughly with a whisk, adding the milk little by little, then whisk until the mixture is completely smooth. Strain into a bowl and finally add the lemon zest. Leave the mixture to rest for at least 30 minutes at room temperature.

2 · Cooking the pancakes
Heat the pancake frying pan on a medium heat. Add a teaspoon of the remaining butter and swirl it around the pan. Pour in a quarter of the batter and rotate the pan so that the bottom of the pan is evenly coated. Cook for 30–40 seconds, then turn the pancake over with a spatula and cook the other side for another 30 seconds. Reserve the cooked pancake on a tray, and proceed with the remaining batter as above. You need four pancakes.

3 · *Preparing the banana garnish and sauce*

In the non-stick frying pan, heat the butter until it starts to foam. Place the whole bananas into the boiling butter and cook them on a low to medium heat for 4 minutes only. Turn them over, sprinkle on the demerara sugar, and cook for a further 4 minutes to caramelize them. Turn over once more and on a strong heat carry on cooking for 2 more minutes: this will caramelize this side as well.

Pour the rum on to the hot bananas and light it. (This reduces the harshness of the alcohol but keeps the wonderful flavour.) When the flame goes out, remove the pan from the heat. With a palette knife, take the roasted bananas out of the pan, very carefully, and place them on a plate. Reserve.

Replace the frying pan on the stove and deglaze it with the lemon juice and water: this dissolves any ingredients left in the pan (such as caramel). Reduce this sauce to 120 ml (4 fl oz) to concentrate the flavour and give it body, then pass through a sieve to get rid of any small pieces of banana. Reserve.

4 · *Serving*

Pre-heat the oven to 180°C/350°F/Gas 4.

Slice the roasted bananas in half lengthways. Place the four pancakes on an oven tray and cover one half of each evenly with the warm roasted banana halves. Fold the other half over the bananas, and place in the pre-heated oven, but for no more than 4 minutes or they will be too dry.

Meanwhile, warm the sauce up in a pan.

Place each pancake on a plate, cover with the sauce and serve.

VARIATIONS

The bananas can be replaced by Granny Smith apples, and the rum by calvados. Follow the quantities and method above.

A scoop of the best Vanilla Ice-cream (see p. 279) would be very nice with this dessert.

C H E F ' S   N O T E S

The egg must be at room temperature when added to the cool butter, to prevent the formation of lumps of fat created by the coldness of the egg.

Adding the milk little by little to the flour mixture prevents the formation of lumps in the mixture. Passing the mixture through a sieve helps to smooth the batter.

Resting the batter at room temperature is important. This prevents the butter in the batter becoming too cold.

Cooking the pancake on a medium heat is important. If the frying pan is too hot the pancake will burn; if the frying pan is too cold, the pancake will be leathery and colourless. Practice makes perfect!

Bananas must be ripe with a yellow skin and covered with brown spots. If green, the banana will be hard and tasteless; if overripe the banana will turn into a 'compote' after cooking.

Time the banana cooking carefully. Only 4 minutes are required to partly to cook the first side of the banana, leaving it still firm enough to turn over to continue the cooking process.

Hot Orange Buns

MAKES 6–8 BUNS

PREPARATION TIME: 5 minutes

RESTING TIME: About 1 hour

COOKING TIME: 12 minutes

SPECIAL EQUIPMENT: 6 large 'bun' moulds, muffin moulds or cake tins which contain about 20 ml ($^3/_4$ fl oz) each.

PLANNING AHEAD: The bun mixture can be made up to half a day in advance and kept covered in the fridge until needed.

INGREDIENTS
40 g (1½ oz) unsalted butter
finely grated zest of 1 orange
finely grated zest of ½ lemon
50 g (2 oz) caster sugar
1 egg
a pinch of salt
1 tablespoon milk
70 g (2¾ oz) self-raising flour

FOR THE BUN MOULDS
50 g (2 oz) unsalted butter,
softened
2 tablespoons plain flour

METHOD

1 · Making the bun mixture

In a medium bowl, cream the butter until soft. Whisk in the orange and lemon zests and the caster sugar. Add the egg, salt and milk, and whisk together again. Fold in the self-raising flour.

Rest in the fridge for at least an hour.

Pre-heat the oven to 180°C/350°F/Gas 4.

2 · Greasing the bun moulds

With a pastry brush, coat the inside of each mould or tin generously with the soft butter and dust with the plain flour. Shake off the excess flour and place the moulds in the fridge for 15 minutes to allow the butter to set.

3 · Cooking the buns

With a tablespoon, fill the buttered, floured moulds up to the top with the bun mixture and cook in the pre-heated oven for about 12 minutes until a light blond colour. The buns should have a spongy texture and a crust should have built up underneath. Remove the cooked buns from the moulds or tin, and allow to cool a little on a wire rack. Serve whilst still warm.

VARIATIONS

The Hot Orange Buns can be served with the Blood Orange Gratin (see p. 286). If the gratin is made with apples, replace the citrus zest in the buns with vanilla seeds, scraped from 1 vanilla pod.

(see p. 286)

CHEF'S NOTES

Creaming the butter with a wooden spoon until soft will allow it easily to absorb the other ingredients such as eggs, flour etc. If the butter has not been softened enough, the mixture might split and will leave you with lumps of butter, which would considerably change the balance of the recipe.

The unsalted butter in this recipe can be replaced by unsalted margarine for those on a vegetarian or dairy produce-free diet.

Self-raising flour can be replaced by plain flour mixed with baking powder. The ratio is 20 g ($^3/_4$ oz) baking powder per 1 kg ($2^1/_4$ lb) flour; in this particular case, 3 pinches for 70 g ($2^3/_4$ oz) flour. If too little baking powder is added, the dough will not rise much; adding too much does not make the dough rise much more, and makes it develop a very strong flavour.

Coating the inside of each mould generously with butter will stop the bun sticking to the mould. Removing the buns from the moulds when cooked allows steam to escape and prevents the built-up crust becoming less crisp.

My Mother's Rice Pudding

FOR 4 GUESTS

PREPARATION TIME: 20 minutes

COOKING TIME: About 1¼ hours

SPECIAL EQUIPMENT: A heatproof and ovenproof pan or dish, 25 cm (10 in) in diameter, with a lid; 4 ramekins, 10 cm (4 in) in diameter, 4.5 cm (1¾ in) in height.

INGREDIENTS
750 ml (1¼ pints) milk
1 vanilla pod
75 g (3 oz) short-grain rice
30 g (1¼ oz) sultanas
3 egg yolks
70 g (2¾ oz) caster sugar
30 g (1¼ oz) unsalted butter

METHOD

Pre-heat the oven to 160–180°C/325–350°F/Gas 3–4.

Place the milk in the pan with the vanilla pod and bring to the boil. Rain in the rice, and stir until it comes back to the boil. Cover with the lid, and place in the pre-heated oven for about 30 minutes, stirring from time to time. Remove from the oven.

Stir in the sultanas and replace in the oven for a further 30 minutes or until tender, stirring from time to time. Remove from the oven.

While the rice is cooking, mix together the egg yolks and caster sugar. Pour a quarter of the cooked rice on to the egg yolk mixture, mixing in quickly. Return to the bulk of the rice and mix in quickly. Discard the vanilla pod.

Grease the ramekins with the butter, and divide the rice mixture evenly between them. Place them in the oven and bake until brown on the top. Serve to your children.

CHEF'S NOTES

It is important to choose the right kind of rice for this dish. Short-grain rice is very much more absorbent than long- or medium-grain rice, and it also has more starch molecules. This contributes to the creaminess of the finished dish.

Raining in the rice and stirring until it comes back to the boil prevents the rice forming a large lump due to its high starch content.

Covering the rice with a lid stops over-evaporation of the milk. It also stops a direct heat browning the mixture.

Cooking the rice in the oven allows a gentle simmering of the rice.

The meringue floating islands consist mainly of protein (from the egg white) and sugar. The fat content of the dish is increased by the vanilla cream which is made with egg yolks. However, both the egg yolks and the milk provide vitamins A, B and D as well as a number of important minerals. Milk is one of the best sources of calcium.

The accompanying raspberry sauce, as well as being a delicious addition, is rich in vitamin C.

Floating Islands
with Raspberry Sauce

FOR 4 GUESTS

PREPARATION TIME: 50 minutes

CHILLING TIME: 4 hours

SPECIAL EQUIPMENT: A large shallow pan for poaching.

PLANNING AHEAD: The whole dessert can be prepared well in advance, about 12 hours.

INGREDIENTS

FOR THE MERINGUE
6 egg whites
250 g (9 oz) caster sugar

FOR POACHING THE MERINGUE
1 litre (1¾ pints) milk
**2 vanilla pods, split
lengthways**

FOR THE VANILLA CREAM
(see also p. 64)
5 egg yolks
**75 g (3 oz) caster sugar
poaching milk**

FOR THE RASPBERRY SAUCE
**250 g (9 oz) fresh
raspberries**
30 g (1¼ oz) caster sugar
a drop of lemon juice

METHOD

1 · Preparing and poaching the meringue
Put the milk and split vanilla pods in the large shallow pan and bring to the boil. Reduce the heat to just below simmering point and leave to infuse for about 5 minutes.

In an electric mixer on medium speed, beat the egg whites to a light peak, then add the sugar. Increase to full speed and beat until firm. Scoop out 12 large chunks of meringue. Poach six at a time in the simmering milk for 2 minutes. Turn them over and poach for 2 more minutes. Remove with a slotted spoon and leave to drain on a small tray. Poach 6 more meringues in this way. Cool and refrigerate.

Remove the vanilla pods from the milk, then strain and reserve, you should have about 500 ml (17 fl oz).

2 · Making the vanilla cream

Make as described on p. 64, whisking the egg yolks and sugar together first, then add the flavoured poaching milk and stir over gentle heat until it thickens. Stir off the heat, then place in a large serving bowl and leave to cool.

3 · Making the raspberry sauce

Save 12 of the raspberries as garnish, then make the sauce as described on p. 281. Reserve.

4 · Serving

Top the vanilla cream in the bowl with the poached meringues, then pour over the raspberry sauce. Place the reserved raspberries on top of the meringues. Serve to your guests.

VARIATIONS

You could sprinkle the meringues with some toasted, flaked almonds and then pour over some freshly cooked runny caramel. The caramel will not last more than 2 hours, so do this at the last moment. Follow the caramel-making instructions on p. 264, using half the quantity stated in the recipe.

CHEF'S NOTES

Simmering allows the essential oils of the vanilla pods to seep out and flavour the milk.

Do not boil the milk otherwise it will make the meringue expand; thereafter it will deflate miserably when cooling down.

Turning the meringue over allows the other side to be cooked thoroughly. The poached meringue should be cooked until firm to the touch.

Floating Islands
with Raspberry Sauce
(see p. 311)

Glossary of Terms

AMINO ACIDS – The building blocks of proteins, characterised by an amino (NH$_2$) group in the molecule. There are 20 different types which can be combined together in many ways to form hundreds of different proteins.

AMYLOPECTIN – A type of starch consisting of up to 100 000 glucose units linked together in a branching chain. Usually found along with amylose in starchy foods.

AMYLOSE – A type of starch consisting of a few hundred glucose units linked together in a coiled chain. Usually found along with amylopectin in starchy foods.

ATOM – The smallest particle of matter consisting of a positively charged nucleus in the centre and negatively charged electrons orbiting around the nucleus.

BLANCHING – A brief form of boiling, involving a cooking time between a few seconds to a few minutes.

BOILING A method for cooking food in rapidly boiling water (100°C/212°F).

BRAISING – Food is cooked in a small amount of liquid in an oven at a low temperature. It may be browned in hot fat first.

CLARIFYING – A change in the structure of a protein in a food (e.g. milk; egg white) brought about by heat (e.g. cooking) or acidity (e.g. milk souring) which results in a change to the food's texture and appearance.

CONDUCTION – The transfer of heat from one molecule to another molecule in a step to step fashion, takes place in liquids, solids and vapours.

CONVECTION – A movement of heat through a liquid (or vapour) produced when heat is applied at the bottom of the cooking vessel (e.g. when boiling). The heat rises and is replaced by cooler liquid descending from the top in a circular fashion, in an attempt to equalize the heat throughout the liquid.

CURING – A method of preserving foods (e.g. meat, fish) with salt, brine or smoke in order to reduce the moisture content and kill or prevent the growth of bacteria.

DEEP FRYING – Food is completely immersed in oil or fat which has been heated to a high enough temperature for it to brown on the outside and cook on the inside.

EMULSIFIERS – Substances which enable water and oil to mix, forming an homogenous emulsion.

ENZYMES – Proteins which control all the many thousands of chemical reactions in plant and animal cells, e.g. starch manufacture, energy production, digestion.

FRUCTOSE – Sometimes known as fruit sugar since it is found naturally in fruit and honey. A simple sugar unit, similar in structure to glucose, but sweeter than both glucose and sucrose.

GLUCOSE – A simple sugar unit containing six carbon atoms linked in a ring, found naturally in fruit and (to lesser extent) vegetables. Less sweet than sucrose. A building block from which larger more complex carbohydrates are built.

GRILLING – Food is cooked at a very high temperature by radiant heat from a single direct source such as a grill or barbecue for a relatively short time. Only one side is cooked at a time.

LACTOSE – Found naturally in milk ('milk sugar'), consists of two simple sugar units linked together: glucose and galactose. Less sweet than glucose, fructose and sucrose.

MAILLARD REACTION – A chemical reaction between a protein and sugar in the same food which occurs at high temperatures and is responsible for the desirable changes in flavour, colour and aroma produced during baking, roasting and toasting.

MARINATING – Food is soaked in a liquid (usually based on oil, vinegar, wine or fruit juice) to tenderize and/or flavour it prior to cooking.

MICROWAVE COOKING – A method for cooking food by microwave radiation (electromagnetic waves with a wavelength longer than visible or infra red light) which causes food molecules to oscillate. This friction is then converted into heat, thus cooking the food.

MOLECULE – Two or more (up to several thousand) atoms linked together to form a distinct unit.

PICKLING – A method of preserving food (e.g. onions, fish) by covering with an acidic solution such as vinegar to kill and prevent the growth of bacteria.

POACHING – Food is cooked in barely simmering liquid (e.g. water, milk, stock) at just below boiling point.

PROTEINS – Consist of thousands of amino acids linked together. They make up the structure of every cell in meat, fish, fruit, vegetables and all other animal and plant foodstuffs. Also make up the structure of enzymes and hormones.

RADIATION – A method of heat transfer from a single heat source (e.g. grill) through the air to the food.

ROASTING – Food is browned by cooking in a little oil either in the oven or on top of the stove then placed in a moderate oven to complete the cooking. It may or may not be basted.

SAUTEEING – Cooking fairly small pieces of food in oil or fat over a moderate heat while stirring to distribute the heat evenly.

SEARING/PAN FRYING – Pieces of food are cooked briefly in a pan over a medium heat to brown the outside.

SOUSING – Similar to pickling but a less acidic solution is used (e.g. for herrings).

STARCH – The major food reserve of plants, it is a complex carbohydrate built up from thousands of connected sugar units. There are two main types which occur together: amylose and amylopectin.

STEAMING – Cooking food in steam over boiling water.

STIR-FRYING – A method for cooking food (usually cut into strips to give a large surface area), in a little hot oil or fat while at the same time stirring and shaking the pan for a brief time so that the food is served al dente.

SUCROSE – Or ordinary table sugar, consisting of two simple sugar units linked togther: glucose and fructose. Found naturally in fruit and vegetables and commercially extracted from sugar cane and sugar beet.

SWEATING – Food is cooked in a small amount of fat or oil in a pan over a gentle heat sufficient to soften it but not enough to brown it.

Index